# AMID ONCOMING STORM

A novel

Copyright © Juliane Weber 2024

All rights reserved. This book or any portion thereof may not be reproduced or used in any manner whatsoever without the express written permission of the publisher, except for the use of brief quotations in a book review.

Portions of this book are works of fiction. Any references to historical events, real people, or real places are used fictitiously. Other names, characters, places and events are products of the author's imagination, and any resemblances to actual events or places or persons, living or dead, are entirely coincidental.

ISBN 979-8-3391-4048-1

Cover design by White Rabbit Arts

www.julianeweber.com

For my parents. For everything.

Ireland
Spring, 1847

# Prologue

HE OPENED HIS eyes suddenly, coming instantly awake. He lay still, listening, but the angry voices he'd heard were silent, gone with the dream that had wakened him.

He turned his head and looked at his wife. She was sleeping peacefully, one hand resting over their unborn child. Her eyelids fluttered and her lips twitched briefly into a dreamy smile, her night-time meanderings quite unlike his own.

The first light of dawn was creeping through the window, a twitter of birds marking the start of a new day. A new day filled with the hope of spring and fresh beginnings—even as the cold hand of despair spread across the land.

He shoved away the covers and slid out of bed, moving silently to the sitting room, where he reclined at the small table and ran a hand across his face.

The sounds of conflict started echoing in his ears, the wailing of the hopeless as they buried their loved ones and were torn from their homes, their desperate pleading going unheard.

He shook his head to dispel the flashes of violence, but his mind would not quiet.

The angry voices rose once more as hopelessness turned to rage—and rage turned to rebellion.

# 1.

I STRETCHED LANGUOROUSLY, content in the knowledge that I didn't yet need to get up. Early pregnancy was making me feel tired and I was glad of the opportunity to rest a little longer.

I placed a hand on my abdomen, which was still flat despite the growing baby inside of me. A deep sense of joy spread through my middle at the thought of the tiny being my body sheltered—a gift given to us despite all odds.

I had almost died a few months earlier when I'd been struck down by fever—the same illness that had taken the life of Margaret and her infant son not long before, cruelly snatching away the wife and child of John, our groom. Part of my parents' household for as long as I could remember, Margaret had been more than just a maid to me. She had been my friend and I had come to care a great deal for her and her young son.

I swallowed heavily at the memory of their loss.

I had wondered since, whether I may already have been pregnant when the sickness took hold of me. I'd heard that expectant mothers were fragile. Perhaps the rigours of creating new life had weakened my body and made me more susceptible to the fever, leaving me at death's door. Then again, Margaret herself had been in good health before she fell ill and yet she had succumbed.

And if I had been pregnant, surely, I would have lost the child, I thought, recalling the numerous miscarriages I had suffered before. Unless...

A sudden chill ran down my spine and I clutched my hands reflexively over my belly. What if I hadn't lost the baby but it had been damaged somehow by the ravages of the fever? Images of malformed children flashed through my mind, the blank stares of feeble-minded others making me take in a sharp breath. Was such a thing possible? Could the new life we'd prayed for been dampened before it had even truly begun?

I forced myself to breathe slowly in and out until my heartbeat began to slow. Most likely—and I fervently hoped this to be true—the child had been conceived soon after my recovery, when Quin and I had turned to each other in desperate need.

I caressed my abdomen once more, imagining stroking a baby's soft head and the curve of its cheek.

A sound at the door made me look up and I met Quin's eyes as he came into the room, closing the door softly behind him.

"You're awake," he said, coming to sit beside me on the bed, a tender look on his face as he placed his hand over mine.

I must still have looked distressed for he frowned. "What's wrong, Alannah?"

I shook my head, not wanting to burden him with my fears. He looked down his nose at me and I shrugged. "I worry about him…or her," I said without looking at Quin.

He tilted up my chin and cupped my face in his hand. "You worry too much."

"There's much to worry about."

He was quiet for a moment, a troubled look flashing across his features as he held my eyes briefly. "That's undoubtedly true." He ran his hands gently over my belly, then down my thighs and up again, pulling up the thin fabric of my nightgown. He lowered his head and placed a soft kiss over our unborn child.

Suddenly, I felt him smile against my sensitive skin. He glanced up at me while running a hand slowly up the inside of my thigh. "But perhaps I can distract you from your troubles," he said, his green eyes glinting with mischief before he lowered his head once more.

FEELING RATHER PLEASED with himself Quin went back downstairs a short time later, the agreeable early morning activity doing much to suppress his own concerns about the future.

In the entrance hall he spotted his valet, Rupert, who was eyeing the small figure standing next to him.

"You know I'm happy to see you, Emmett, but...well...what in the world are you doing here?"

Emmett, so addressed, looked down and shuffled his feet, avoiding his brother's eye.

With his family residing in London, nobody had expected Emmett's appearance at Glaslearg a few days before, least of all Rupert. In the excitement following Emmett's unannounced arrival—and the news of Alannah's pregnancy—Emmett had thus far managed to avoid explaining the circumstances of his visit, but it appeared Rupert was now demanding answers.

"Um...is there any breakfast?" Emmett asked instead, darting a quick glance at Rupert.

"Don't think you can distract me," Rupert growled, nevertheless leading Emmett toward the kitchen.

Interested in hearing the boy's story Quin followed the siblings. Finding his employer suddenly behind him Rupert gave a quick bow before giving his brother a meaningful look to do the same.

Quin waved his hand. "Do continue. I must say, I am rather intrigued myself to hear what brought you to the sticks of Ireland, Emmett."

Emmett cleared his throat. "Ah..."

"Well?" Rupert raised his brows.

"Let the boy eat first, Rupert. He's nought but skin and bones." The cook, Mrs O'Sullivan, placed a steaming bowl of oatmeal in front of Emmett, having first assured herself Quin would eat with Alannah when she came downstairs. "Ye've travelled a long way, haven't ye?"

Emmett looked relieved at this respite, beaming at the cook as he sat down at the table. "Oh aye. 'Twas a most arduous journey."

"*Arduous*. Hmph." Rupert slid onto the bench beside him and accepted his own breakfast. "What I want to know is why you came here in the first place."

"Aren't ye glad t' see me?"

"I've said I was and so I am. But for you to arrive by yourself and without a word from mum and dad, it's...well...it's strange is what it is. So, out with it. Why have you come to Ireland?"

"Well...I..." Emmett trailed off, stirring his oats mechanically.

"Yes?" Rupert was having none of it, leaning menacingly toward his brother, spoon hovering forgotten over his bowl.

"Ye see I...ah..."

"Did you do something foolish and get sent away?" Rupert suggested.

Emmett fidgeted on his seat. "Well...um..." He threw a glance toward Quin, who nodded encouragingly. "It weren't exactly foolish but...ah...well...maybe a little."

"Go on then."

"Ye see, my friend Hugh and I, well, we heard of...of a place..."

"What kind of place?" Rupert asked, unable to hide his impatience.

"Um...well...a place where men...well where they go t'...um...hmph..." Emmett's cheeks went bright red, and Rupert's eyes suddenly flew open, his spoon clattering to the tabletop.

"You mean...a *bawdy house*? You went with your friend to a bawdy house?"

Mrs O'Sullivan gasped and threw Emmett a shocked look.

"We was only curious," he said dismissively. "We wanted t' see the ladies, is all."

"You wanted to see the ladies," Rupert muttered to himself, shaking his head. "Who told you about this place? And what were you thinking going there?" Before Emmett could answer Rupert went on, "You got caught, is that it? And that's why mum and dad sent you away."

"Ah...not exactly."

"How exactly was it, then?" Rupert demanded.

"Well, when we got there, we couldn't see nothin'. So we snuck t' the back o' the house. We heard some strange noises and was just tryin' to look through one o' the windows when someone grabbed the back o' me shirt. I yelped and tried t' run away but couldn't."

"What happened then?" Mrs O'Sullivan asked, her work forgotten as she listened intently to Emmett's tale.

"Before I knew it, I'd been shoved through the door and int' the house."

"You were alone?" Rupert interrupted. "Where was your friend?"

"He managed t' get away."

"Hmph. Go on."

"The man who'd caught me was snarlin' at me when a woman arrived wi' another man. She seemed upset t' see me there in the passageway but then the other man gave me a strange look and said he didn't need t' see no more." Emmett glanced back and forth between his brother and Quin before going on. "The man who'd caught me sniggered and then started draggin' me up the stairs. He said if I didn't want t' end up locked away I'd do as I was told, twistin' me arm for good measure. Then 'e shoved me int' a small room with a bed, the other man followin'."

Quin sucked in a deep breath. He wasn't sure if he wanted to hear the rest of Emmett's story. It didn't matter, though, as Emmett evidently had no intention of stopping now.

"The other man, he pulled a chair in front o' the door. Then he turned back t' me and gave me that strange look again, makin' me skin crawl. And when 'e came closer and told me t' undress I thought I knew what 'e was about." A bright red flush spread across Emmett's cheeks, which was echoed by Rupert, who was sitting stock-still, his jaws tight with tension. "When I didn't move and he tried t' do it for me, I knew I 'ad t' get away."

"Did you?" Rupert croaked, his hands clenched into fists.

Emmett nodded, making Quin and Rupert exhale as one, while Mrs O'Sullivan fanned her face with her hand.

"It wasn't easy, mind. I was screechin' and hollerin' for help, and tryin' to kick 'im, scratch 'im, anythin' I could, but he threw me ont' the bed. I thought I was done for when he started comin' nearer but then I spotted a candlestick on the table next t' the bed. It was one o' them tall ones, wi' the candle almost burnt away. I grabbed for it just as he lunged for me, crackin' 'im on the head with it. Except I hit him in the eye instead, and he let out a terrible shriek, blood pourin' down 'is face."

Quin glanced at Rupert, whose own face was masked in shock. Whatever story he'd been expecting his brother to tell, this clearly wasn't it.

For Emmett, though, the telling seemed something of a catharsis, the words pouring out of his mouth faster and faster as he went on, Mrs O'Sullivan clucking along in sympathy.

"I was starin' at 'im, the candlestick still in me 'and, when I heard the door rattlin' like. I saw then someone was tryin' t' come in but couldn't budge the chair wedged under the handle. I thought o' pullin' it away but then I remembered the man who'd caught me and the woman who'd given me away like a sack o' meal, and I figured I wouldn't get no help from them. So I turned back int' the room, which was a good thing too because the other man came at me with 'is arms outstretched, snarlin' like a demon and lookin' like one too."

Emmett suddenly jumped up from the bench. "I tripped 'im up, I did, so he fell ont' the floor. But then I still 'ad t' get away. Only I couldn't go out the door, so I went for the window and smashed it with me candlestick." Emmett demonstrated the motion with one hand, his face aglow with excitement.

What might have been a terrifying experience for some seemed to have been a great adventure for him, Quin thought.

"There was a thin ledge," Emmett continued, "and I managed 't climb down from there."

"And when you came home and told mum and dad you'd been to a bawdy house in what was no doubt one of London's worst neighbourhoods they sent you away to Ireland," Rupert concluded, his eyes narrowed at his brother.

Emmett slowly shook his head. "Ah...not quite."

"What else?" Rupert raised his hands, exasperated.

"I managed t' sneak back int' the house without 'em noticin' I'd been gone." Rupert opened his mouth to say something but was forestalled by Emmett. "But I 'adn't realised I'd been followed."

"Followed?"

"Aye. By the fellow I'd bashed over the head. He was waitin' for me outside the house the next day after everyone'd gone t' work. And what a fright I got too, wi' his head all wrapped around wi' a scarf that covered one eye, and the dried blood all over one side of 'is face."

Mrs O'Sullivan tutted. "What did ye do?"

"He'd got hold o' me arm, so I bit 'is hand until he let go. Then I ran back int' the house, with 'im after me hollerin' 'bout *an eye for an eye* and…and worse."

"Did ye send for the police then?" Mrs O'Sullivan asked, patting Emmett on the arm.

He shook his head as he flopped back onto the bench. "I told 'im I would. Yelled it right out the window at 'im but…well 'e grinned at me and told me t' go ahead…for 'e *was* the police. And the way 'e said it, I knew it were true.—Besides, who'd listen t' the likes o' me anyway?"

Rupert frowned. "So this man, this constable, he meant to hurt you…maybe even…" He cut off and clamped his lips together briefly. "And he knew where you lived…"

"Aye. So I 'ad t' get away, d'ye see?"

"Aye, I can see that now. Mum and dad were right to send you here."

"Um…aye…aye they were."

Rupert gave his brother a curious look, but Emmett avoided his eyes and fidgeted with his sleeve. When Emmett flashed Rupert a sideways glance, the valet suddenly paled. "Emmett! Mum and dad *did* send you here, didn't they?"

"Um…"

"Emmett!"

The boy looked down onto his lap. "Well, not exactly…"

"Not exactly?"

Emmett lifted one shoulder, making Rupert's eyes go even rounder. "Emmett, you told me mum and dad knew where you were!"

"And so they do. I left 'em a note, didn't I?"

"You left them a note?" Rupert looked wildly around the room, as if seeking inspiration for dealing with his insufferable relation.

"Aye, I did! I've been learnin' me letters, 'aven't I?" Emmett raised his chin in defiance.

Rupert scoffed. "And what did the note say, then? *Mum, dad, I've gone to Ireland, love Emmett*?"

Emmett's cheeks went bright red, which had a rather alarming effect on Rupert, who leapt from his seat in an explosion of breath.

"D'ye mean t' tell me ye travelled 'alfway across Britain on yer own without anyone knowin' about it?" Rupert's usually more cultured accent was rapidly deteriorating to its Cockney roots. Emmett opened his mouth to respond, but Rupert shut it for him with a glare. "How did ye do it?" he demanded. "Without any coin?—Did ye steal the fare t' get here?"

Emmett rose once more from his own seat and scowled. "I did not!—I hid away, I did!"

"You hid away?" Rupert shook his head slowly back and forth, looking dazed. "We 'ave to send you back!" he bellowed suddenly before turning toward Quin. "We have to send him back, sir!"

"Ye can't, can ye?" Emmett said before Quin could get a word in. "It's much too dangerous on me own!"

"Too dangerous…on your… But that's how you got here in the first place!" Rupert's face was slowly going puce in the heat of battle with his irascible brother.

The brother in question shrugged. "Ye didn't know it then, did ye?"

"*I* didn't know?"

"Aye. And now that ye *do* know, ye'd never send me back t' England on me own."

Rupert sputtered alarmingly at this logic, making Quin hope he wasn't about to have an apoplexy. He decided it was time to intervene. Before either of the Joneses could open his mouth again, Quin lifted both hands.

"What we're going to do forthwith is send a letter to your mother, assuring her you're safe. She must be worried sick about you, Emmett." Quin gave the boy a long look, making him droop in shame.

"I did leave a note," he said in a small voice.

"So you did." Quin nodded sympathetically. "Still, mothers tend to worry." From what Quin could tell from observing his pregnant wife, this maternal trait seemed to emerge before the baby was even born. What Emmett's mother must have felt reading his pitiful explanation for his disappearance, Quin tried not to contemplate.

"Are ye goin' t' send me back, sir?" Emmett's youthful face was masked with misery. Clearly, he could think of no worse punishment.

"That will depend largely on what your parents have to say about it."

"I'll work, sir!" Emmett pounced on Quin's vague response. "I could be a…a stable lad!"

Rupert emitted a loud snort. "You? A stable lad? When you know not a thing about horses?"

"And how much d' *you* know about horses?" Emmett retorted, stemming his hands on his hips.

"More than *you*, I'm sure! Besides, I'm a *valet* not a stable lad." Rupert spat out the term with contempt and snootily lifted his chin.

Emmett defiantly stuck out his own chin. "I can learn!"

"I'm sure you can, Emmett," Quin interrupted the pair, "and I dare say, there's always plenty to be done on the estate, horses or no. But I can hardly allow you to stay here against your parents' wishes. If they ask me to send you back to London I shall have to do so, I'm afraid."

"But what about the man what's after me?" Emmett made one last attempt.

"We shall deal with him in due course. But we must await your parents' decision first."

Emmett sighed, making Rupert finally take pity on the boy and drape an arm around him.

"I shall pen a letter to your mother," Quin said, "telling her you've arrived safely at Glaslearg…and discreetly explaining the reasons for your hasty departure." He paused, catching Emmett's eye. "Shall I also convey your profound regret for your foolish actions and the anguish you've caused her?"

Emmett's cheeks flushed as he looked down at his shoes. "Yes, sir."

"But perhaps you'll add a few words of your own to the end?"

Emmett nodded silently before following Rupert to the door.

"At least I'll be far away when mum reads that letter," Quin heard him grumble under his breath as he left the kitchen.

Once the brothers had gone and Mrs O'Sullivan returned to her duties, Quin rubbed a hand over his face. Was this what parenting would be like? Constantly having to worry about forthcoming mischief and cleaning up the ensuing mess? If so, he wasn't sure he was ready for it.

"Quin?"

He looked up as Alannah came through the door, immediately feeling guilty. She'd told him she'd been feeling nauseous since the start of the pregnancy and here he was preoccupied with the distant future. Perhaps it wasn't only mothers who tended to worry, after all.

"What is it?"

Alannah's voice made him tear his eyes away from her abdomen, where the bump of their growing baby would soon become visible.

"I'm alright," she said, misunderstanding his look.

"I'm glad to hear it." He got up and pulled her briefly to him. "Are all children troublesome, do you think?"

Alannah laughed at the question. "Many, I'm sure.—Have the Joneses given you trouble, then? I just passed them on my way here. Emmett looked rather subdued."

"And so he should." In a few words Quin told her about the boy's adventures, making her eyes go ever wider.

"Emmett can count himself lucky for getting away unscathed! But poor Mrs Jones! She must be beside herself with worry."

"I expect so."

Alannah gave him an amused look. "And you expect our own child to give us such trouble?"

"Hmph."

"You realise it'll be a few years until we have to concern ourselves with such things," Alannah said.

"You're right." Quin laid a hand over her belly. "Something so small can hardly cause much mischief."

"Mischief, no, but sleepless nights and constant worry about its welfare."

"Well thank you ever so much for brightening my mood."

Alannah laughed and wrapped her arms around his middle. "You'll be a wonderful father.—And deal with all challenges as they come."

Quin smiled and kissed her on the forehead. "If you say so it must be true."

# 2.

HOPING TO BE allowed to stay in Ireland Emmett quickly set out to inveigle himself into the household by trying to prove his usefulness. And while it was true that he barely knew one end of a horse from the other, he was perfectly capable of mucking out stalls or doing any number of other menial tasks required around the estate.

He soon became fast friends with Benjamin, a former Dublin street urchin who'd come to live with them some time before. The two boys were frequently found with their heads together, usually joined by Conor, the son of one Glaslearg's tenants. Naturally, the trio occasionally got up to the expected mischief, but were usually kept in check by a stern word from Mrs O'Sullivan.

Quin found he quite enjoyed having Rupert's brother around, his exuberance often bringing a smile to Quin's face. In fact, it was becoming increasingly difficult for him to imagine sending the boy back to England. With Alannah feeling much the same the two of them often chose to share a meal with their staff in the kitchen rather than eat a more formal dinner in the dining room by themselves.

On one such occasion Emmett barely got around to eating, so many questions were pouring out of his mouth.

"But how'd ye know when the wheat is ready t' harvest?" Having assisted on the fields that morning he now wanted to know everything there was to know about agriculture.

"When the seed heads have turned a golden yellow and there's no more visible green," Alannah answered patiently.

"Ye can also test the grain," Mrs O'Sullivan added as she placed a platter of steaming vegetables onto the table. "Ye rub the seed head between yer hands t' release the grain. If it's hard when ye bite it, the wheat is ready fo' the harvest."

"Hm." Emmett nodded his head thoughtfully. "And when's that supposed t' be?"

"At the end o' summer," Benjamin said, grinning at Emmett when he gave him a surprised look. "I've learned a thing or two about farmin' since I've been 'ere, too."

"It'll be summer soon," Quin said, looking forward to the long hours of daylight.

"And Bealtaine will be coming up then too."

Quin looked up in some surprise at Rupert's comment. "Bealtaine? Since when are you interested in pagan rituals?"

Although Rupert had been terribly excited about coming to Ireland with Quin several years earlier, he'd always been a little sceptical of some of the less than Christian practices to be found in his new home—much like himself, Quin had to admit.

Rupert's cheeks went pink as he avoided the eye of Finnian across from him. The young Irish footman had often mocked the valet about his very English demeanour.

"I enjoy a good festival as much as anyone, sir," Rupert said defiantly. "And I have been here for a while now. But as it is, Ger…I mean, a…a friend was telling me all about the ancient fire feasts and…well…"

Benjamin sniggered and elbowed Emmett in the ribs. "A *friend*, he says." He gave Rupert a knowing look, making the young man's face go even redder, while Finnian smirked at his obvious discomfort.

Emmett ignored the byplay, his eyes widening in fascination. "Fire feasts?" Unlike his brother, he seemed to have no qualms about Ireland's outlandish beliefs.

"There are four of them," Alannah told him before glancing briefly at Rupert, who was studiously examining the tabletop, his ears still glowing. "They mark the beginning of spring, summer, the harvest season in autumn, and winter."

"And Bealtaine marks the beginnin' o' summer?" Emmett guessed, making Alannah nod. "Are we havin' a Bealtaine fire feast then?" he asked, practically vibrating with excitement.

Quin caught Alannah's eye as Emmett started bouncing up and down on his seat.

"Oh, can we, sir, please?"

"Please, sir?" Benjamin joined his voice to the plea as he mimicked his friend, the two of them resembling a pair of crazed hens upon their perch.

Quin laughed. "You realise things are rather subdued out here in the countryside. Nothing like the festivals of the ancient Celts, I'm sure."

"Oh, but we can make it so!" Emmett jumped to his feet and rounded on Rupert. "What did Geraldine tell ye then?" he demanded.

"Um...well..." Rupert sputtered. He shot a glance at Quin before quickly looking away, making Quin suppress a laugh as Alannah's mouth turned up at the corners.

"We do celebrate Bealtaine, Emmett," she assured the boy, effectively directing his attention away from his brother, who sagged in relief.

"Ye do?" Emmett sucked in a breath before his face split into a wide grin. "Me first pagan festival... What d'ye think mum will say when she hears of it?"

Rupert looked like he'd rather not find out what their mother would have to say about it.

"Considering your mother's reaction to your running off to Ireland," Quin said drily, "you may want to keep the pagan festival to yourself."

A letter from Emmett's mother had been delivered the week before, which she must have sent soon after his disappearance. Beneath her genuine concern for his welfare was the unmistakable threat of a thorough thrashing upon his safe return. And once Quin's missive arrived at her doorstep, there was every possibility Emmett would find himself on his prompt way back to England, Bealtaine festival or no.

The same thought must have occurred to Emmett himself for a look of dejection appeared on his face. "I 'ope she lets me stay here."

"I hope so too, mite," Rupert said, patting his brother's arm. "You're a good lad...even if you don't always think before you act."

"If she tries t' send ye back t' England ye can always pretend her letter never got here," Benjamin suggested, making Emmett brighten up.

Seeing the looks on Quin and Alannah's faces, though, they both went bright red and looked down at their shoes.

"I do hope the Bealtaine festival will be soon," Emmett said, peeking out at Quin from beneath his lashes. "Afore me mother sends me packin'!"

AS IT WAS, Emmett's mother did not send him packing. The dreaded letter arrived a few days later, its appearance making Emmett turn rather green. Though the letter was addressed to him, Quin invited the brothers to attend the reading, their sombre expressions making the occasion resemble the reading of a will. Emmett seemed not to breathe throughout, his eyes going ever wider as his mother's relief at finding him safe morphed into a thorough dressing down. I held my own breath, waiting to hear if she would insist on his return. Not so, though. While she questioned the intelligence and judgement of her youngest son, Mrs Jones agreed that Ireland was likely the safest place for Emmett under the circumstances—if we would indeed be willing to take such a troublesome lad as he into our household.

The troublesome lad in question seemed ready to slide off the chair at the conclusion of the reading. "She said I can stay.—Did she say I can stay?" Emmett turned anxiously to Rupert, lest he'd misunderstood.

"She said a few other things too," his brother said dryly, "but aye, she said you can stay."

Emmett gave a great whoop and leapt into the air.

"You'd think he'd been told he was off on holiday," Quin observed in some amusement.

Watching Emmett launch himself into Rupert's arms, his face aglow with happiness, I thought I understood. "He wanted to be with Rupert."

I felt a tightening in my chest, recalling a time when I'd had a brother I adored. Two years older than I, Kieran had been my closest friend when we were children. We'd been inseparable for a time, until disillusionment and hatred had caused a rift to come between us as we got older. And just when we'd started finding our way back to each other he'd been permanently snatched away—murdered by Martin Doyle, an old ally who'd thought Kieran had betrayed him.

Quin reached a hand across to me, squeezing my fingers lightly. His eyes met mine and I gave him a fleeting smile. I had lost my brother but had found Quin, and he'd been there for me throughout.

I sighed, wishing I could have kept them both.

"And t' think I might 'ave missed the festival!"

Emmett's voice brought me back to the present and I laughed. "What would you have done if your mother had insisted you return to England?"

Emmett grinned. "Pretend I was sick and only return after? Or hide away in the barn until the last o' the month?"

"You must be very excited if you'd go to such lengths," Quin said.

"I've ne'er been more excited in me life!" Emmett agreed as he dashed toward the door. "And I'm goin' t' find out all there is t' know about Bealtaine now I can stay!—Ah, if I may, sir?" He blinked at Quin, hand on the doorhandle.

Quin raised one brow. "If you may leave the study or if you may stay at Glaslearg?"

Emmett's eyes went wide, and a look of horror bloomed on his face as he seemed to realise Quin hadn't yet given him permission to live with us at the estate.

"Both, sir," the boy squeaked.

Quin was silent for a moment, lifting his chin as he assessed the new potential resident, who swallowed heavily and flattened himself against the door.

At last, a smile broke out on Quin's face, making Emmett sag with relief. "You may, Emmett. Welcome to Glaslearg."

# 3.

"D'YE THINK THE name comes from the god Belenus? Or is it just a Celtic reference t' the Bealtaine fires?"

"Well…" I started responding to Emmett's questions but got no further.

"They do say as Belenus is a mighty god who rules over life and death, so it makes sense t' ask for his blessing for the crops and livestock goin' int' summer, no?"

"I suppose…"

"But the fairies must also be kept happy, o' course." Emmett nodded madly to himself. Suddenly, though, he clapped his hands over his mouth. "Ah, I mean the Sidhe…" He glanced around suspiciously, lest one of these creatures come to exact revenge for being called an offensive name.

I gave him a curious look, making him flush.

"Not that any o' that is *real*, though," he said, not meeting my eyes. As a good English Protestant, he knew he shouldn't be paying too much attention to pagan gods and fairies, but the topic—like so many others—had quite fascinated the boy since stepping foot on Irish shores.

I smiled, recognising a fellow inquisitive mind. "Who have you been talking to?" I asked, fascinated by the knowledge the boy had acquired in such a short time.

"Oh, everyone! But Grandfather O'Reilly specially, and some o' the other older folks too."

"Well, you'll be sure to inform us of all the correct procedures for the festival then, won't you, Emmett?"

"Oh yes, ma'am, I did say I would." He pulled himself up to his full height and puffed out his chest. "And will we be havin' a bonfire as high as the barn then?"

I laughed. "I rather doubt we'll manage one quite as large as that but I'm sure it will be a night to remember, nonetheless."

IN THE END, we had not just one bonfire but two, on Emmett's insistence.

"It's t' allow the livestock t' run between the fires," he informed Quin, who nodded gravely as he perused the site. Having overseen the construction of the stacks of wood and peat that morning Emmett had insisted on showing us the results of his efforts before we returned for the celebrations that evening.

Quin caught my eye and his lips twitched. Emmett had been chattering almost incessantly for the past hour, regurgitating every piece of information he'd gathered about Bealtaine, between spouting other bits of Irish folklore.

"Just like the ancient Celts used t' do," Emmett went on. "It's said they herded their cattle between the fires to their summer pastures on Bealtaine eve."

"Why would they do that?" Benjamin, who'd come up behind Emmett scrunched up his nose, looking sceptical.

"I dunno."

"Well, what's the point o' tellin' us about it then?"

Emmett glared at Benjamin, who narrowed his own eyes in turn.

"I for one find it fascinating," Quin said quickly. "Perhaps you could regale us with a few more interesting titbits?" He cocked his head toward Emmett, who visibly brightened at the suggestion.

"Oh, yes, sir! Did ye know that ye're supposed t' leave out a pot o' water the week before May eve, when ye bring it int' the house to ward off colds in the comin' year?"

"Hm. We're a bit late about it if so."

Emmett grinned. "No, sir. I put one out the moment I learnt about it, didn't I, and hid it in the barn."

"Oh well done," I said. "We'll be sure to remain in good health then.—You know, my grandmother used to swear that washing her face with dew before sunrise on May Day assured her of a good complexion."

"D'ye think that works?" Benjamin asked, studying my face.

I lifted one shoulder. "I can't say I've tried it myself, but she did look remarkably youthful even when she died, so perhaps there is something to it."

"But gettin' the first water from the well on May Day does bring good luck," Emmett said, nodding earnestly.

"How are all the people supposed t' get the first bucket o' water on May Day?" Benjamin asked scornfully.

"They can't, can they? That's why ye have t' try t' be the first."

"But…"

Quin rolled his eyes. "Mrs O'Sullivan told me that she needed to skim the milk today, otherwise we'd have no cream for the next year."

"No cream?" Benjamin looked horrified. "For the next *year*?" A lover of all things sweet, he was so distracted by the thought that he seemed to forget all about the impending argument—which was no doubt what Quin had intended.

"That would be a right shame," Emmett agreed, licking his lips before looking across at Benjamin. "We might go see if she's done the skimmin' already, just t' be sure."

Thus reunited by their quest of saving the estate's sweetmeats, the two boys stalked off toward the house.

Laughing, Quin and I followed them along the trail that led to the estate's outbuildings and the manor house beyond. It was only a short walk from the empty field where the festivities would take place.

When the time came to return there a little later, Emmett was practically demented with excitement.

"Will we be havin' a human sacrifice?" he demanded, having popped up next to me as we gathered with the staff in the courtyard before setting out.

"Um…I rather hope not," I said. Next to me, Quin tried to hide a grin, with only limited success.

"Oh." Emmett's lips turned down in disappointment. "Grandfather O'Reilly did tell me the Celts used t' choose someone t' sacrifice at the Bealtaine fires for the gods each year."

"And would you be honoured to be chosen for such a task today?" Quin asked, cocking his head in Emmett's direction.

"Me?" The boy's eyes went wide. Clearly, he hadn't thought of the practice in quite such personal terms before. "I…well…"

Quin chuckled and patted Emmett on the head. "Not to worry, young Emmett, we shan't be sacrificing anyone tonight.—Although I can't say I won't be tempted," he added as Conor and Benjamin came shrieking toward the courtyard from the stable, pelting each other with what looked like horse apples.

"Conor. Benjamin," Quin called, making the delinquents come up short, looking guilty. "You are going to clean up this mess before you come anywhere near the festivities. Otherwise, I may just allow Emmett to have his human sacrifice after all."

Benjamin gasped and Conor swallowed heavily, before the two of them glanced at each other and bolted back toward the stable as one.

Laughter broke out around us, while Quin himself looked rather smug as he started leading the group toward the path.

"Working on your parenting techniques, are you?" I asked.

"I have yet to see an effective technique that doesn't involve threats or bribery."

"Are those your years of experience talking?"

"I'm just observant.—Besides, I've been on the receiving end of a few such techniques myself."

"Really?"

"Oh yes. My father wasn't averse to taking a tawse to my bum when the occasion merited it."

I tried to picture Quin's father, the very proper Baron Williams of Wadlow, bending Quin over his knee and burst out laughing at the thought.

Quin gave me an affronted look. "So much for womanly sympathy."

I patted his arm. "At least the experience seems to have paid off. You've turned out a most charming young man."

"Hmph. Thanks ever so much."

I laughed once more, and Quin smiled. "In truth, it usually sufficed to threaten me with not being allowed to ride my horse...or worse, going to bed without supper! It was the rare occasion when my father got angry enough to give me a good leathering. Although that didn't stop him from showing his disappointment in me in general."

He shrugged. Unmet expectations and bitterness had long been the cause of a troublesome relationship between father and son. Fortunately, this had improved to a degree after our visit to London the year before, when they'd resolved some of their differences.

"My mother was always more prone to bribery," Quin went on, a nostalgic expression on his face. "I recall one occasion when she offered me the temptation of an unlimited quantity of dessert after supper if only I'd catch up on my sorely neglected schoolwork. Four hours later and a terrible stomach ache at bedtime, and I rather wished I'd left the schoolwork to rot and taken the strap instead!"

"And how will you discipline your own child?" I asked, running a hand across my abdomen. "Will it be bribery or threats?"

Quin took my arm and tucked it into the crook of his elbow. "Neither one," he said, making me give him a quizzical look. "I'll simply let *you* do the disciplining while *I* spoil the child rotten."

I shook my head in amusement as I followed Quin along the path, wondering what our son—or daughter—would be like growing up. Would the child be even-tempered and docile or lean toward rebellion? I thought I myself must have been something in between. Usually happy to be accommodating, I had nevertheless had a stubborn streak when it came to things I wanted, one that extended to my interest in science and learning in general. Fortunately for me, my father had always encouraged my thirst for knowledge, beyond what most girls were exposed to.

Perhaps we'd have a daughter of a similar mind, who would go on to do wondrous things, one of very few women to make a mark in a man's world.

I sighed, knowing such a future was unlikely. Besides, I thought, the child might just as easily be a boy. Would a son follow in Quin's footsteps, joining the army and risking his life in some mindless war in a far-distant part of the empire? That thought made my heart speed up and I quickly tried to push it aside.

I was glad to see we'd reached the meeting point at the edge of the field, where I looked around to distract myself. Most of the tenants had made their way there from their cottages at the other end of the estate, some bringing along chairs or blankets in handcarts or with the help of the occasional mule. While the children darted back and forth, the adults stood or sat companionably in small groups as new arrivals looked for a comfortable spot to spend the evening, calling out greetings.

Having dispensed our own welcomes, we found an empty patch of grass, where Quin spread the large picnic blanket he'd brought from the house. In the process of handing me down to the blanket, he was distracted by a loud noise coming from the empty field. We both paused and watched as several older boys attempted to leap over the stacks of peat and firewood, whooping raucously.

Quin gave them a sceptical look. "I thought the fires are meant to be lit before one starts jumping over them."

"Perhaps they're practising," I suggested. I winced as one of the boys landed short of his target, ending up sprawled on the ground among a clattering of sticks and peals of laughter from his friends.

"Well, let's hope that practice does indeed make perfect before they have flames to contend with!"

I nodded, rather hoping Mrs O'Sullivan had brought something to treat burns.

"Mr Williams! Mr Williams, come look!"

Emmett rushed up to Quin, twitching madly with excitement. Impatient with our slow progress, he had dashed ahead of us to the field and had clearly discovered something most fascinating.

"You come too, Mrs Williams!"

"Oh, alright." I paused once more in the process of sitting down and took Quin's arm instead.

Emmett led us between the other revellers, toward the edge of the nearby stream. He ran ahead to the small whitethorn bush that grew there, which was sparkling in the sun's low rays. As we got closer, I could see that the bursts of colour came from numerous ribbons and ornaments draped across the foliage.

"It's a May bush!" I said, clapping my hands together in delight. I reached out a finger and set a small flower garland swinging. "We used to have one at the house every year—although that was only ever a few sprigs. My father always collected them for us." I felt a sudden pang of longing for my father, wondering why I hadn't kept the tradition alive after his death.

"It's t' ward off the little people." Emmett's voice pulled me back to the present as Conor and Benjamin came up behind him.

Conor looked gravely at his friend. "Aye, Emmett. For ye don't want 'em meddlin' with yer crops and livestock!"

"No, we certainly wouldn't want that," Quin agreed.

Benjamin wrinkled his forehead in contemplation. "D'ye think that's what's happened the last few years then? That there's not enough people keepin' the hill folk happy and stop 'em from causin' mischief?"

"Perhaps there's something to it," Quin said, catching my eye.

No doubt there were indeed those who blamed Ireland's fairies for the famine that had wreaked havoc across the land these past two years, causing thousands of people to starve and succumb to disease. I compressed my lips briefly, trying to shake off the thought. It was far too late to appease any supernatural creatures now. We could only hope the worst was finally behind us.

Benjamin ran his fingers along one of the ribbons hanging from the tree. "In Dublin, they used t' decorate a pole on May Day," he said, dismissing his previous concerns. "I saw it the once."

"A pole? Don't they have any trees in Dublin?"

Benjamin scowled at Conor's remark. "O' course they have trees. They just used a pole, is all. Besides, the pole came from a tree, didn't it?"

Conor opened his mouth to respond but was cut off by Emmett, who seemed always to have a question about everything. "How'd they decorate it? Not with eggshells!" Emmett extended a hand to a delicate arrangement of painted eggshells adorning one of the whitethorn's branches, stopping just short of touching it.

Benjamin shook his head. "Mostly ribbons. But I did hear an old man say they used t' hang it with a pair o' breeches and a hat, and the like."

"Breeches and a hat?" Conor scoffed. "What sort o' decoration is that?"

"None at all. Twas the prize for the man who managed t' climb the pole."

"I'd 'ave climbed up there in no time," Emmett declared, puffing out his skinny chest.

Benjamin grinned. "Not if the pole was soaped up t' make it more difficult, like the old man said it was."

Emmett's eyes widened. "But they didn't climb the pole at all when you saw?"

"No. Although there was much of a hullaballoo around it even so."

"Go on," Conor said. "What'd they do then?"

Benjamin waved an airy hand, clearly enjoying the attention. "There was dancin' and races atop donkeys or on foot...oh and folks tryin' t' leap and run in sacks. But the best part"—Benjamin paused dramatically as Conor and Emmett leaned toward him in anticipation—"was when the pig was released."

"The pig?" Conor scrunched up his nose while Emmett's mouth dropped open.

"Aye," Benjamin said. "Let it loose right in the middle o' everyone, they did. For someone t' catch it. And they soaped up its tail, too, after shavin' it, t' make it more difficult."

Benjamin mimicked trying to grasp something slippery, stumbling forward with his hands outstretched. Conor whooped, setting off the others. Before long the three boys were rolling on the grass, laughing so hard that tears were streaming down their cheeks.

"Well, I don't think anyone's brought a greased pig today," Quin said drily.

This statement seemed vastly hilarious to the boys, for they set off again. Shaking his head in amusement Quin glanced toward the rest of the gathering, before giving me a questioning look. I nodded and followed him to our picnic blanket.

Looking at the sun I thought it was almost time to light the bonfires. When the boys joined us a short time later, they seemed of the same mind and started pestering Mr Connell, who was traditionally in charge of this important part of the proceedings. Having given his consent, Benjamin, Conor and Emmett eagerly herded the others to the edge of the field.

When everyone was gathered, an expectant hush fell among the onlookers. With his knack for showmanship Mr Connell chose this moment to slowly make his way down the space between the two piles of peat and firewood before turning toward us, the burning brand in his hand held high.

"*Bíonn an saol cadránta in amanna,*" he called out in a clear voice. "*Mar a chonaiceamar.*"

I leaned closer to Quin to translate. "Life can be cruel at times. As we have seen."

All around us, faces became drawn in remembrance of those who had suffered—and those who still did.

"*Ach níor chaill fear an mhisnigh riamh é.*"

"But while there's life there's hope."

"*Go gcuire Dia an t-ádh ort!*"

"May God put luck upon you!"

With this Mr Connell lowered the brand, first to one pile then the other, until flames flickered across the kindling. Two columns of smoke started rising against the darkening sky and I imagined the ancient Celts standing at just such a bonfire, chanting to their long-lost gods, asking them to bless their crops and livestock as the summer began.

"Will we be selectin' a May King and Queen?" I turned reluctantly away from the flames, toward Benjamin's eager voice. "I did see it done that time in Dublin."

"Why not. Who would you suggest?"

"I think Rupert ought t' be king," Emmett put in with a wide grin as he observed his brother, who was standing a short distance away next to a group of girls. By the look on the valet's face, he was rather enamoured with one of them, throwing her shy glances but quickly dropping his eyes when she looked his way.

"And Geraldine can be his queen!" Conor batted his stubby eyelashes and made kissing sounds with his lips, causing him and Emmett to erupt into laughter.

Benjamin frowned. "Why can't *I* be the king?"

"You?" Emmett eyed him critically, clearly finding him wanting.

"I suggested it!"

"D'ye really want t' be kissin' a *girl*?" Conor looked horrified at the thought.

"Who says I 'ave t' kiss anyone?"

"But a king needs a queen! And kissin's what married people do, ain't it?"

"Hmph. It's only pretend anyway!"

"And a good thing too," Emmett said. "Otherwise ye'd have t'...you know." His eyes widened and his mouth turned down in a grimace of distaste.

"Eugh." Benjamin seemed suddenly to remember they weren't alone for he threw me a sideways glance as his cheeks turned bright red. The other boys were soon similarly affected, and they quickly made mumbled excuses and hurried off.

My breath exploded as I let out the laughter I'd been struggling to hold in. "It seems they've picked up on a few of the finer points in life."

"It's not surprising," Quin said. "Emmett's already visited a brothel after all." He grinned, revealing the small dimple in his left cheek, before pulling me close and kissing me soundly.

"What a disgusting thing to do," I said once he'd released me, looking around surreptitiously.

"I can think of a few others that are even more disgusting."

"Can you, then?"

"Indeed. Would you care for a demonstration a little later?"

"I believe I would.—Oh look!"

Benjamin, Conor and Emmett had ambushed the unsuspecting Rupert and were dragging him toward the bonfires, chanting "All hail the May King!" at the top of their voices. The spectators soon took up the cry, leaving Rupert little choice but to wait—in obvious mortification—as they went to collect his queen. When he saw who the boys had singled out Rupert's cheeks went as red as Benjamin's had been a moment before. The latter seemed to have gotten over his disappointment at not being May King himself, instead looking rather relieved as he watched Rupert fidget and squirm.

I smiled as Queen Geraldine, who was of course the Miss O'Hagan Rupert had been admiring for some time, shily placed her hand in his. The valet's face took on a look of extreme astonishment before he suddenly beamed dreamily. He straightened his shoulders and puffed out his chest, seeming suddenly quite content with this turn of events.

Before long the newly elected May King and Queen were leading their subjects in a jolly dance, laughing as they skipped past the bonfires and the May bush, its bright ribbons fluttering in the breeze.

"A game, sire," a breathless voice called out from the crowd once the dancing had come to an end.

"A game?" Rupert stroked his chin in thought. He bent toward Geraldine and the two of them conferred for a moment. "Is there a bell to be found?" The king looked expectantly around but was met with shaking heads.

"Hmm."

"I'll fetch one, King Rupert." Emmett dashed forward and, before anyone could say a thing, had raced off toward the house.

While waiting for the boy to reappear, Rupert called together those men eager to participate in the impending contest. After some discussion an agreement was reached, and the group dispersed briefly once more. When they returned to their king, each man was carrying some kind of fabric which he used to bind his eyes—all except one, who was designated the bellringer and given the small silver bell Emmett presented a minute later, huffing and puffing with exertion.

The scene set, the men were soon stumbling across the empty field, hands outstretched as those with blindfolds sought to catch the bellringer. Whoops of delight from the onlookers accompanied their fumbling attempts, interrupted by the odd shout as one or two lurched too close to the fire. Nimble and quick, the young man with the bell dashed between his would-be-captors, becoming ever more confident as he evaded their grasping fingers, taunting them by ringing the bell behind their backs.

When one of the men finally seized the bellringer by an outstretched arm before he could escape, the crowd erupted into raucous applause. The victor roared in satisfaction as he yanked off his blindfold and snatched away the bell. Recognising Finnian, I laughed. Gangly and awkward, the footman hardly seemed capable of such a feat as he had shown.

Sweating freely but glowing with pride Finnian presented his trophy to the king. As he gave Rupert an elaborate bow, he glanced furtively at Geraldine, making me lift one brow. Finnian and Rupert had come to blows about a girl in the past. The two young men appeared to be getting on reasonably well since then and it would be a shame for their truce to come to an end once more.

Queen Geraldine, though, having courteously congratulated her champion, looked adoringly at her king. I hoped her affections would remain thus focused.

Finnian would simply have to look elsewhere.

Fortunately, affairs of the heart seemed far from his mind at present. Bolstered by his recent success Finnian appeared to feel himself invincible, for he soon gathered other young men as brave as he and set out in determination toward the bonfires. With an idea of what they were about I glanced at Quin, who shrugged, while across from me, Mrs O'Sullivan only shook her head.

The bonfires had burned down somewhat by now, but I held my breath as the first of the young men took a running leap over the flames. He cleared the pyre to whoops of delight and was quickly followed by the next gallant hero and the next.

As the crowd cheered on their champions, they were suddenly joined by a pair of four-legged beasts, driven by a whooping Emmett and his friends.

"It's the livestock, sir," Emmett yelled before having to come to a stop as the two mules stubbornly dug in their hooves, refusing to move any closer to the flames.

The boys pushed and pulled, cajoling and yelling, but to no avail. I opened my mouth to tell them they might have done better to select more compliant animals when one of the mules brayed loudly and leapt with all fours into the air, its back hooves narrowly missing Benjamin, who'd been standing by its hindquarters.

Benjamin stumbled and landed heavily on his backside as the mule shot through the narrow gap between the fires, its panic causing the second animal to join its fellow on its mad dash across the empty field. Before long they'd both disappeared over the hill, a trail of dust following in their wake.

With whoops of delight, Conor and Emmett turned to Benjamin, wide grins appearing on their faces as they helped him get to his feet. Conor thumped Benjamin's back in congratulations before they moved further away from the fire.

"What on earth did you do to that mule?" I asked as the boys came closer.

"Uh…"

I saw Benjamin place a hand behind his back and narrowed my eyes. "Benjamin?" I demanded, making him reluctantly withdraw his hand.

I gasped. "Is that a hatpin? Why would you bring a hatpin to a bonfire? Where did you even…? Oh, never mind," I muttered, watching the boys shuffle their feet.

Just then a hand shot out, grasping Benjamin by the shirtfront and yanking him off the ground.

"What d'ye do t' my mule?"

The outraged voice belonged to Mr Murphy. Usually grim, the tenant's face was now wreathed in fury, an expression that didn't improve one bit when Quin tried to persuade him to release his foe.

"The boys will collect the animals directly," Quin assured him, "and make sure they're in good health." Quin aimed a long, withering look at the three troublemakers, before turning expectantly to Mr Murphy.

The man snarled but finally let go of Benjamin's shirt, pushing the boy away from him in disgust. Giving each of them a final glare he stomped off, ignoring Quin and me.

"You might want to steer clear of Mr Murphy," Quin advised the boys drily. "He's not a particularly jovial fellow—nor a very forgiving one, I suspect," he added under his breath. I supposed he was remembering his confrontation with Mr Murphy about his poor treatment of his wife and children—Mary Murphy, who worked at the house as a maid, having let slip a few comments about her husband's abusive nature. Quin hadn't wanted to challenge the man but had given in when I'd pleaded with him to think about Murphy's children. As expected, Mr Murphy had been deeply affronted by Quin's thinly veiled implications and probably hadn't forgiven Quin for calling him out.

"Who does the second mule belong to?" Quin asked, visibly trying to maintain his composure.

The boys remained silent, fidgeting and shaking their heads while avoiding Quin's eye. He gave me an exasperated look.

"You'd best hope it's someone who remembers being young and reckless himself.—Now go fetch those poor animals and coax them back to their masters."

Needing no further encouragement, the boys dashed off across the field, huddling close together in unison.

Quin looked after them for a moment before shaking his head. "What is it we were saying recently about troublesome children?"

"That they can't be avoided?" I suggested, making Quin narrow his eyes.

I laughed. "You can't tell me you never caused any mischief as a child."

"Well…no." He cleared his throat. "But I never stuck a mule with a hatpin!"

"Well, that's something," I said, patting his arm.

"Hmph."

He tucked my hand into the crook of his elbow, and we started ambling toward the river. Sidestepping an energetic group of revellers testing their strength in wrestling contests, we passed Grandfather O'Reilly, who was sitting on a wooden stool, looking at the sky. Our greetings went unheard as the old man stared up at the waxing moon, sprouting grey eyebrows drawn together on his wrinkled forehead.

"Perhaps he's trying to divine the weather," I said softly.

Quin gave me a curious look.

"It's said one can predict the coming summer's weather by taking careful note of the sky and the moon at Bealtaine. The direction and the strength of the wind and the amount of rain, all are said to be signs of things to come."

Quin glanced at the hunched figure behind us before turning back to me and squeezing my hand. "Then let us hope the signs are most auspicious today."

I nodded silently. After repeated seasons of want, divining the future seemed to have its limitations.

A sudden shout caught my attention, just as Quin pulled me deftly out of the way of a horde of children that came barrelling in our direction. Brandishing long green strands like swords, they chased each other to and fro, making a hellish racket.

"Are those nettles?" Quin asked, eying the fronds dubiously.

"Och, aye, sir." Mrs O'Sullivan had come up next to us and cocked her head toward the spectacle. "The children collect 'em for the soup.—Ye must eat nettle soup thrice in May if ye want t' prevent the rheumatic in the comin' year," she informed Quin, waggling a finger in front of him.

"I see. Might I assume the soup will be on the menu tomorrow then?"

"O' course, sir! It is the first o' May after all."

"Hm." Quin seemed distracted, probably trying to recall if he'd had nettle soup every first of May since he'd arrived in Ireland. "Well, the children seem to be enjoying the collection method, at any rate. Although I wonder if any of the nettles will survive the battle."

"Och, aye, there'll be enough t' use." Mrs O'Sullivan smiled, her round cheeks plump like red apples. "Let the little ones have their fun."

Watching the children as they raced across the empty field, I suddenly had to stifle a yawn. Quin put an arm around me and kissed me on the forehead.

"Shall I take you back to the house?"

I started shaking my head but was interrupted by another jaw-cracking yawn.

"I suppose you'd better," I said in resignation. "Growing another person seems to be sapping me of my energy."

"I'm not surprised," Quin said as he started leading me away, nodding to Mrs O'Sullivan in parting. "Oh, I almost forgot." He turned abruptly, pulling me back toward the bonfires. "We mustn't forget the brand to relight our hearth fire."

I gave him an amused look. "I see you've resigned yourself to embracing Ireland's outlandish customs."

"This is one of the tamer ones," he said and chuckled, making me recall his scepticism when he'd first encountered some Irish beliefs—well-known and beloved traditions to me but strange and superstitious to an Englishman born and bred.

"If the fires hadn't all been put out before our departure I wouldn't have to bother," he said with a wink.

Having reached the bonfires, he quickly lit a brand before we bid farewell to the revellers milling about and got underway.

"I suppose there is something soothing about such a ritual," he took up our earlier conversation once we were back on the path to the house. "A rebirth of sorts, the ending of one season and the beginning of the next, symbolised by the flames."

"A transition one hopes will bring forth bountiful rewards."

"Indeed." Quin squeezed my hand. Anxious thoughts about the next harvest were never far away. "Will the bonfires be kept burning throughout the night?"

"Oh yes. Emmett will insist on it, having learned the Bealtaine fires are traditionally kept burning until sundown of the first of May. He told me so a few days ago, terribly concerned there wouldn't be enough fuel for such an undertaking."

"I suppose you assured him everyone on the estate would contribute."

"I did. But that didn't stop him from enlisting the help of Benjamin and Conor to scour the countryside for firewood for the rest of the day."

"So that's where they disappeared to. You know, it seems to me Emmett would make an excellent scholar, what with his inquisitive mind and all."

"An inquisitive mind, yes, but also a pair of legs that can hardly keep still.— But now that you mention it, I *can* imagine him clambering over ancient building sites, trying to dig up long-lost secrets. Perhaps he'll become a scholar of antiquities."

Quin smiled. "Perhaps. What I know for sure, though, is that Emmett will be the first to get his hands dirty when it comes to scattering the ashes from the bonfires over the fields."

I laughed. "You're right. Remind me to make sure the washtubs are placed outside so the boys can clean up before coming into the…h…h…"

The last word went under as I tried unsuccessfully to stifle yet another yawn. Fortunately, we'd reached the house by now. Quin led me through the door and deposited me on a small chair in the entrance hall.

"Wait here," he said, before dashing up the stairs with the burning brand in his hand.

I nodded mechanically, too tired to ask questions. When he returned a few minutes later, he swept me up into his arms.

"Oh," I said, nestling against his chest as he carried me to our room, where the freshly lit fire was crackling companionably.

He placed me gently on the bed and I closed my eyes, dimly aware of him removing my shoes. When he started unfastening my dress, I lifted one lid. "You wouldn't be taking advantage of me, would you?"

He chuckled. "Only if you want me to." One large, warm hand slid slowly up my stockinged calf and to my thigh, where it lightly caressed bare flesh.

"Hm." I closed my eyes again and pulled him toward me until his mouth met mine. I felt rather like I was underwater, my limbs slow and heavy, all sensation pinpointed to where Quin's skin touched mine. We swayed together on the tide as he undressed me slowly, a gentle brush of his lips here, a lingering touch there while his own clothes disappeared. He kissed my eyes, my cheeks, the hollow of my throat, his hands all the while caressing me as his body covered mine, until at last we both sighed, and I drifted peacefully off to sleep.

# 4.

WHEN I WOKE up the following morning—admittedly rather late—the house seemed strangely empty. Wandering into the kitchen I found Mrs O'Sullivan chopping the nettles for the promised soup.

"Where is everyone?" I asked after we'd greeted each other.

"Och, the boys are off tendin' the bonfires and the master was called out t' inspect a crumblin' bit o' wall on the McAndrews' cottage. Now it's no wonder t' me the wall is a' crumblin', the McAndrews' home bein' nought but an earthen hut, but all folks must choose their own way o' course."

Judging by the look on her face she clearly disapproved of the McAndrews' decision to remain in one of the old mud huts rather than build a new stone cottage upon Quin's arrival on the estate. I knew the McAndrews had forgone the more modern building as they'd felt it wasn't necessary for just the two of them when they'd only use it to sleep in but decided to change the topic.

"Ah, and where are Rupert and Finnian...and Denis?" I knew Mary wasn't coming in today as I'd given her the day off but had expected to encounter the three servants who resided in the manor house with us.

Mrs O'Sullivan gave me an amused look but suddenly yelped, pulling her hand away from the nettles. "Prickly beasties," she said, inspecting her thumb briefly before getting back to work. "I expect Denis is attendin' Rupert." I looked at her in some confusion, making her chuckle. "It seems our May King was a bit taken with his new role and drank too much o' the ale—and perhaps a few stronger things besides."

"Oh dear."

"Not t' be outdone by his rival, Finnian isn't farin' much better.—Although he's had t' empty the chamber pot but the once." She grinned, revealing a few missing teeth. "Mr Williams kindly allowed the two o' them t' spend the day in bed."

I laughed, although I couldn't help feeling a little sympathy for the two young men, what with the nausea that so often assaulted me these days. I hoped it would soon come to an end. Perhaps as a portend of just such an occurrence, I found myself feeling suddenly ravenously hungry.

"There's fresh baked bread on the table," Mrs O'Sullivan said, as if divining my thoughts, waving a meaty hand toward a covered tray. "With a crock o' butter and an egg just boiled."

Not needing further encouragement, I sat down at the table and uncovered my breakfast, my mouth watering at the sight. I closed my eyes in bliss a minute later, as I bit into the soft bread, revelling in the taste of the creamy butter slathered onto the thick slice.

"I could eat this entire loaf," I said between mouthfuls, sprinkling a bit of salt onto the butter.

Mrs O'Sullivan smiled as she placed a steaming teapot in front of me. "Go on then. But do eat the egg as well, it's good for the growin' babe."

Boiled egg and several slices of bread duly consumed and washed down with a sweet cup of tea, I thanked Mrs O'Sullivan and made my way across the entrance hall to the study. I sat down at the desk, where I spent some time perusing the ledgers. Having been involved in the running of my family's estate before my father's death I also took an active role in Glaslearg's affairs. Fortunately, Quin welcomed my assistance and we had become comfortable in spreading the workload between us.

With the beginning of summer, there were kitchen crops to be sowed, seedlings to be tended and livestock to be cared for. Battling encroaching weeds and banishing destructive pests throughout the growing season meant the farmer's job was never done—even more so in the years since the first failed potato harvest, when every ounce of edible produce gleaned during harvesting could mean the difference between life and death.

I shook my head to rid myself of such maudlin thoughts. Unlike many other estates, Glaslearg had weathered the storm in relative comfort. With a good acreage of arable land given over to the growth of wheat and other grains—and our willingness to share with those in need—none of our tenants had gone hungry, even when their own fields had failed to produce a single edible potato.

I got up to look through some of the records on the shelf beside the desk. While Quin and I agreed that it was unquestionably our duty to assist those living on our estate in times of need, the last few years had been cutting into Glaslearg's finances. Giving away a good portion of our own crops instead of selling them on the British market meant a loss of income. But with hardly enough food grown to feed their own families, much less any surplus to sell at the local market, the tenants simply had no money to give us in return—although most insisted on repaying us in any way they could.

I ran my finger down a column of numbers and sighed, reminding myself we were still faring better than many.

Three brisk knocks on the door made me lift my head. "Come in," I called as I placed the ledger on the desk.

I had been expecting a friendly face and compressed my lips when I was instead presented with Mr Murphy. True to form he wore a deep scowl, which didn't improve when his eyes flicked across the room and found only me.

"I'm lookin' for Mr Williams," he barked in Gaelic.

"Good day to you, Mr Murphy," I responded in the same language, forcing myself to give him a pleasant look. "Can I help you?"

"Hmph. When is he back?"

"I'm sure I can assist you just as well as my husband," I said, ignoring the question.

"Will ye do somethin' about them devils then?" he demanded.

Realising he must be referring to Benjamin and the other boys and the previous night's incident with the mule, I tried to assuage his concerns. "I'm sure Mr Williams will give them a stern talking to, if he hasn't done so already."

"A talkin' to? Ha! A good beatin' is what they need!"

I took a deep breath, trying to calm my rapidly rising temper. "I realise you're upset, Mr Murphy, and rightfully so, but please be assured the matter will be dealt with and that the children will be made to understand they behaved inappropriately."

Mr Murphy growled. "Posh! A good beatin' is what they need, I tell ye. It's the only way t' deal with the likes o' them!"

"Just as you like to deal with your own children?"

As soon as I said the words, I knew I'd made a mistake. Murphy snarled, his face going purple as he lunged toward me, one hand curled into a fist. I took a hasty step back and came up hard against the edge of the desk, toppling backward as my heart leaped into my throat. It started hammering violently when Murphy lifted his fist and leaned over me.

"How I deal with me own children is none o' your concern!" he snarled, spittle flying.

I swallowed heavily but made myself lift my chin. Mustering every ounce of resolve I had, I started pushing myself up from the desk, forcing him to move back. Our eyes locked and for a moment I thought he really would hit me, smashing his fist into my face. And in that instant, I was hurtled back into a dim stable as I fought for my life, Martin Doyle's knuckles bruising my flesh and his existence marring my soul.

Time seemed to stop along with my breathing until at long last, Murphy stepped back.

My legs wobbled and would barely hold me upright, but I straightened slowly to my full height—which was one or two inches above his own. "I will ask you to leave now, sir," I said, trying to suppress the tremor in my voice.

Murphy's lips pulled back into a grimace before he spun away and stormed toward the door.

As soon as he was gone, I collapsed onto the chair in front of the desk, my body shaking in reaction. I gripped the armrests, wiling myself to breathe, for I was gasping in shallow spurts that were making my head spin. Over and over, I felt the heavy blows of fists upon my face and the cold hard edge of a knife pressed against my throat, my chest filling with terror in remembrance of being trapped by my brother's killer. Black spots appeared before my eyes and I leaned forward, letting my head hang down between my knees.

Slowly, slowly, my breathing returned to normal, but I stayed curled into a ball, trying to banish all thoughts of that dreadful day and to focus on the here and now.

"Alannah?"

Somewhere far away I heard Quin calling my name.

"Alannah?" This time his voice was filled with concern. "What is it?"

A hand gripped my shoulder and I flinched. He let go and kneeled before me, reaching out tentatively to stroke my hair.

"Is it the baby?" he asked in little more than a whisper.

I shook my head and heard a deep intake of breath. Quin cautiously lifted me until I was sitting upright. Seeing my face, he pulled me into his arms, one hand running up and down my back.

"What happened?"

"I was...remembering. Doyle..."

His hand stilled. "Ah.—It was like...you were there again, in that place..." His voice sounded distant, and I glanced at his face. His eyes were hooded, like he was seeing something that wasn't there.

"It's happened to you?"

"It has," he said softly. "I wake sometimes, from dreaming, sure I'm on the battlefield. The enemy coming at me, so slowly I should surely be able to save myself...but I never can."

"Does it ever stop?"

He was silent for a heartbeat. "I'll let you know if it ever does."

His arms tightened around me once more and I closed my eyes, leaning against his chest.

"You are safe now. He is dead." He kissed me on the forehead and stroked the back of my head. "Remember that in those moments."

I nodded silently as the last of my dread drifted away and I felt myself anchored to the present once more. Quin shifted his leg and I realised he was sitting on the carpet, leaning against the desk with me on his lap.

I ran a hand along his cheek. "And you remember you survived—to come to Ireland and to find me."

His mouth turned up at the corners before descending onto mine. "It's a journey I would repeat a hundredfold," he whispered against my lips.

"Do you think we'll sit on the floor in each other's arms once the baby is here?" I asked a moment later.

Quin chuckled. "I would hope so! And I doubt the baby would object.—Although I'm not so sure about the staff." He glanced toward the door, which was standing half open.

"It's a good thing they're otherwise occupied then," I said, nevertheless sliding off his lap.

"Are you alright now?" Quin asked, his eyes searching mine as he helped me to my feet. I nodded and he smiled, giving my hand a brief squeeze. "Did Mr Murphy come by the house earlier? He stormed past me on my way back, looking even more bad-tempered than usual."

"He did. He was looking for you."

"To complain about his mule, no doubt.—I suppose he demanded punishment?"

"Yes. He insisted the boys deserve a good beating."

"And perhaps they do.—Although not likely the kind Mr Murphy would administer." Quin frowned and I flushed, recalling what I'd foolishly said to the man. "What is it? What did he say to you?"

"It's more what I said to him." Quin lifted one brow. "I implied he...um...likes to take his anger out on his children."

"Well you're not wrong but..." Quin stopped talking when I looked down, refusing to meet his eyes. "Alannah? What happened? What did he do?"

"He um..."

Quin gripped my arms, sudden fury rolling off him in waves. "Did he lay his hands on you?" he hissed.

"Not exactly."

"But he threatened to. Is that it?"

I glanced up at Quin's face. His jaws were tensed, muscles bunching in his cheeks. "Is that what made you think of Doyle?"

I dropped my eyes once more, making Quin breathe in heavily through his nose. Abruptly, he spun away from me and started heading toward the door.

"Where are you going?"

"To throw Murphy off my land!"

"But you can't!"

"Of course I can! I'm the landlord."

"Quin, wait!" I followed him to the door and grasped his forearm. It was hard as steel, his hand tensed into a tight fist. "He has a contract, legally binding paperwork. You can't evict him as long as he pays the rent."

Quin snorted. "No magistrate would rule in his favour. I have every right to evict the man when he's threatened my wife!"

"But Quin..." I tugged hard on his arm before he could step into the entrance hall.

"What?"

"You can't evict him!"

"Alannah..."

"Think of Mary! Think of the children! If you evict Mr Murphy, you evict all of them." Quin's nostrils flared as he looked down at me before glancing back toward the entryway. "Where will they go? How will they live? Especially now..."

Quin pulled his arm out of my grasp. "So you expect me to do nothing?" he growled.

I shook my head. "Talk to him, shout at him...hit him even, if you must.—But don't condemn the innocent!"

He was silent for a moment, his lips pressed together into a tight line. "I'll go *talk* to him then," he said at last before disappearing out the door.

I watched him go, a prickling feeling starting at the back of my neck. The front door closed behind him with a dull thump, and I wondered what would come of this day in the end.

BY THE TIME Quin arrived at the Murphy's cottage he was even more enraged than when he'd left Alannah standing in the study, pleading for mercy.

How dare the man threaten his wife? After all they'd done for him. Not only had Quin assisted the family in building a stone cottage and ensured they were secure in their tenancy, but he'd hired Mrs Murphy to work at the manor house to help her husband pay off his debts. And when the blight arrived in Ireland Quin hadn't hesitated to share the estate's produce with the Murphys, whose own potato harvest hadn't been sufficient to feed the family.

"Ungrateful sod," Quin muttered to himself as he reigned in Gambit and slid off the saddle.

There was no-one tending the field and so he marched toward the door but paused before knocking, trying to calm his temper by taking a few deep breaths.

He couldn't hear any noises coming from inside the cottage and wondered where the children were. Perhaps Mary had taken them on an errand on her day off, Quin thought. In fact, he fervently hoped so, as it would make the confrontation with Mr Murphy all the easier if the two of them were left alone.

Then again, the presence of Murphy's family might deter Quin from throttling the man.

"Hmph." He rapped briskly on the door, glaring at the wood under his knuckles.

A scuffling on the other side told him someone was home, and he waited in growing annoyance until the door was finally opened in response to his third knock.

Mr Murphy stood in his shirtsleeves, looking none too pleased at the interruption to his day. When he recognised his visitor, uneasiness flickered briefly across the man's face, but he soon resumed his usual scowl, stepping forward to block the doorway and crossing his arms over his chest.

"Mr Murphy, as a paying tenant on my estate you have the right to voice your grievances," Quin began without preliminaries, "but if you ever threaten my wife again in any way, I shall throw you off my land." Quin purposefully loomed over the shorter man, his eyes boring into Murphy's. "You will stay away from her and deal only with me in the future. Do you understand?"

A muscle in Murphy's jaw twitched but he didn't say anything.

"It is only because of my wife's concern for your family that I am permitting you to stay here," Quin continued.

Murphy's nostrils flared in obvious fury as their eyes locked in silent battle.

The sound of voices broke the tension and Quin glanced toward the edge of the cottage, where Mary and the children were just emerging. Spotting the two of them in the doorway a look of dread flashed across Mary's features. She murmured something to the children, and they quickly scuttled off.

"Mr Williams," she said cautiously, "is anything amiss?" Her eyes flickered between her husband and her landlord, her face pale and drawn.

Before Quin could respond Murphy barked something to her in Gaelic, causing her to hunch her shoulders. She dropped her eyes and gave Quin a brief curtsy before inching past Murphy into the house. The sight made Quin clench his hands into fists. "Let me remind you, Mr Murphy, it is out of concern for your *wife and children* that I am allowing you to continue calling Glaslearg your home—against my better judgement! I sincerely hope you remember that."

Without another word Quin turned his back on Murphy and stalked toward his horse. He swung into the saddle seething with anger, not only at Murphy himself but also at Alannah, for insisting he not evict the wretched man when he deserved nothing less.

He urged Gambit to a gallop and raced along the path. Instead of heading directly to the manor house, he veered toward the river, pounding along its bank until at last, he felt some of his fury fade away. Breathing almost as heavily as the horse he slowed to a walk, consciously taking note of his surroundings for the first time.

It was a beautiful day, with the sun shining down from a sky scattered with wispy clouds. Birds and insects flitted through the air and the season's new growth dotted the landscape with every imaginable shade of green. The reeds on the riverbank swayed in the breeze, while the shallow water bubbled alongside.

It was imminently peaceful, and Quin finally felt himself relax.

As much as he wanted to see the back of Mr Murphy, he knew Alannah was right. Mary and the children didn't deserve to suffer for his sins. Quin would simply have to tolerate the man and hope he'd keep his temper under control.

He sighed, doubting Murphy would do any such thing. He could only pray the man would refrain from using his fists.

# 5.

DESPITE THE UNPLEASANT scene in the study on the morning after the Bealtaine festival I managed quite quickly to push Robert Murphy and his unsavoury character to the back of my mind. Mary and the children seemed well enough—and I hoped they would stay that way—and we had little to do with the man on a daily basis, for which I was grateful.

And so, as that year's summer began I felt hopeful about the future. The weather remained fair, not plagued with the almost constant rainfall of '45, when the potato harvest had failed for the first time. Although the living conditions of Ireland's poor were unlikely to improve much in the near future we could at least hope for a successful harvest this season to ease their burden.

The unmitigated disaster of a third successive failure could scarcely be imagined.

I did my best to keep such thoughts at bay, marvelling instead at the changes to my body as the baby grew and started turning somersaults inside of me as it prepared to come into the world in a few months' time. I still worried, occasionally, about the baby's health but with no signs to the contrary I chose to believe everything would be well—and managed to hold onto that belief for most of the time.

The birth, too, flitted frequently across my mind. I wondered what it would be like to experience such a life-altering event, sometimes with a sense of eagerness at meeting my son or daughter, sometimes with a sense of panic at all that could go wrong. But as my abdomen swelled with life I managed to keep these fears under control as well.

Quin's father sent his well-wishes from London, as did Quin's friends from Dublin, while Mrs O'Sullivan clucked over me like a mother hen, with the other servants not far behind. My heart lifted at the thought of the many people who cared for us, including my former tutor, Mr Henderson, who also lived in London.

I picked up the flat, rectangular package included in the letter from Mr Henderson that had arrived that morning, turning it over in my hands. It was wrapped in paper, with the words *Fry's Chocolate* stamped on top. With a smile I set it aside, looking forward to having a cup of drinking chocolate with my breakfast the next day.

Knowing my fascination with the natural world Mr Henderson's heartfelt congratulations on the impending birth of our first child were followed by a list of discoveries he'd learned of over the last few months. Settling comfortably into my drawing room seat I was soon immersed in a wondrous world.

*It is the most marvellous thing,* he wrote. *A new planet has been discovered! The German astronomer Johann Gottfried Galle made the extraordinary discovery after the planet's existence had been predicted by the man's French compatriot, Urbain Le Verrier, some time before. That one could do either of those two things is simply a marvel to me! Imagine predicting the presence and position of a celestial body using only mathematics. How, I ask you? How is such a thing possible? And the telescopic power required to identify a planet thousands upon thousands of miles away... The mind boggles! But back to this most wondrous of discoveries: It is said the planet is seen as a small blue-green dot by telescope and has thus been named Neptune after the Roman God of the sea.*

*How many more planets may yet be discovered, I wonder? And will I still be alive to hear of them? Ah, but if only we could be granted immortality, if for no other reason than to learn more of the universe's splendid secrets!*

*Speaking of which, I was fascinated to hear more about the substance ether—which my friend Sir Linklater (I'm sure you'll recall him, the fellow with the dangerously sharp points to his moustache) told us about when you visited me in London. Apparently, the ether has now been successfully used by several surgeons during operations, and seems most effective at putting patients to sleep. With the patients immobile and their pain dulled, the surgeons are far better able to perform their task, making for far more successful surgeries—and considerably less discomfort for the person whose flesh is being cut into, I would imagine!*

*Oh, what wonders surround us every day! I could shout it from the rooftops, as I know you will well understand, my dear Alannah, the beauty of the world around us and all we can learn from it having ever fascinated the two of us.*

*But even the man-made world holds much fascination, of course. Take the recent invention of a hydraulic crane by my countryman William Armstrong, for instance. Such a contraption is likely to have an enormous impact on the world, once it is employed in hoists at docks and machinery in mines to ease the work of labourers. Whether the crane may yet replace the work of these labourers (like so many other inventions already have), making the men's usefulness obsolete and leaving their pockets empty is a debate I shall enjoy having with you when we see each other again.*

*Many labourers must have been employed, though, to complete the building of a two-mile-long railway bridge over the Venetian Lagoon in Italy, which I read about just a few days ago. A most extraordinary feat, indeed. If such developments continue the entire world will surely soon be covered in railway tracks and roads, crisscrossing the countryside, allowing travellers to go speedily wherever they wish. While such ease of travel is an exciting prospect I do wonder about the impact the ever-expanding built-up areas will have on the natural world.*

*But such is the price of progress!*

*I hope I have given you some stimulating topics to contemplate over the next few days while you go about your business.*

*I have included with my missive a bar of Fry's Chocolate, which is not, as you no doubt will have thought, intended for drinking but rather for eating in its current form. It is a newly invented moulded chocolate bar that I assure you is well worth the effort required for its procurement (which was considerable!). I suspect you will find the taste most delectable (as I do) and would advise you to sample the delicacy without delay!*

I set aside the letter, thinking perhaps I ought to do as I was told. I picked up the bar of chocolate, fascinated as much by it as by everything else Mr Henderson had written. Having indeed believed the chocolate to be intended for drinking—drinking chocolate being the only type of chocolate I was familiar with—I slowly unwrapped the paper, revealing a dark brown bar moulded into neat squares within. I broke off a piece with a satisfying snap and placed it delicately on my tongue. The intense but sweet taste of chocolate exploded in my mouth and I closed my eyes in bliss. Leaning back in the armchair I thought I might be tempted to go to the ends of the earth to obtain more of this heavenly delight.

When I opened my eyes a short time later Quin was standing at the entrance to the drawing room, wearing an amused expression.

"Whatever that is I want some of it," he said, coming closer and nodding toward the slab of chocolate.

I offered him a piece and he inspected it briefly before putting it into his mouth.

"Mm. That *is* delicious, although perhaps not quite as delicious as your face might have led me to believe." He grinned, dimple showing. "When you look like that, it's usually because of something *I've* done…and done well."

I laughed, giving Quin a sly look. "Do I dare compare the two?"

"I would advise against it!" Looking slightly affronted he bent down and kissed me thoroughly, leaving me a little breathless.

"Point made. But you must admit this chocolate is delectable. Much richer than the drinking variety."

"It is that. No doubt all of London will soon be salivating after these bars and *Fry's* will have a hard time meeting the demand."

"If that isn't already the case," I said, recalling Mr Henderson's purported difficulties in obtaining this particular sample. "But it's a good problem for a manufacturer to have, isn't it?"

"I suppose so. But what will you do, now that you've had a taste?"

"I'll have to beg Mr Henderson and your father to send me some more," I said and laughed.

"Ah, so Mr Henderson sent you this sinful delight." Quin's eyes twinkled before inspecting the bar of chocolate once more. "And how is your former tutor?" he asked, setting the slab aside.

"He's well. And he's told me about the most fascinating discoveries."

I started getting up and Quin gave me a hand. Once I stood in front of him he cocked his head, looking me over.

"What is it?"

"Pregnancy suits you," he said, a soft look on his face. "You're glowing."

"For now." I ran a hand over my belly. "Until I'm the size of a house and careening into everything in my path."

Quin chuckled and offered me his arm. "I doubt it will come to that. Now come along. You can tell me all about these fascinating discoveries over our dinner."

# 6.

"WE'VE BEEN INVITED to a house party," Quin said two weeks later, having retired to the drawing room at the end of the day. He'd just left the study, where he'd gone through several letters that had arrived late in the day.

"A house party?" Alannah looked surprised as she sat down in one of the wingchairs next to Quin.

"It's when the well-to-do gather at someone's country house," he said, "to spend an inordinate amount of time in frivolous pursuits."

Alannah gave him a long-suffering look. "I am familiar with the concept, thank you. I simply can't recall the last time I went to a house party.—Whose house are we meant to be visiting in any case?"

"The family of Ollie's new bride."

"Oh."

A speculative expression appeared on Alannah's face as she contemplated the prospect of spending a few days with Oliver Penhale's wife. They'd attended the wedding of Quin's friend the year before and while Alannah had declared herself happy for the couple, she'd had some reservations about the bride. Although Anne Cartwright professed herself to have fallen madly in love with unassuming Ollie, that hadn't stopped her from being rather free with her flirtations elsewhere, including on her wedding day—behaviour that had struck Alannah, and Quin himself, as odd.

"And where is this family home?"

"Near Kingscourt, on the Meath border."

"That's about halfway to Dublin from here."

"So Ollie assured me.—Still, perhaps I should decline the invitation."

"Decline the invitation?" Alannah repeated, surprised. "Why ever would you do that?"

"It's only that…" Quin broke off, his eyes dropping to the small swell of her abdomen, making Alannah give him an irritated look.

"I am not ill, Quin, only pregnant. I'm sure a few hours' travel will do me no harm."

Quin nodded but was still unsure.

"Any number of pregnant women are continuing with their daily lives as we speak," Alannah insisted, her voice strongly tinged with irritation.

"I don't want anything to happen to you," Quin said. When Alannah opened her mouth to object, he leaned forward and took her hands in his, squeezing her fingers lightly. "Or the baby."

He held her eyes for a moment as understanding flashed across her features. With the numerous miscarriages she'd had before Quin couldn't help but worry.

"Nothing will happen to us," Alannah said softly, gently caressing the fabric of her skirts. "I know it."

Quin gave her a crooked smile before pulling her out of her chair and onto his lap. He kissed the top of her head as she leaned against him.

"I'm sure you're looking forward to seeing your friends," Alannah said after a short silence, running a hand over his chest. "I assume Ham and Archie will be there too?"

"They will."

Quin couldn't deny he was indeed eager to see his friends. They'd met at officers' training years before and had kept in touch ever since, even when Quin had been stationed in India and gone to war in China. He'd visited the three of them several times in Dublin, Oliver Penhale, Hamilton Wolstenholme and Archibald Bellinger having been sent to the military outpost there some time before Quin's own arrival in Ireland.

"I wonder what the Cartwright estate is like," Alannah said.

Quin shrugged. "All I've been told is that the manor is called Cornac House. I don't know much about the Cartwright's circumstances…although their townhouse in Dublin is certainly nice enough."

"Will you take Rupert?" Alannah leaned back a little so she could look up at him.

"I suppose so. A man must travel with his valet, not so?" He grinned and stuck out his chin.

"And a woman must travel with her lady's maid?"

"Hm." The only maid they had was Mary, who performed any number of services around the house, and for Alannah. She could hardly come with them to the house party, though, with her own family to take care of—even would her disgruntled husband allow it. Before Quin could think of an alternative Alannah continued.

"What about Emmett? Will we take him too?"

"Why not? He'll certainly be up for it. And we may as well arrive in style, with an entire entourage by our side—as befits a future baron and his baroness." Quin chuckled at the thought, making Alannah smile.

"Oh, I forgot to ask: when is the house party supposed to take place?"

"In three weeks." He looked toward the double doors that led out onto the portico and the last rays of sunshine that illuminated the lawn. "It looks to be turning into a pleasant summer. Let's hope it will stay that way for a few more weeks."

# 7.

WITH ALL THERE was to do on the estate in early summer—much like throughout most of the year—everyone was busy over the next few weeks. Many of our tenants had been hired to work Glaslearg's fields alongside their own, and the land was bustling with activity. The crops needed to be weeded and fertilised, the small herd of sheep needed to be sheered and dipped against parasites and disease, and the hay needed to be cut and set out to dry along with the peat—all this in addition to the daily chores of milking cows, collecting fresh eggs, mucking out stalls and the like.

Quin helped where he was needed, not afraid to get his hands dirty, although he was mostly involved in overseeing the work being done, which was a role he both enjoyed and was good at. With Glaslearg having no hired overseer to take the reins in his absence we did wonder how the estate would fare during the impending house party. We quickly realised, though, that there was little need for concern. Glaslearg's tenants had been caring for their own fields their entire lives and didn't need constant supervision, and Mrs O'Sullivan was more than capable of running the household. We had no doubts she and our other staff members could deal with any small difficulties that might arise during the week or so we would be away.

With the estate humming and thriving around us the days flew by at an alarming rate. Before I knew it I found myself in the carriage as we made our way to the Cartwright estate at the end of June.

The ride was comfortable enough to begin with, but several hours later, the rattling of the wheels over country lanes was starting to take its toll. By the time we finally arrived at Cornac House my back was aching terribly. I couldn't prevent a small groan from escaping my lips as I stepped down onto the driveway, making Quin give me a worried look. I waved off his concern while trying to stretch my tense muscles without his notice. Fortunately, several liveried servants had arrived to greet us, diverting his attention.

I looked around the courtyard and found I had to make a real effort not to gape at the opulence of my surroundings. The Cartwright's house—if such a term could be used to describe the place—was an impressive three-storey edifice with a multitude of chimneys and even a small tower with crenelations at the top. A broad staircase led to the front entrance from the courtyard, which featured an array of blooming flowerbeds with several statues and a sizeable fountain that bubbled enthusiastically at the newly arrived guests.

While Rupert and John assisted the estate's servants with removing our luggage from the carriage roof, I could hear Emmett and Benjamin whispering excitedly behind me. After some discussion Quin and I had decided to also take Benjamin along to the house party, thinking Emmett would enjoy the company. The boys had been inside the carriage with us, while the valet and the groom had ridden up front, John having taken the reins. With Emmett and Benjamin together there was, of course, the danger of the boys getting up to mischief and I hoped they wouldn't be so overwhelmed by their circumstances that they'd forget themselves entirely and do something foolish. Seeing the delight on their faces, though, I couldn't regret our decision to bring them on what would no doubt be a great adventure for them.

Turning my attention to the bustling activity that had sprung up around me I realised several people were waiting to receive Quin and me. The first of these was an older gentleman whose mouth was turned down at the corners, whom I recognised as Mr Cartwright, the father of the erstwhile bride and owner of the estate. He quickly remedied his expression as we got closer, greeting us heartily. Quin thanked him for the invitation, which the man acknowledged with a quick nod and an easy smile. When he glanced at his son-in-law, though, who'd come up next to him, the scowl reappeared on the older man's face. It was gone in an instant, but I wondered about the relationship between the two.

I was distracted from my thoughts when Oliver Penhale and Hamilton Wolstenholme rushed forward to thump Quin on the back and kiss my hand. Seeing the joy on Quin's face I felt my own spirits soar in his friends' company. In another moment I found myself embraced by a bear of a man as he bussed me enthusiastically on the cheek. I laughed when he released me, looking fondly up at the towering form of Archibald Bellinger while he grinned from ear to ear. Never a stickler for proprieties Archie ignored the disapproving looks of some of those around us as he greeted Quin and me warmly.

"And congratulations on the happy news," he said with a wiggle of his eyebrows and a knowing look at Quin.

I felt my cheeks flush but thanked him graciously before darting a glance at Mr Cartwright, who didn't seem terribly pleased—either with the display of affection he'd just witnessed or Archie's reference to my pregnancy, a topic upper class ladies and gentlemen did not broach in public. Ignoring Mr Cartwright's expression, I turned toward the ladies who were waiting for my attention.

"Mrs Penhale," I greeted Ollie's wife, a voluptuous redhead with a dusting of freckles across her nose.

I wasn't sure what sort of reception to expect and was a little surprised when she clasped my hands. "Oh, it's Anne, please. We're practically family." She lifted her chin toward Quin and the other men, who were talking animatedly among themselves, not caring the least that they stood in the middle of a courtyard.

I smiled and agreed we could perhaps forgo the formalities before turning to Anne's mother and younger sister, whom I'd met briefly at the wedding. The two women looked nothing like Anne, both being willowy and dark-haired, almost identical in appearance aside from their age. And while they greeted me courteously enough, there appeared to be little of Anne's lively personality in her female relations.

Miss Colleen Cartwright expressed herself delighted to see me again, all the while looking me over from the top of my head to the bottom of my shoes in such an unashamed assessment of my physical attributes that it took me aback. When her green eyes—the only feature she shared with her sister—finally met mine I gave her a long look, making her purse her lips but show no other signs of having committed a social blunder.

"I hear you live in the country, Mrs Williams," she said, her nose wrinkling at the thought.

"We do, yes," I responded brightly, making her titter.

"How lovely."

"It is lovely, I agree." I waved a hand at our surroundings. "Is it not?"

"Well yes, certainly, for the weekend or a short holiday. But who would choose to live here all the time, so far from society?—But of course we must all do as we prefer." She gave me a condescending look that required me to take a deep breath.

Fortunately, I was saved from answering by the appearance of Quin, who performed a neat bow before greeting the Cartwright women. Colleen's demeanour changed visibly as she assessed Quin's form, leaning toward him and offering her hand. When he released her, she smiled, batting her eyelashes.

"I'm charmed, Mr Williams."

"Likewise," Quin said, before throwing me a brief glance.

"Come, let me show you to your rooms," Anne said, stepping in front of her sister, whose features drew together at the interruption.

A flash of annoyance rippled across Anne's face, but she quickly hid it as she started leading Quin and me toward the house. Steering us through numerous halls and corridors she chatted merrily about the history of the manor, which had been in her family for generations, handed down to her father from her great grandfather, the Viscount Egglestone. With more money and properties than he knew what to do with the viscount had bequeathed Cornac House to his youngest daughter's son, the present Mr Cartwright, whose own father had also left him a fine townhouse in Dublin, thus ensuring the Cartwright family lived in comfort.

Anne paused, giving me a bright smile at this conclusion, compelling me to congratulate her on her family's success. She thanked me kindly before coming to a stop in front of a particular door, announcing we'd reached our quarters.

And fine quarters they were, indeed, the suite consisting of a sizeable bedroom and private sitting room, as well as a separate dressing room with all the trimmings. Our luggage had already been brought up and Anne bid us farewell, inviting us to join the family and remaining guests for dinner a little later.

I sighed gratefully as I sank into a wingchair once she'd left, glad to have some time to rest after the long journey. Running my fingers over the fabric on the armrests I noticed it was a little frayed.

Quin touched my arm, a look of concern on his face. "Are you alright?"

I nodded. "Just a little tired."

"Why don't you lie down?"

"I think I might," I said, suppressing a yawn.

He gave me a hand to pull me up from the chair. Seeing me arch my back in discomfort he dug his knuckles into the muscles along my spine, making me moan.

"If you carry on like that, we won't make it down to dinner," Quin murmured close to my ear.

I laughed. "We still have a little time."

He gave me a speculative look before shaking his head in regret. "Rest," he said, leading me toward the bed. "We can always continue a little later."

Too tired to argue I kicked off my shoes and lay down. Quin pulled a woollen blanket over me, and I closed my eyes, drifting off almost immediately.

It seemed like only a moment later when a gentle touch on my arm woke me. I blinked up at Quin in some confusion, trying to remember where I was.

"It's time to get dressed for dinner," he said, giving me a hand to sit up.

I yawned as he rang for one of the maids to assist me, ignoring my protestations that I was perfectly capable of dressing myself. Since I had brought no lady's maid—not having such a personage at my disposal—our hosts had insisted I make use of one of theirs. Relenting, I went to the dressing table, where I sat down. There was a thin crack across the mirror, which made the top of my head look a little distorted, and I blinked owlishly at my reflection for a minute or two.

When the maid arrived my lingering tiredness finally drifted away, and I found I was quite looking forward to spending time with Quin's friends. I was also curious to observe Ollie and his wife after what I'd witnessed at the wedding—although I wasn't so sure about interacting with the rest of her family.

It was thus with a mixture of anticipation and apprehension that I descended to the dining room on Quin's arm. We were greeted cordially by our hosts—Mr Cartwright seeming to be in a better mood than earlier—before the assemblage was led to the table, which was lavishly set. I noticed, though, that the carefully polished furniture was nicked here and there and that the heavy drapes at the windows were faded, which nevertheless did little to diminish the opulence of the room.

As befitted a proper dinner party the men were attired in fine dress coats while the women dazzled in silk and lace, none more so than the beautiful Miss Colleen Cartwright, who was seated across from me. Clearly used to being admired the young woman pouted and tittered to best effect, confident in her role as the centre of attention.

I plastered a smile to my face as I listened to her prattle on between courses. While I, too, could appreciate her handsome appearance, I had realised within moments that there was little substance underneath.

"Tell me, Mrs Williams," she said at one point, "have you ever visited London?"

"I have, yes. My husband and I travelled there last year to visit his father."

At this declaration Colleen seemed on the verge of clapping her hands together in glee but managed to restrain herself just in time. "How wonderful! How fortunate you are, to be married to an Englishman!" She eyed Quin admiringly before looking back at me.

I gave a surprised laugh, having never heard such a sentiment expressed before—in fact, the opposite had been true as far as my brother was concerned. Loathful of English interference and oppression throughout the course of Ireland's history Kieran had deeply resented Quin for his Englishness at the start of their acquaintance. It was only shortly before Kieran's death that the two of them had developed a genuine affection for each other.

I suddenly had to swallow heavily as I tried to push the thought of Kieran's loss aside.

"You must tell me everything!" Colleen demanded, oblivious to my momentary disquiet. "For I have not had the pleasure of visiting that great city myself."

Her face drooped at this terrible lack before perking up again as I started telling her about our time in London, regaling her with a few anecdotes I thought she might find amusing. She was particularly interested in local fashion trends and everything to do with high society, insisting I tell her precisely which members of the peerage I'd been privileged enough to lay eyes upon. With the list being disappointingly short, though, the conversation soon ran its course, leaving us stranded in silence while the others chatted on around us.

I was just trying to think of something else to say when a frown appeared between her shapely black brows.

"Why *do* they discuss such a topic at dinner?" she asked, darting a glance toward Quin and Archie, who were lamenting the failure of the public works.

"Perhaps because it's a topic that affects all of us living in Ireland?" I suggested.

Her eyes widened. "The public works? Affect *me*?" She gave a small shake of her head. "What could any of that possibly have to do with *me*?"

I opened my mouth to answer but realised it would be a futile exercise. Miss Cartwright seemed to be a woman intimately involved with her own interests. She clearly did not consider the suffering of others to be her concern, even when it affected a large portion of the Irish populace. Indeed, I doubted she even knew what the public works entailed, much less that the system was collapsing because the need for work and pay had long since outstripped what prime minister Lord John Russell and the British government could provide.

With hundreds of thousands of Irishmen desperate to support their families under spiralling food prices, the relief works had been costing the British millions, but to little effect—already malnourished, and often ill, the labourers staggered to work every day, only to push themselves to the brink of collapse performing menial tasks to make a pitiful and wholly inadequate wage that was often late in being paid. Even when bad weather curtailed the men's ability to perform their given tasks, most insisted on continuing anyway, despite the fact that they'd get only a fraction of their pay under such circumstances—any minimal amount was better than not getting paid at all if they did not work. Realising the system was deeply flawed and no longer sustainable, the relief commission had ordered the dismissal of thousands of workers across Ireland.

"Nothing, I'm sure," I said in a soothing voice, making Miss Cartwright visibly brighten.

Anne, who was sitting a little further down the table, caught my eye, and I hoped my rapidly growing disdain for her sister didn't show on my face.

"Mrs Williams…Alannah, I had meant to compliment you earlier on your gown," she said. "The blue brings out the colour of your eyes. The effect is quite lovely."

She appeared sincere in her admiration and so I smiled, wanting to tell her the gown was one of my favourites. In fact, I'd been delighted that Mary had managed to take it out in the seams to accommodate the growing baby, as I might otherwise have appeared at dinner in a drab day dress—no doubt to the horror of my hosts.

Before I could so much as thank Anne for her kindness, however, Miss Cartwright patted the emerald fabric of her own dress. "It's for the same reason that I'm wearing the green silk. I do believe it is quite becoming." She batted her lashes to good effect, drawing attention to what was undoubtedly a striking pair of green eyes, lined with thick, dark eyelashes and enhanced with a touch of kohl.

It was not the beauty of her appearance that struck me, though, but rather her inability to allow anyone's attention to stray from her person.

"It certainly is," I agreed, unable to prevent a little scorn from colouring my voice.

A spark of irritation flashed across her face, but she quickly replaced it with a slightly more pleasant expression, which I did my best to return, reminding myself I was a guest in her family's home.

Fortunately, she was soon distracted by her mother, allowing me to breathe a sigh of relief. Noticing Anne watching me I felt my cheeks flush, but a corner of her mouth twitched, and she gave me an amused look. I returned the look with a lifting of one shoulder, making her laugh.

Ollie, who was sitting between the two sisters glanced at his wife at the sound. He started to smile but when Anne's eyes met his, he abruptly looked away, causing her own smile to disappear. There was a brief pause before Anne turned her attention back to me and launched into a series of questions about Glaslearg.

I answered courteously, pleased at her interest, all the while wondering about the peculiar interaction I'd just seen. Should the Penhales not still be floating in marital bliss? But perhaps they'd simply had an argument before dinner, I thought as I caught sight of Anne's father, who was sitting at the head of the table looking rather grim once more. With a family like hers there must certainly be plenty of fodder for quarrels.

I almost laughed at the absurdity of this observation but resolved to watch Ollie and Anne a little more closely.

By the time the dessert was being served my interest was truly piqued.

At the wedding breakfast I had noticed the bride in mild—yet to my mind inappropriate—flirtations with several male guests. Now, though, the former Miss Cartwright barely glanced at any man other than her husband, her eyes straying frequently to Ollie even while she was in conversation with someone else. Ollie, on the other hand, hardly looked at his wife at all, although his mouth often formed a tight line when she spoke, before he caught himself, resuming his casual air in an instant.

Gone was the young bridegroom who had barely been able to believe his own luck, utterly enthralled by his beloved's every move.

Naturally, their behaviour now did not lack in decorum. They remained entirely civilised with each other and those around them, and a less keen observer may not have noticed anything amiss. I *had* noticed, though, and found myself speculating about what may have happened between the pair. And not only between the bridal pair but also between the recent bridegroom and his newly acquired father. For Mr Cartwright had appeared quite jovial throughout dinner—except when Oliver Penhale was involved. Having observed Ollie and his bride for the past hour it had become clear to me that her father's expression soured whenever he looked at the younger man.

Engrossed in the trio's strange behaviour I hadn't paid attention to my table companion, who now cleared his throat, evidently waiting for me to respond to something he'd said.

"I beg your pardon, Mr Cartwright, could you please repeat that?"

A distant cousin of Anne's father, Mr George Cartwright had been introduced to us before dinner. With his red hair and freckles he resembled Anne in appearance and seemed nice enough, although he looked a little annoyed with me now.

"Certainly," he said shortly. "I was asking whether your husband plays cards."

I glanced at Quin, who was once again deep in conversation with Archie. From what I could tell they were now discussing the likelihood that the soup kitchens the government had recently introduced would provide sufficient rations for the vast number of destitute people across Ireland, including those previously reliant on the public works. Having already come far too late for thousands in the worst affected areas I thought the probability of adequate relief was limited, especially so, as the largely ignorant head of London's treasury, Charles Trevelyan, and the rest of the British government were still refusing to put a ban on Irish grain exports—for the questionable reason of trying to prevent feelings of insecurity in those involved in the grain trade and the "permanent injury" such discouragement would cause to Ireland as a whole. That the famine itself was causing far greater injury to the Irish people seemed not to have occurred to Trevelyan and his fellow politicians.

"Yes, my husband does play cards," I said, suddenly dismayed that we could be sitting here at an ostentatious dinner party casually talking about card games when countless people continued to suffer every day. "Although he doesn't have many opportunities to do so at the estate."

"Then perhaps he will agree to a game or two during his stay at Cornac House." Cartwright's face brightened at the thought.

"Perhaps. Are you an avid card player then, Mr Cartwright?"

"Oh yes. A little wager always bolsters the mood, doesn't it?"

"I imagine that depends on whether the wager is won or lost," I said drily, making Cartwright give a small chuckle.

"Right you are, Mrs Williams. Although one must always live in hope of a win!" His face took on a slightly dreamy expression and I wondered how frequently he lived in hope rather than reality. Placing foolish wagers and gambling entire fortunes on myriad games seemed to occupy many a gentleman's time—not always to their gain.

Unaware of Cartwright's particular situation, though, I nodded politely.

He didn't reveal much about himself, but we spent the remainder of dinner in pleasant conversation before the ladies retired to the drawing room, leaving the men to their cognac and cigars.

Thinking I'd prefer staying behind with the men, I reluctantly followed our hostess through the house. Like the dining room, the drawing room was large and opulent, filled to bursting with imposing furniture, the walls decorated with tasteful works of art. As before, though, I noticed a few small signs of neglect—a threadbare cushion here, a notched floorboard there—which were rather in contrast to the seeming perfection exhibited by the women of the house. Mrs Cartwright and her youngest daughter floated into the drawing room with a haughty air, and I wondered what in the world we would talk about.

With some apprehension I sat down next to Anne and Mrs Lewes, an elderly aunt of Mr Cartwright who'd also arrived at the estate that afternoon, along with her middle-aged spinster daughter. Beyond a few pleasantries at dinner, I hadn't spoken to the pair, and hoped they weren't of the same ilk as the Cartwrights, else the evening would turn out to be a long one indeed.

"The tea will be served presently," Anne's sister declared before perching herself elegantly on the edge of a settee, her hands folded on her lap as if she were sitting for a portrait.

As I murmured my thanks, I caught Anne's eye. She smiled at me, and I smiled back, thinking perhaps I ought to make an effort to get to know her a little better. From what I'd seen at dinner, there appeared to be more to Mrs Penhale than I'd first assumed.

For the time being, though, the conversation was a little stilted, commencing with the inevitable discussion of the weather. This continued until everyone was equipped with a cup of tea, after which Anne regaled the visitors with a few more anecdotes about Cornac House—much to the evident tedium of her mother and sister. While I found it fascinating to learn that Mr Cartwright's grandfather, the Viscount Egglestone, had won the estate in a round of whist the previous century, Colleen's expression made me think she'd be rolling her eyes at any moment. And perhaps she might have done so if the men hadn't arrived fortuitously to provide her with better entertainment.

This entertainment proved to be short-lived, however, as the two Cartwright men declared they would be turning in and had only come to bid the ladies a good night.

"I'm afraid I'm worn out," George Cartwright lamented. "The journey to get here has quite taken it out of me." He looked around the drawing room with regret, his eyes eventually coming to rest on Quin. "But we must have that card game tomorrow night, Mr Williams. I insist upon it!"

Quin inclined his head. "Certainly, Mr Cartwright. I shall be looking forward to it. And I do hope you rest well tonight."

Mrs Cartwright soon declared herself to be as exhausted as her husband, which allowed the remaining ladies to make their excuses and head up to bed. I found I was quite looking forward to my own rest. It *had* been a long journey to get here, and I was tired, despite my earlier lie-down.

Quin saw me to our room but had no intention of sleeping just yet.

"I'll have a few more drinks with Ollie and the others before I join you. You don't mind, do you?"

I shook my head. "Not at all." I stifled a yawn, my eyes watering at the effort. "I doubt I can stay awake for more than five minutes in any case."

Quin chuckled, pulling me gently into his arms. "I'll help you undress then," he breathed into my ear, making me wonder if I might have the energy to stay awake a little longer after all.

Having to suppress another yawn, though, I decided it was a lost cause. Indeed, as soon as I was stripped down to my chemise I collapsed onto the pillow and was asleep before Quin had even left the room.

QUIN SMILED AS he quietly closed the door behind him. He'd been tempted to stay with Alannah and coax her into some private entertainment, but she'd clearly been exhausted and needed to rest—not only for herself but for the growing baby.

As always, the thought of his impending fatherhood was slightly startling. He wondered if he'd still feel the same after the birth or whether holding his child in his arms would let him slip comfortably into his new role, ready and able to take on parenthood and all its challenges.

With his thoughts wandering, he made his way through the house, hoping he wouldn't get lost. He'd declined the assistance of a footman, sure he'd be able to find his way back to the drawing room from their quarters. The corridors seemed deserted, with most of the house's occupants having gone to bed. The light of the few lit sconces flickered as he walked past, reflected here and there by swords and other ornaments that adorned the walls. No gas lighting in this old mansion, he thought, wondering what it would cost to modernise the enormous edifice. But perhaps Mr Cartwright was simply old-fashioned like Quin's father, who remained sceptical of such an innovation despite its ever-spreading use.

It wouldn't surprise him if Cartwright declared himself of the same mind as the baron, recalling how the man's face had lit up when Quin had mentioned that his father had fought under Wellington against the French. Cartwright had been practically giddy with excitement, almost spilling his cognac in his eagerness for Quin to elaborate on the campaigns the baron had been involved in during the Napoleonic wars.

For a man who'd never served in the army himself, he showed a surprising interest in military matters.

But perhaps it was precisely because he'd never been on active duty that Mr Cartwright found warfare so fascinating. Quin recalled his own enthrallment with the topic when he was growing up, based on his father and grandfather's thrilling stories and his own desire to achieve military glory and follow in the baron's footsteps. It was only once he'd experienced the horrors of war for himself that he'd started seeing things a bit differently.

And since resigning his commission, he had no desire ever to set foot on a battlefield again.

Realising he'd reached the drawing room by now Quin shook off the thought. He opened the door to find Ollie, Ham and Archie waiting for him. At least one good thing had come out of his military career, he mused, with the friends he'd made for life.

"What do you say to a game of billiards?" Ollie asked as soon as Quin entered the room.

"I say lead the way to the table."

It was thus that Quin and his friends found themselves comfortably ensconced in the spacious billiards room of Cornac House on a warm night in June while the remaining inhabitants were tucked up in their beds. Quin hadn't played the game in some years and was looking forward to testing his skills— and catching up with Ham, Ollie and Archie besides.

A footman delivered a tray with a decanter of whiskey and four glasses before bowing out of the room, leaving the four of them alone. Ollie poured them each a glass and toasted to their health.

"Say what you will about the Irish," Ham said with a sigh of satisfaction after he'd downed his portion, "but they do make a fine drink."

"They do that," Archie agreed. "Now, who's up for a game?"

After some discussion it was agreed that Archie would go up against Ollie, as their host, with the winner keeping the table and the remaining players alternating after that. The first two contenders selected their cues and Archie made a great show of flexing his shoulders and arms while Ollie placed the two cue balls on the table.

"You don't stand a chance," Archie said, puffing out his chest as he looked down at his smaller opponent.

Ollie rolled his eyes. "Just get on with it."

Archie grinned at Ham and Quin before getting into position at the end of the table next to Ollie. With a loud crack the two men sent the balls flying along the green felt before they bounced against the cushioned railing and rolled back toward the baulk.

"Huh. Will you look at that." Archie's face was a mask of surprise as he contemplated the two cue balls, which had come to rest near the starting point, the white ball with the black dot closer to the cushion than the plain one.

Ollie shrugged nonchalantly and selected the winning cue ball for the game. Whatever size advantage Archie may have had, it quickly became apparent that Ollie had the better touch, dispatching cannons and hazards in rapid succession while Archie could only watch in amazement. For every five scoring shots Ollie made Archie managed only one, and in no time at all the smaller man had reached the target of three-hundred points.

Quin looked at Ham, who waved a hand toward the table. "After you, Quinton."

Thinking he would be lucky to get in a single shot before Ollie won his second game Quin replaced the balls on the table and picked up a cue.

Archie, meanwhile, was evidently in need of a restorative. "Have you done nothing but play billiards since you resigned your commission, Ollie?" he asked while refilling his whiskey glass.

Surprised, Quin turned toward Ollie, who was leaning against the mantel. "You resigned your commission? When?"

"About four months ago."

Quin wondered why Ollie hadn't told him but asked something else instead. "Why?"

"I decided I needed to be able to spend more time with my wife." A small frown appeared on Ollie's face at this statement, making Quin cock his head.

"And are you?"

Ollie was silent for a moment before answering. "I was…"

"But you aren't any more?" Quin had noticed that Ollie was a little subdued at dinner but thought it was simply being surrounded by some of his taxing in-laws. Perhaps there was more to it, though.

Ollie held Quin's eyes briefly before shaking his head.

Quin took a step closer to his friend and laid a hand on his arm. "Is everything alright?"

Ollie stood up a little straighter. "Of course, it is. I am able to live quite comfortably off my family's estates and my own investments, so there's no need to worry."

Quin knew Ollie came from a wealthy family and would have no difficulties forgoing his army pay, but that had little to do with anything. "That's not what I meant." He leaned toward the shorter man, giving him a meaningful look.

At last Ollie sighed and waved a hand at Archie. "Pour me another whiskey, will you?"

Archie obliged and Ollie wasted no time tipping back his head and downing the fiery liquid, coming up with his eyes watering. The others dispatched their own drinks in a similar fashion before looking expectantly at the recent bridegroom.

"Everything was grand at first…or at least I thought so." Ollie pursed his lips as he paused. "I suppose I was blinded to the truth."

"What was the truth?" Ham asked, wrinkling his forehead.

Evidently, he and Archie weren't privy to all the details of Ollie's personal life. Ham reached for the decanter again, making Quin give him a surprised look. Undeterred, Ham poured another round.

"That she married me for my money."

"Ah." Quin nodded. Marriages of convenience were hardly unheard of among the upper classes, but he supposed it would have been a blow for Ollie to discover Anne had married him for financial reasons when he'd thought he'd made a love match.

"Are you sure?" Archie asked, banging his glass onto the sideboard and eyeing the remaining whiskey. Turning back toward Ollie he cocked his head. "I thought there was more to it than that."

"So did I…but…well I asked her. And she admitted it."

Archie huffed while Ham shook his head slowly from side to side.

"There was much crying and wailing of course," Ollie continued, "and then she tried to convince me it had been a mistake…"

"The marriage?" Archie's eyes went wide at the thought.

"That, too, I suppose, although she said she regretted not telling me the truth."

"Hmph." Archie splashed more whiskey into their glasses before pointing a finger at Ollie. "How much has she taken you for?"

Ollie looked down, his cheeks going red. "It was just small amounts here and there to begin with. She told me her father had made a bad investment and needed a little to tide him over until he got back on his feet." He raised his eyes, which were filled with disappointment. "But then she admitted the man was deeply in debt and about to lose his country house." Ollie lifted his hands in resignation before dropping them as his shoulders slumped. "That's when I confronted her, and she told me the truth.—That she had planned to use me from the start."

Archie scowled as he handed Ollie his glass while Ham continued to shake his head. Quin clapped Ollie on the back, not sure what to say.

"Why didn't you tell us any of this before?" he asked at last.

Ollie gave a deep sigh. "I suppose I was embarrassed. After everything…"

"This is precisely why I am not married!" Ham announced, his words a little slurred.

Archie nodded emphatically. "You wouldn't get your heart broken by a mistress…or a strumpet for that matter.—In fact, there's a fine establishment in Dublin I can recommend," he added, digging an elbow into Ollie's side. "Just ask Quin here."

Archie caught Quin's eyes and laughed before launching into the tale of how the two men had ended up in a Dublin brothel in the dead of night, bruised and bloodied from their alleyway adventures.

"You should have seen Quin's face when the harlots started undressing him so he could bathe." He put on a shocked expression and clutched himself intimately. Although Ham and Ollie must have heard the story several times before they roared with laughter, swaying only slightly.

Quin grinned. "I wasn't sure if it was bathing they were after or something else."

"Something else," Ham declared, "definitely something else!"

"Fortunately for me, I don't require something else from anybody else besides my wife."

"You lucky bastard," Ollie said and hiccupped, looking down into his empty glass.

Archie snatched it from him and refilled it to the brim. "Yours might come around," he said as he gave the glass back to Ollie, "and realise she's in love with you after all."

"I'll toast to that," Ham said before going over to the billiards table and picking up a cue. "Now, who's up for another game?"

"You should play against Ollie," Quin said, "he won the last round."

"Here." Ham lobbed one of the cue balls toward Ollie, who stared at it as it flew past him and thumped against the wall, before belatedly sticking out his hand.

"You've got the reactions of a dead horse," Archie said drily, examining the dent in the panelling.

Ollie lifted one shoulder. "I'm paying for it." He came to stand next to Archie and ran his fingers over the damage. Suddenly, he snorted. "I'm paying for it." Laughter fizzed through his nose, slowly at first before breaking loose in loud gales that had him holding his sides as he bent over. "I'm paying for it!"

Quin looked from Ollie to Ham and Archie, who were eyeing their friend in some bewilderment, as he was doing himself. Before long, though, all four of them were hooting with laughter, their eyes watering at the effort.

When at long last they stopped, Quin sat down in one of the armchairs by the fireplace. "You'll be alright, Ollie. Even when your wife is being less than civil toward you, you'll have the three of us to keep you company."

"I am a lucky man," Ollie said in a dreamy voice before his eyes rolled up into his head and he collapsed onto the rug, making the others burst out laughing once more.

# 8.

THE FOLLOWING DAY, I woke up to a groan coming from the large, warm body next to me. Opening my eyes, I saw Quin holding his head in both hands, a torturous look on his face.

"Is it morning already?" he croaked.

"It is. And it appears to be a beautiful day."

This statement was met with another groan. "That's debatable."

I laughed. Feeling suddenly wide awake I got out of bed and went to the window, where I cracked open the curtains to look outside. Our room was equipped with an imposing view, and I felt my spirits soar at the sight of the luscious lawn and gardens, and the sizeable lake that sparkled in the distance.

"Must you open the drapes?"

I looked toward the bed, where my husband was lying in a pile of misery with one hand over his eyes, before turning back to the curtains and the sliver of scenery revealed by the inch-wide opening. Shaking my head, I pulled the fabric firmly closed once more before making my way to the garderobe.

"Good morning," I said to the baby as it wriggled and squirmed, pummelling my bladder to best effect. With the pressure of the growing baby noticeable even now I wondered how I would feel shortly before it was due to be born, imagining my belly extending over my toes as I waddled through the house.

When I came back to the bed, I found Quin in no better condition than before.

"Shall I ring for some coffee?"

He made a face and opened one eye a slit. "I suppose you'd better." Not a devotee of the black brew, Quin nevertheless respected its restorative properties. He must have had quite an evening, I thought, tugging on the bellpull. I'd seen him in his cups before but had never known him to feel quite so wretched the next morning.

While waiting for the coffee to be delivered I went to the dressing room, deciding I was perfectly capable of getting dressed without the assistance of one of the maids. As I was finishing a knock sounded on the sitting room door. I thanked the footman and took the tray he'd brought to the bedroom, where Quin was just sitting up. He shuffled to the edge of the bed, swaying slightly, his hair sticking out in all directions.

I smiled at the sight, earning myself a look of resentment. I quickly poured the coffee and handed him a steaming cup. He grimaced but drank dutifully, pausing only briefly between sips to blow on the hot beverage. Replacing the empty cup on the tray he yawned and rubbed a hand over his face.

"Remind me never to drink whiskey again."

"Perhaps you shouldn't drink quite *so much* whiskey again," I suggested wryly. "I'm fairly certain fine whiskey is meant to be *sipped* not gulped."

He nodded absently, before yawning again and stretching out his arms. Finally, he shook his head briskly and opened his eyes wide, announcing he was ready to go down to breakfast. I gave him a sceptical look but assured him he appeared entirely restored, making him narrow his eyes at this clear falsehood.

With his face scrubbed and dressed in fresh clothes he did look much better, although his eyes were still a little bloodshot. Descending to the breakfast room I noticed that he wasn't the only one who'd had a rough night, though. Archie and Ham wore glazed expressions as they contemplated the foods on offer, while Ollie staggered in a little later, looking like he'd barely been to bed.

I exchanged an amused glance with Anne, who threw her husband a wistful look.

"I trust you all slept well," Mrs Cartwright said brightly once everyone was seated.

Sounds of agreement echoed around the room, with some, I was sure, genuine in their affirmation.

Mrs Cartwright smiled, the picture of perfection, making me wonder what time she'd woken up to achieve such magnificence. Colleen, too, had not a hair out of place in her elaborate style and could easily have walked into any drawing room in London without a moment's hesitation.

I felt a little shabby in comparison but shook off the thought, turning my attention to Mrs Lewes and her daughter, whom I'd found to be pleasant companions despite their unassuming appearance.

"What a lovey day it is," Miss Lewes said, her plain round face lighting up as she looked out the window. "Perhaps we could arrange for a walk and have a picnic by the lake."

I was about to voice my enthusiasm for the suggestion when Colleen announced, "We'll set up a pavilion on the lawn," her tone leaving little room for argument. With the discussion clearly at an end she turned her attention back to her breakfast.

Miss Lewes and her mother looked at each other briefly, the younger woman clenching her jaws in irritation. She didn't say anything, though, and the rest of the meal passed pleasantly enough.

After breakfast Quin and his friends disappeared—presumably to recover from the lingering effects of the night before—while I headed toward Cornac House's library. I'd assured Anne I would be perfectly fine on my own and, indeed, I found that I needed no company as I browsed through the Cartwright's modest collection of books. It was imminently peaceful in the wood-panelled room, with a few dust motes floating in the soft rays of sunshine that fell through the window, and I was glad to spend some quiet time there by myself.

When we all convened again midday the promised pavilion had been erected on the lawn behind the house. It contained several scattered chairs and picnic blankets, as well as two large tables covered with an array of food and drinks, far more than our small party was likely to consume.

Colleen clapped her hands together in delight. "Isn't this lovely?"

I nodded slowly. While it was indeed lovely, with the sun shining down on the expansive landscape and the gentle breeze whispering through the large canvas structure, I would have preferred seeing a little more of the estate after our recent arrival. And I especially would have preferred being given the opportunity to voice my opinion instead of being told what to do.

With a shrug I sat down on one of the chairs and accepted a cool glass of lemonade from a footman, while Quin reclined on a picnic blanket next to Ollie. Both men looked much improved since this morning and quickly struck up a lively conversation before being joined by Archie and Ham, who were carrying heavily laden plates. I found I was not even remotely hungry after the large breakfast we'd had not too long before and wondered how they could possibly eat again so soon.

"And they 'ave a lake! *We* don't 'ave lake.—Why don't we 'ave a lake?"

I smiled at the sound of Emmett's voice behind me. He and Benjamin were being employed to do menial tasks around the estate during our stay and were clearly impressed by their surroundings.

"I don't know," Benjamin answered. "We'll 'ave t' ask Mr Williams.—Don't ask 'im now!"

Emmett huffed at being prevented from approaching his master but did as his friend had said. He threw a quick glance at Quin as he walked past him to collect some empty plates but did his best to ignore him otherwise—an effect that was entirely wasted when Quin thanked him for his efforts, making the boy beam from ear to ear.

"How about a game of cricket?" Mr Cartwright said suddenly, looking around at the men of the party, most of whom bobbed their heads enthusiastically.

"Why not?" Quin said. "That's another thing I haven't done in some years."

"Don't worry, Quinton," Archie said as he hefted himself off the ground, "we'll remind you of the rules to refresh your memory. Unfortunately, there isn't much we can do about the physical decline that comes with old age."

"An age that *you* haven't reached, of course, being all of five months younger than I."

Archie grinned. "I *am* younger. That's all that counts."

"Didn't all of you just eat?" I asked sceptically.

Ham waved a hand. "It'll take a while to set up. Plenty of time for a few more bites." He popped a small savoury into his mouth in illustration and gave me a wink.

After a lengthy discussion the men decided that the six of them were insufficient for a decent game and roped in a few of the servants to increase their number. Hearing this, Emmett and Benjamin crept closer to the group, begging in small voices to be allowed to join as well.

George Cartwright shook his head. "Cricket is a game for *men*," he said, patting Benjamin's bright red hair.

While the gesture was likely meant in consolation Benjamin scowled in outrage. Looking toward Rupert he opened his mouth, no doubt to lament the unfairness of the valet being allowed to play, when he and Emmett were not. He quickly snapped it shut, though, when Quin gave him a stern look. Still glowering, the two boys stalked off to the far side of the pavilion, where they stood muttering to each other, clearly disillusioned with the state of the world.

In the meantime, the others had finally decided on the teams and the proud sportsmen sauntered off onto the lawn, which was to serve as the playing field for the afternoon. One of the footmen was sent in search of a pair of bats and wickets, which nobody really knew where to find, making the man square his shoulders in determination. While he headed off on his quest, Ollie and George set about measuring the length of the pitch, the exact placement of which required further debate.

Watching all of this I was beginning to see what Ham had meant by his comment about the set-up. If they continued in this vein, it would be evening before they even got started.

It was in fact mid-afternoon when the footman finally reappeared with the box of equipment, which he brandished as if presenting the company with a long-lost treasure, his cheeks going pink in response to the applause his arrival incited. There was still further delay, though, as it was decided which of the two teams would bat first, and then, in which order the batsmen and bowlers of each team would have a go.

By the time the men had finally taken off their jackets and the first ball bounced onto the pitch I found I had worked up quite an appetite myself. Indeed, in the peculiar way of pregnancy, I was suddenly ravenously hungry and eagerly helped myself from the generous selection.

I sat back down with my plate but jumped at the sound of a loud crack. I looked in some bewilderment toward the cricketers, where Archie had just dispatched the ball onto the far side of the lawn.

"The ball is solid, you know," Mrs Lewes informed me, "not like the inflated pigs' bladders children like to play with."

"Oh." Kieran hadn't played much cricket when we were younger, and I only had a vague understanding of the sport. I watched the game with greater interest, wondering if I would be able to swing a bat.

"My brother's friend got hit with a cricket ball once," Mrs Lewes continued. "Right here." She indicated her temple with a forefinger. "Dropped like a stone and never got up again."

I gasped.

"It never stopped any of them from playing, though," Mrs Lewes dismissed the matter, accepting a fresh cup of tea from one of the maids.

The present players seemed equally unperturbed by the possibility of injury or death, cheering and cajoling as the ball flew back and forth, sweating freely in the summer sunshine. With another loud crack Archie sent the ball sailing over Mr Cartwright's head. Setting off down the pitch the large batsman grinned at Ollie as the two of them ran between the wickets.

"They look ridiculous," Colleen said, watching her father scramble after the ball. She wrinkled her nose at the state of his shirt, which showed dark patches under the arms.

"They're enjoying themselves," Anne said, smiling at her husband, who was taking his place before the stumps.

Ollie puffed out his chest, a look of determination on his face as Ham came running toward him with the ball. Ham hurled the dark red orb onto the pitch and Ollie swung wildly, making it fly into the air, where it seemed to hang for a moment before starting its descent. One of the footmen came racing forward, snatching it up just before it hit the ground.

A loud cheer went up from the fielding side. Ham thumped the footman on the back, making the man break into a wide grin, which was mirrored by Quin, who'd been given the role of wicket keeper. He caught my eye briefly before returning to his position behind the stumps as the next batsman made his way onto the pitch, Ollie departing with drooping shoulders.

Colleen sniffed, looking suddenly bored. "How long is this going to go on?"

"It's difficult to say with cricket," Mrs Lewes said. "It could be a few hours, or it could be several days.—But since they don't have full teams of eleven players it shouldn't take all that long I should think."

"Well, that's some relief, I suppose."

Colleen didn't *look* terribly relieved, and I wondered if she'd had any other plans for the afternoon. Then again, I thought it was entirely possible that she simply didn't like watching other people have a good time without her.

"It's a beautiful estate," I said, trying to change the topic.

Anne beamed at me at the praise. "It is. I love coming here."

"It's nice enough," Colleen said with a dismissive wave of her hand, "but I much prefer the city."

How anyone could prefer the crowded and often filthy confines of a city to the crispness of the open countryside was beyond me, but I didn't say anything. "Does the estate have any tenants?" I asked instead.

Anne nodded. "My father rents out a section of land on the other side of the lake. There aren't many tenants, though, and…well a good number of them have had to leave in recent months." She sighed as she looked into the distance.

"It's been a difficult few years for the Irish people," I said, wondering whether the tenants had left voluntarily or been evicted by Mr Cartwright because they hadn't been able to pay their rent.

"It certainly has been.—How are you faring on your own estate?" Anne cocked her head as she waited for my answer, seeming genuinely interested—unlike her sister, who had an annoyed look on her face. Her mother, in conversation with the Leweses, paid us no mind.

"All in all, we're faring fairly well," I said. "A good portion of Glaslearg's land is given over to our tenants and Quin and I have done our best to assist them where we can, especially over the last few seasons. We've been fortunate enough to have had a good grain yield from our own fields, which has been invaluable."

I saw Colleen wrinkle her nose at my comment but ignored her.

"We don't grow any crops of our own here," Anne said, "only the potatoes the tenants produce on their small parcels of land. And with recent harvests being insufficient, many have gone to nearby towns and cities seeking better fortunes."

"One can only hope they find them there. The failed potato harvests have been a devastating blow to Ireland's poor."

Colleen suddenly huffed into the ensuing silence. "They shouldn't complain so," she snapped, frowning in disgust.

"About being poor?" Anne asked, an incredulous look on her face.

Her sister rolled her eyes. "About their precious potatoes.—I'm sick of hearing about it. Growing a few less isn't going to kill them!"

I gaped at Colleen, so shocked that my mouth hung open, an expression mirrored by her sister. Evidently more familiar with Colleen's abominable opinions Anne regained her composure first.

"It's hardly just a few less, Colleen. And a poor potato harvest *is* going to kill them if they have no other food to eat and *starve*, you ignorant fool!"

Colleen gasped and placed a hand to her bosom. The sisters glared at each other for a moment before Colleen turned away abruptly and stomped toward the house.

"How dare you?" Mrs Cartwright rounded on Anne, her face like thunder, having clearly heard her daughters' last exchange. "You will apologise to your sister at once!"

"I will do no such thing, mother!" Anne lifted her chin in defiance. "Colleen is ignorant, selfish and cruel, and always has been. I am tired of letting her get away with it!"

With a gasp and a huff of her own Mrs Cartwright followed her daughter in her flight, leaving the pavilion in an awkward silence.

"I'm sorry," I said at last, thinking I shouldn't have brought up the topic.

Anne shook her head. "Don't be. This was a long time coming."

"You're right Anne. Your sister *is* ignorant, selfish and cruel."

I looked in surprise toward Mrs Lewes, having forgotten she was there.

"Just like her mother," she added with a sigh, making Anne's eyes go wide. "I warned your father not to marry her but"—she lifted one shoulder—"I suppose he thought she was quite the catch." She suddenly turned to me and gave me a stern look. "You be sure to instil some discipline in your own child, Mrs Williams, for you do not want to be reaping the consequences of a lax upbringing!—Now, all this fresh air is making me tired. I shall go and have a rest." She got up and started walking away but stopped next to Anne. "Do not fret, child, all will be well."

Anne looked down and her aunt patted her arm before heading toward the house.

"I am very glad I'm plain," Miss Lewes said, having sat silently throughout the encounter, "for I have never been in danger of becoming so conceited."

"My mother always favoured Colleen," Anne said quietly, "probably because she reminded her of herself. Beautiful, willowy, elegant—all the things I am not. There was nothing she wasn't allowed to do…" She paused briefly. "I used to envy her but now…I feel nothing but relief."

"And so you should," Miss Lewes said as she got to her feet, "for beauty is fleeting. And those who are left with no redeeming qualities once it is gone may yet find themselves regretting who they allowed their appearance to become." With those words she took her leave, intending to join her mother in an afternoon respite.

"Are you alright?" I asked Anne, who was looking rather forlorn.

She started to nod but broke off suddenly.

"Familial confrontations can be deeply troubling," I said, recalling the many times Kieran and I had disagreed—sometimes vehemently so.

"Yes, that's true." She looked toward the lawn, where the game had come to a halt while the men stood in a circle, arguing about something. Finally, she sighed. "I judge my sister harshly. But I am no better than she."

"What do you mean?" Although Anne and I were by no means close, I knew which Cartwright sister I'd prefer spending my time with.

"Ollie." She lifted her chin toward her husband, who was waving his arms in the air as the discussion continued. "You may have heard…" She clamped her mouth shut before going on. "I'm not sure what he might have told Quin but…well…the truth is, I married Ollie for his money."

I hadn't heard this from Quin and raised my brows—although I wasn't all that surprised, having observed the pair's strange behaviour since their engagement. Watching Anne now, though, and recalling the previous night's dinner party, I had my doubts.

"It's not an uncommon reason for matrimony," I said cautiously.

"I know but…well I made him believe I cared for him."

"And do you?"

She gave a jerky nod. "I do now. I...I love him." A tear rolled down her cheek and she brushed it away impatiently. "It was my mother's idea. She'd noticed him at social events...fawning over me as she called it...and made a few enquiries. When she found out he owned a substantial fortune she encouraged me to...to encourage him."

"And you did."

"I did. Although I didn't want to at first." She looked at me searchingly, imploring me to believe her. "But father...well, he'd gotten himself into debt, you see. So I had no choice." She glanced toward her father, disappointment flashing across her face.

"I see."

"And of course, such a match would never do for Colleen, for she is destined for far greater things." She looked toward the men once more. "But Colleen can only dream of a man as wonderful as Ollie.—And now I've ruined our chance at happiness."

"Why don't you talk to him? Tell him how you feel."

"I've tried. He won't listen."

"How long has it been since he found out the truth?"

"A few weeks."

"Ah." Suddenly I understood their strange behaviour the previous evening—Anne's desolate glances at her husband and Ollie's stubborn refusal to acknowledge her more than necessary, not to mention her father's resentment of the man on whom he found himself financially dependent. "Ollie just needs a little more time," I said, patting Anne's hand. Having experienced male stubbornness before I didn't think all was lost.

"Do you think so?" She lifted hopeful eyes toward me before looking back at Ollie, who was heading to the pavilion with the other men.

"I do." I nodded emphatically, giving her fingers a squeeze. "At least the strained relationship between the three of you now makes sense."

Her eyes went wide, and I cleared my throat in some embarrassment. "I'm sorry, Anne, I…"

She shook her head. "Don't be. I just hadn't realised it was so obvious."

"It wasn't. It isn't. It's only that…um…I've been watching you a little more closely than is considered entirely polite."

Anne laughed, which quite transformed her features. While she might consider herself the plain Cartwright sister, there was much to speak in her favour—not least of all her far more pleasant personality.

"Thank you, Alannah," she said, making me smile at her as the cricketers descended upon us, still arguing vociferously.

"Your leg was clearly in front of the wickets," Ham was saying, pointing a finger at Archie, who was shaking his head.

"The ball was spinning away from the stumps, meaning it was no leg before wicket."

"It hit your pad," Ham insisted, thwacking the top of the knee-high protective gear Archie had strapped to the front of his legs.

"The ball was not pitched directly in line with the wickets," Ollie added his voice to the argument. "And its trajectory would have carried it past the stumps. Whether it hit Archie's pad or not is irrelevant."

"Since we have no umpire the fielding team should make the call!" Ham insisted.

"I saw it clearly from where I was standing," Ollie claimed, having watched the game from the edge of the lawn after being bowled out.

"Well of course you would say that. You're on Archie's side!"

"Now, now. Why don't you three calm down and have a nice, cool drink," Quin said, coming up behind Ollie. He glanced briefly at me and rolled his eyes before turning back to his friends, who allowed themselves to be shepherded toward the refreshment table, with only a moderate amount of grumbling.

Anne watched them go in amusement. "Ollie is very competitive."

"I think they all are. I wonder if they'll continue their game or just keep arguing for the rest of the afternoon."

"Watch out!"

The shout from the lawn made us both look up, just in time to see the cricket ball sailing toward us. Anne shrieked and dove from her chair, while I bent forward and stuck my arms over my head. When I heard a clattering behind me, I leapt from my chair to assess the damage. The ball had struck one of the serving platters, sending it crashing to the ground and scattering pastries everywhere.

I looked toward the lawn, where Benjamin was standing with a bat in his hands, his deathly pale face in stark contrast with his red hair. He opened his mouth, but no sound came out, and he snapped it shut again, swallowing heavily as he stared at the adults with wide eyes.

"Are you alright?" Ollie rushed from the drinks table where the men had been congregated, crouching in front of Anne where she'd landed on one of the picnic blankets.

She nodded, allowing herself to be pulled up into his arms, making me smile briefly. Clearly, all hope was not lost for a happy future together for the Penhales.

Having assured himself that I, too, was unharmed, Quin marched toward Benjamin, who was still standing motionless with the bat in his hands, and Emmett, who was trying unsuccessfully to hide behind his friend.

"What the devil do you think you're doing?" Quin growled.

"Um..."

"Ah..."

"We...um..."

"Well..."

"Sorry, sir," the boys finally managed in unison, looking down.

"You could have hurt someone!" Quin hissed at the delinquents, who stared at their feet, shuffling uncomfortably back and forth. "If you're going to take a swing with a cricket bat without permission then at least swing away from the crowd of people!"

"Yes, sir."

"Now, go apologise to Mr Cartwright and his guests and clean up the mess.—And I'll deal with you later!"

Benjamin and Emmett exchanged frightened glances before heading toward the pavilion, their shoulders slumped. Almost immediately, the Cartwrights started berating the boys, making me feel a little sorry for them. I was about to go and lend them my support when Quin took a few steps closer to me, looking me over from head to toe.

"I'm fine," I assured him once more.

His eyes fixated on my growing belly. "What if the ball had hit you?"

"It didn't."

"But…"

"Nothing happened," I said a little more forcefully. "Besides, you can't lock me away until the baby is born!"

"I suppose not."

The expression on Quin's face made me think he'd like to do exactly that. I huffed in irritation and the corner of Quin's mouth twitched in amusement.

"Perhaps we'll simply have to find a few more enjoyable activities we can safely perform indoors."

I cocked my head. "Perhaps."

Quin laughed and pulled me briefly to him, kissing the top of my head. "I'm glad you're not hurt." When he released me, he glanced toward the others and sighed. "I'm afraid I'll have to go mete out some punishment. It would hardly do for the boys to get away with this unscathed."

I nodded as I turned back to the pavilion, where Mr Cartwright was in the middle of a lecture about the gentlemanly conduct that was essential to the game of cricket—and the utter lack thereof displayed by Benjamin and Emmett with their thoughtless and dangerous antics.

"It's just not cricket!" George Cartwright declared, looking down at the drooping figures in front of him while Rupert patted his brother's back.

When at last the Cartwrights deemed the boys to have been sufficiently rebuked, Benjamin and Emmett quickly collected the scattered edibles before slinking up to the house. Quin followed them at a short distance, squaring his shoulders, clearly not looking forward to his role in the afternoon's theatrics.

Quin's departure prompted a hearty debate among the remaining cricketers as they discussed what to do about the game. It was eventually decided that a suspension was warranted in order for optimal playing conditions to be restored. Agreeing to reconvene at the pavilion in an hour the Cartwrights and their guests started walking away, while the footmen and a pair of maids began setting the pavilion to rights.

Anne came up next to me as I reached the path that led to the house.

"Would you care to join me for a cup of tea?" she asked hopefully.

"I would, thank you. Let me just find someone to tell Quin where I am."

Having sent Rupert in search of Quin, Anne and I retired to her sitting room. It was smaller than the one in the suite Quin and I had been assigned but cosy enough, with the afternoon sunlight streaming in through the large window overlooking a patch of greenery on the side of the house.

With none of the restraint from the day before hindering our conversation Anne and I chatted amiably, finding we had much in common. The more we talked the more I liked her and sincerely hoped she'd be able to work out her differences with Ollie.

"He's a stubborn man," she said with a sigh when I said as much. "Once he's convinced himself of something it's difficult to persuade him otherwise."

"That's a trait he shares with many of his sex.—Still, I do believe that he'll come around. If his reaction in the pavilion this afternoon is anything to go by, he still cares for you deeply."

Anne's features softened. "Then I shall talk to him tonight and insist that he hear me out." She gave me a wry smile. "I may have to use some underhanded means to ensure he listens to me, but I think I can come up with something." The suggestive look that appeared on her face made me blush.

She laughed, leaning forward and clasping my hands. "I can't tell you how glad I am to have found someone to talk to. When I tried to raise my concerns with my mother, she simply dismissed me, insisting I had no right to complain. I married into money, after all, so what more could I want?"

"What more indeed? Do I take it your parents' marriage was one of convenience then?"

"I can't really say. I believe my father has always been smitten with my mother but as for her..." Anne paused briefly before continuing. "The way she berates him about every little thing makes me doubtful she ever had any real feelings for him."

"I'm sorry."

Anne waved a dismissive hand. "They each made their own choices in life. And some of my father's choices have been...well..." Her mouth compressed briefly into a tight line. "But that's not what *I* want. I want...more."

"And you'll have more," I said, nodding earnestly, "you'll see."

QUIN PULLED HIS cravat away from his neck, wondering why the devil he was wearing the dastardly thing when he'd been playing a game of cricket.

When he finally managed to free his throat, he tossed the piece of fabric aside and took a deep breath.

"That's better," he muttered to himself, reaching for the whiskey decanter on the sideboard. He paused momentarily, recalling his wretched state that morning but soon shrugged, deciding a small amount wouldn't hurt.

Sipping wouldn't do, though, and so he gulped down the fiery liquid and sighed.

The game itself had hardly seen him break a sweat, situated behind the wickets as he'd been. It was the act of retribution he'd been forced to inflict thereafter that had caused his heart to beat wildly in his chest.

Having followed Benjamin and Emmett to the servants' quarters, he'd intended to give them an earful about their dangerous behaviour and banish them to the house for the next day or two to think about what they'd done. It quickly became apparent, though, that this was insufficient as far as the rest of the staff was concerned. With several of the servants having witnessed the boys' antics themselves—and the rest having presumably been informed of the details—it was the general opinion that nothing but physical punishment would do under the circumstances. None of them had said so outright, of course, for they wouldn't dare tell a baron's son what to do, but the wide eyes and expectant expressions had spoken volumes.

It was thus that Quin had found himself conducting his first thrashing—on not one but *two* miscreants, and with an audience to boot—which had left him perspiring freely and desperately longing for a drink.

Returning to the sitting room in his quarters he was quite glad of the solitude afforded by Alannah's absence. He still had about half an hour before he was to meet the others to resume their game, and so he sat down on one of the padded wingchairs, leaning his head back and closing his eyes.

Both Benjamin and Emmett had taken the ten crisp lashes across their backsides stoically and had sworn afterward never again to do anything foolish.

Quin snorted, wondering how long it would take until they got up to further mischief and whether the thrashing they'd received that afternoon would have had any effect at all in preventing it. He thought about his own childhood, trying to remember whether the threat of the tawse had ever put him off anything. Truth be told, he wasn't sure, although he could recall the threat of his father's tongue-lashing leaving him quaking in his boots—which left him contemplating the general efficacy of corporal punishment versus its alternatives.

Lost in thought his eyes wandered leisurely to the small timepiece over the mantle, only to fixate suddenly on the clock hands. He jumped up from his seat, glancing briefly at the crumpled cravat lying on the floor but deciding to leave it where it was as he dashed toward the door.

By the time he made it to the pavilion the others were already waiting for him.

George Cartwright looked down his nose at Quin. "Give the boys a good talking to, did you, Williams?"

"Of course." Quin cleared his throat. "Shall we?"

The men spent a few more hours on the pitch, battling it out well into the evening. Quin found he was quite enjoying himself, even though the unaccustomed exercise was likely to make him feel stiff the next day. Whether Mr Cartwright would even be able to get out of bed in the morning was questionable, his face red as he laid aside his bat and finally declared an end to the day's game.

"But it isn't over yet," George grumbled, evidently wanting to see the contest through to the end.

They'd agreed to a single innings per team, and the match would be decided once the remaining batsmen had been dismissed or the batting side reached the target of runs amassed by their opponents earlier. With the nature of cricket being what it was, though, it was difficult to say how long it would take for either outcome to occur.

"We can resume tomorrow," his cousin said, mopping his face with a white handkerchief. Clearly, the older man was exhausted. That he'd managed to play as long as he had was astonishing.

George didn't argue further but continued muttering to himself as he made his way to the house.

Quin followed more slowly with his friends, enjoying the long summer day. Back in his rooms he was delighted to see that a bath was already being prepared for him.

"I was watching from the window," Alannah said, standing on her toes to kiss his cheek. "When it looked like you were done for the day I rang for a maid."

Sinking into the warm water a little later Quin sighed in contentment, thinking there was something to be said for the leisurely activities conducted by many a British gentleman. While he bathed Alannah told him about the argument between the Cartwright women and her conversation with Anne.

"Ollie *does* think she married him only for his money. He told me so yesterday evening."

"But it's not true. Or at least, even if it was true, it's no longer the case. She cares for him deeply."

"I think he feels the same. But I suppose they're both too stubborn to admit it," Quin said, thinking he ought to get out of the tub soon if they were to make it to dinner.

"She did say she'd speak to him tonight." Alannah took a towel off the washstand when Quin started standing up.

Stepping in front of him she ran her eyes appreciatively over his bare chest, making him lift his chin. "See anything you like?"

Her gaze slid lower, and a smile quirked her lips. "I do." Looking back at his face she handed him the towel. "Perhaps we can leave dinner early and have dessert in our room."

"I think that's an excellent idea!"

Quin grinned, contemplating forgoing dinner entirely and skipping straight to the promised dessert. His stomach growled as if in protest, reminding him he'd only had a few morsels to eat at luncheon. Resigned, he got dressed, hoping they'd both be able to stay awake long enough later to enjoy their time alone. For dinner was turning into a rather late affair, although the sun was still hovering just above the horizon as they all took their seats, the late summer sunset making for a long day.

Besides being late dinner was also exceedingly awkward, with the two Cartwright women blatantly ignoring Anne, while Ollie looked bewildered between the three, clearly none the wiser as to the cause of the strife. Clearly, Anne's determination to speak more freely with her husband hadn't come to fruition just yet. As for Anne's father, Mr Cartwright scowled intermittently at the spectacle but said nothing, instead reminiscing with Mrs Lewes about long-gone relatives. Alannah tried to distract a visibly drooping Anne by drawing her into conversation with the younger Miss Lewes, while Quin found himself having to rebut the advances of George Cartwright, who seemed determined to lock himself into a room with Quin and his friends with a pack of cards for the rest of the night.

Having promised him a game the evening before Quin felt compelled to agree to at least one round but knew it would never end there. And as much as he enjoyed playing a hand of cards, he also very much enjoyed the feeling of his wife's naked body against his skin—an experience he was unwilling to forgo for the prospect of winning a few pennies.

He was just considering suggesting they set a time limit for their evening's entertainment when the butler entered the dining room bearing a folded note on a small silver tray. He stopped next to George, who took the piece of paper, looking a little puzzled. Reading the note his eyes went wide and he swallowed heavily.

"Is everything alright?" Mr Cartwright asked.

George looked up and cleared his throat. "Yes…yes, certainly. Just…um…a small matter brought to my attention from…ah…my man of business." He waved the note in the air before depositing it in his jacket pocket. "But I'm afraid I have to leave." He pushed back his chair rather forcefully and got up.

"Now?" Mrs Cartwright glanced in some surprise toward the window, where darkness had fallen.

"I'm afraid it can't wait." With a rather haunted expression on his face George bid his hosts farewell, barely meeting the eyes of the rest of the party. In a matter of minutes, he'd disappeared.

Quin exchanged a look with Ollie.

"Well, that was rather unexpected." Mr Cartwright huffed but soon perked up again. "Much like Lord Nelson taking his ship out of the line to attack the Spanish at the battle of Cape St Vincent." And with this, Anne's father launched into a deferential account of Britain's famous admiral and his daring feats,

Cousin George's abrupt departure already forgotten. "And to think what he achieved even after losing the one arm! Decisive victories at the battle of the Nile and, of course, the battle of Trafalgar, which put to bed any hopes Napoleon had of invading England." Mr Cartwright proudly raised his chin as if he'd commanded the British navy himself.

Archie caught Quin's eye, making him smile.

Oblivious to the exchange, Cartwright sighed. "If only the great man had survived the battle to be received at home as the hero he was.—It was a sad day when news of his death arrived on our shores, quite clouding the news of his victory." A faraway look appeared on Mr Cartwright's face as he perhaps remembered hearing about the triumph and tragedy that was the battle of Trafalgar when he was a young man.

"A hero he may have been," Mrs Cartwright said, making a moue of distaste, "but he quite besmirched his character by taking up with that vulgar Emma Hamilton."

"Nelson was powerless to resist her advances," her husband was quick to defend his champion. "That damned trollop led him astray!"

Mrs Cartwright gasped. "How dare you use such language in my presence?" She placed a hand to her breast, clearly outraged. Colleen, too, was staring at her father in shock.

"I for one think she showed gumption, to go after what she wanted." Mrs Lewes nodded to herself even as the Cartwright women looked ready to faint. "And Emma Hamilton did far more with her life than simply entice Britain's most famous admiral into her bed."

Colleen's cheeks went bright red, while Mrs Cartwright sputtered, fanning her face with her hand as she struggled for breath. "This is not appropriate dinner conversation!" she finally managed, glaring daggers around the table.

Quin wondered what occasion *would* be appropriate to speculate about the private habits of some of Britain's most famous—or infamous—personalities but decided not to ask.

With another dramatic expulsion of breath Mrs Cartwright rose from her chair, declaring that she would retire for the night, obediently followed by her youngest daughter. The two women stormed out of the dining room with barely a backward glance, making Quin contemplate how much social niceties had declined over the course of the past two days.

By the end of the house party, they might be lucky if they managed to wish each other a good day.

After an awkward silence Mr Cartwright announced that he, too, would be heading to bed, thus effectively putting an end to the evening's proceedings. Quin hoped the Cartwrights had separate bedchambers, for the man was unlikely to receive a warm reception from his wife. He suppressed a grin at the thought, barely stopping himself from laughing out loud when he met Archie's eye.

He managed a reasonably civilised leave-taking from the Leweses and bid his friends goodnight before leading Alannah to their quarters.

"Do you think Mrs Cartwright will allow her husband into her bed?" Alannah asked, making him chuckle as he closed the door to their sitting room and removed his jacket and waistcoat.

"I doubt it. I suspect she's already locked the adjoining door or sent him packing to the stables."

Alannah laughed. "Poor Mr Cartwright. He certainly doesn't have it easy with the women in his life."

"Mmm." Quin came up behind her and nuzzled her neck as he started undoing the buttons of her dress.

"Mrs Cartwright and Colleen are terribly judgemental people. And prudish, to boot."

"Fortunately, I don't suffer from the latter defect to my character," he said, demonstrating as much by pushing the dress down her arms so it fell to the floor. Slowly, he ran his hands over her breasts and down the swell of her abdomen.

"It's a wonder Anne turned out the way she did," Alannah said, her voice a little breathless.

"Indeed." Quin let his hands wander a little lower, his fingers sliding over the slippery fabric of her shift. Alannah laid her head back against his shoulder and he kissed her below the ear, making her shiver.

Turning her around he captured her mouth with his own while he wrapped his arms around her. Still holding her close he led her to the bed, where he drew her down next to him. They lay facing each other, her growing belly pressing against his abdomen.

She looked down briefly. "Will you still want me in your bed a few months from now, when I'm even bigger with child?"

"Of course. It's my child, after all. And you're my wife." He kissed her again, while trying to remove his shirt.

She smiled. "I'm glad. Although it might be a little difficult to…" She cocked her head, making him chuckle.

"We'll just have to be a bit creative," he whispered into her ear as he pulled her close once more.

# 9.

"CAN'T WE JUST have breakfast sent up here?" I looked with longing at the sitting room and its comfortable chairs.

Quin laughed. "We might. But I for one have no intention of holing up in here for the next two days. I *do* intend to ignore the Cartwrights' antics for the remainder of our stay, though, and enjoy spending time with my friends.—And I'm sure if you put your mind to it, you can do the same." He stepped toward me and offered me his arm.

"I suppose so." With some reluctance I let him lead me into the hall and down to the breakfast room.

I was relieved to see the Cartwrights hadn't yet arrived. As I was greeting the Leweses, Anne, Ollie, Ham and Archie came into the room.

"You're looking happy," I said to Anne while the men wished each other a good morning. A soft blush appeared on her cheeks. "Do I take it you and Ollie have reconciled?"

She nodded and took hold of my hand. "I told him everything, just like you said.—Thank you, Alannah." She gave my fingers a light squeeze before turning to Ollie, who guided her to her seat, his face aglow as he looked at her.

"At least somebody's in a good mood this morning."

Quin's voice by my ear made me look toward the door, where Mrs Cartwright was just entering with her nose in the air. She was followed by her daughter, who was wearing precisely the same haughty expression on her face.

As if suddenly recalling themselves to their surroundings both women broke into wide smiles when they reached the table, extending their heartfelt greetings to their guests.

"Laying it on a bit thick, aren't they?"

Archie's grumbled comment beside me made me want to laugh out loud and I quickly looked down to hide my face.

"Mr Cartwright sends his apologies," Mrs Cartwright said, regally sweeping the skirts of her morning dress aside as she took her seat. "He's feeling rather under the weather."

I glanced sideways at Quin, who quirked his brow. No doubt the poor man was suffering the after-effects of having been berated by his wife.

Once the obligatory sympathies had been dispensed the party settled down to their breakfast. Taking Quin's advice, I tried to ignore Colleen and her mother, who were making a great show of exuberance, praising the excellence of the food and going into raptures over the splendidness of the weather, clearly trying to compensate for the awkwardness of the day before.

"Speaking of the weather," Anne said, ignoring her sister as she looked toward Miss Lewes, "I do believe today is an excellent day for that walk down to the lake."

Colleen pouted her lips while Miss Lewes' face lit up. "I would like that very much."

With the rest of the company declaring their agreement it was decided we would set out within the hour.

"Wasn't I saying on our way to the breakfast room earlier that an outing to the lake would be just the thing today?" Mrs Cartwright looked expectantly at Colleen as she got up to leave after the meal.

Colleen gave her mother a startled glance but nodded dutifully. "Of course." She headed toward the door, narrowing her eyes when Anne walked past on Ollie's arm. Seeing me watching her she quickly rearranged her features and gave a tittering laugh. I let my eyes linger on hers for a moment longer before sweeping into the hall, glad I needed to endure only two more days in her presence.

As for the rest of the company, those same two days hardly seemed adequate.

The thought made me smile at Anne as I came down the stairs with Quin a little later. I was about to tell her how much I was looking forward to spending the afternoon with her when there was a commotion at the front door. I looked at Quin, who shrugged and followed Ollie toward the source of the noise. In perfect understanding Anne and I did the same, rushing across the tiles to keep up with the men's longer strides.

We found the butler standing at the threshold, one hand gripping the side of the door as if he were about to slam it shut, the other being waved vigorously back and forth as he hissed at someone on the front steps. When I came closer I could see there were several people crowded before the Cartwright's country house, their heads bowed and backs stooped. The sense of dejection emanating from the group was palpable and my heart ached at the sight of the rags that covered the women and children who had clearly come there to beg.

"You must leave," the butler snarled in a low voice. Glancing behind him his eyes widened when he saw he had an audience. "I'll be rid of them presently, sir," he said to Ollie before turning back to the beggars. "Leave!" he growled once more, pointing a finger into the distance. "How dare you come here? And to the front door as if you were worth something!"

Some of the women were not cowed, though, taking a step closer and peering into the house with desperation in their pleading eyes.

"But sir…"

"Please…"

"The children…"

"Go, now!" the butler demanded and started shutting the door.

"That won't be necessary, Everts," Ollie said, coming up next to him and giving him a pointed look.

The butler's lips compressed ever so slightly as he let go of the door and bowed his head. "Of course, sir."  He stepped back, his face expressionless as he awaited instructions.

"Go tell Cook to prepare a basket of food," Ollie told him as he stuck a hand into his jacket pocket, "and see it's handed to these needy folks."

While Everts rushed off to do his bidding Ollie came up with a few coins, which he gave to an older woman with a pinched face. Her stick-thin arm protruded from her sleeve as she stuck out her hand to grasp the money Ollie could so easily dispense with but for her might mean the difference between life and death.

Looking at the emaciated appearance of the people in front of me I felt my throat tighten. I threw a helpless look at Quin, who was rootling in his own pockets. He handed over what he found before stepping back with a sigh and taking my hand, squeezing my fingers briefly.

"What is going on here?"

I turned toward the voice behind me and met the gaze of Mrs Cartwright, who looked dismayed at the spectacle playing out on her front stairs.

"Get these beggars out of here!" she demanded of nobody in particular while behind her, Colleen wrinkled her nose in distaste.

"Not just yet," Ollie said, "I've ordered a basket of food to be prepared for them."

"A basket of food?" Colleen gaped at Ollie as if he'd made an outrageous suggestion.

"Indeed. Food is what they are lacking," Ollie responded much more calmly than I would have managed.

Colleen huffed. "Disgusting," she muttered as she turned away.

"Yes, you are," I said under my breath before looking around a little guiltily. Luckily, nobody seemed to have heard me.

Within a few minutes the butler reappeared, carrying a large basket filled with bread and other edibles, which he handed to the elderly woman with a haughty expression on his face. She murmured her thanks and the group started shuffling away. Everts closed the door behind them in what was almost a slam, clearly pleased to have dealt with the nuisance that was Ireland's hungry populace.

The rest of us made our way back to the staircase, where the remaining house guests had by now congregated, including Mr Cartwright, who claimed to have experienced a precipitous recovery from his earlier ailment. He kept throwing weary glances at his wife, though, who in turn was ignoring him completely.

Feeling a little subdued after the encounter with the beggars I followed the others through the house and onto the terrace. Stepping into the sunlight I tried to shake off my gloomy mood, determined to make the most of what was turning into a lovely day.

"It's so beautiful here," Anne said next to me as we reached the stone pathway, pulling my attention from my thoughts.

"It is," I agreed.

And it was true. The grounds were spread out before us, the carefully manicured lawn looking like a bright green carpet that led down to the lake, which sparkled in the sunshine. The sky was vast and blue, with only a few wisps of clouds floating on the gentle breeze.

"I always loved coming here as a child," Anne said, a nostalgic expression appearing on her face.

With my own spirits lifting once more we ambled companionably along the path that cut through the edge of the lawn. There were a few trees dotted here and there, casting their shadows over the irregularly shaped stones at our feet.

I saw Anne throw a furtive glance at my abdomen. Her cheeks reddened when she noticed me looking at her, but I smiled encouragingly.

"How does it feel?" she asked hesitantly.

"It feels wonderful," I said. "To feel the baby moving inside of me, to be able to bring forth new life." I gave Anne a wry look. "Mind you, having him perform somersaults isn't always very comfortable."

Anne laughed.

"Or her," I said softly.

"Do you mind? Whether you're having a boy or a girl?"

I shook my head. "One day I'm sure I'm having a boy, then the next I'm convinced it's a girl. But no, I don't mind either way...after all the trouble we've had to get here."

"Trouble?" Anne gave me a surprised look.

Nodding, I told her how difficult it had been for me to become pregnant, and to stay so.

"I'm so sorry, Alannah," she said, her eyes filled with compassion. She was quiet for a moment. "I never thought about such a thing. I knew the confinement could be dangerous, of course, but..." She glanced ahead of us, to where Mrs Cartwright was walking with Colleen at the head of the party. "My mother...she would never talk about such a thing. She never talks about anything of importance."

I lifted one shoulder. "It's not unusual.—One might think being pregnant was something to be ashamed of, the way society insists on women hiding their growing bellies and using euphemisms to explain away the miracle of life."

Anne laid a hand to her breast and batted her lashes dramatically. "Oh darling, are you *increasing*?"

"Yes, dear, I'm in a *delicate condition* to be sure."

We both burst out laughing, making Mr Cartwright jerk his head in our direction. I watched his stiff back as he trailed after his wife and daughter.

"It's only because men like to think of women as virtuous and pure, traits that are not quite in keeping with acts performed in the marital bed—of which men do not wish to be reminded in public."

Anne blushed before glancing behind us, where Ollie was walking with Quin and the others. Catching her eye a dreamy expression appeared on Ollie's face.

"I'm only glad I live in the countryside," I said, adjusting the ribbons of my bonnet as the breeze made the ends flutter across my face, "else I'd be expected to wear tight corsetry every time I wanted to leave the house." I took a deep breath, pleased to be able to draw the fresh air into my lungs without constraint.

"God forbid a pregnant woman should look pregnant!"

"Even though that's much better for mother and child."

"Oh?" Anne gave me a quizzical look, making me nod.

"I had a tutor as a child, Mr Henderson. With both of us being equally fascinated by the natural world we've kept in touch ever since he moved back to London. Having learned of my pregnancy, he informed me that his friend, an eminent physician, was adamant that pregnant women should wear no restrictive garments, as this could pose a danger to the mother and the growing baby.—In fact, Mr Henderson made me believe his friend was quite exasperated with women refusing to heed such advice."

"Hm." Anne looked down, placing a hand on her abdomen. "Then I, like you, shall be one of the few women to heed his advice when the time comes."

She smiled at me as we reached the edge of the lake. When Ollie and the others caught up Anne walked over to him while I stood next to Quin.

"Are you feeling alright?" he asked. The sun was shining into his face, making his green eyes sparkle.

"Yes," I said, wanting to lay my hand against his cheek.

He held my gaze and I reluctantly settled for a touch of his fingers as his hand reached for mine. We stood side by side for a moment, looking out across the water, which lapped gently against the grassy bank. There was a clump of bushes to one side, which rustled with the sound of birds flitting through its branches.

"Why don't *we* have a lake?" Quin asked suddenly.

I laughed and he gave me an affronted look. "You sound just like Emmett," I said.

"I do?"

"Indeed. I overheard him complaining to Benjamin yesterday that we don't have a lake at Glaslearg."

Quin chuckled. "Well, we do at least have a river—which lends itself equally well to a spot of swimming."

He gave me a penetrating look and I felt my cheeks flush, remembering a few private assignations we'd enjoyed at Glaslearg's waterway.

"Who's going swimming?" Archie's voice broke into my thoughts.

"Nobody," Quin said, still grinning at me. "It would hardly be fitting amongst mixed company." He looked at Archie, who was eyeing the lake in contemplation.

"Then perhaps a little later," Archie said, "when the ladies have retired for the night." He gave me a wink.

"Perhaps," Quin agreed, offering me his arm and leading me toward the picnic area the servants had set up under the branches of a rather lonesome tree.

He deposited me on a wooden folding chair next to the Leweses before joining Archie and Ham.

"This was a wonderful idea," I said to Miss Lewes. "It's beautiful here."

She smiled at me but didn't say anything.

"Have you been here before?" I asked, looking between the two women.

It was Mrs Lewes who answered. "We have. But not often.—Mr Cartwright doesn't entertain much."

"I see." I supposed Mr Cartwright's lack of social engagements might have something to do with his financial difficulties.

The sound of laughter reached us from the lake, where Ollie and Anne were standing on the bank with their heads close together. Mrs Lewes caught my eye.

"It's nice to see Anne so happy," she said. "She hasn't always had it easy."

The arrival of a footman bearing drinks stopped me from responding. I thanked him and took a sip of the cool syllabub, enjoying the sweet liquid as it slid down my throat.

"I think she's made a good match," Mrs Lewes continued once the footman had left. "Just like you have yourself." She gave me a questioning look, making me nod. "Such a union shouldn't be taken for granted," she advised before glancing at her daughter, sadness flashing across her features. "It's never guaranteed."

I looked across at Quin. "No, it isn't."

"I had that with my own husband." I turned back to Mrs Lewes, whose eyes were hooded, peering into the past. Suddenly, she laughed. "Of course, if he were here with us still, he'd be somewhere over there by now." She waved a hand toward the far side of the lake.

I narrowed my eyes, unable to make out anything but grassland and a few patches of moss.

"Well, not necessarily *there* exactly," she amended, "but knee-deep in a bog at any rate."

"Knee-deep in a bog?"

"Oh yes, he found them quite fascinating."

Not sure what could possibly be so fascinating about bogs, I gave her a curious look.

"It all started when he was a young man and had just inherited his father's house. It wasn't anything grand like this." She lifted her chin in the direction of the manor house. "Just a simple cottage in the countryside of Kildare, surrounded by bogland."

Miss Lewes smiled at her mother, clearly enjoying hearing tales about her father.

"He and his friend and neighbour were out one day cutting peat, just a normal part of life. My husband told me it had been the end of a long day when his friend let out a terrible scream, causing Mr Lewes to scramble out of the bog, just in time to see the man disappearing over the nearest hill."

"What happened?" I asked, leaning forward.

"My husband didn't know, so he crept cautiously toward the spot where his friend had been working, holding his peat cutter high above his head." She paused dramatically and I held my breath. "That's when he saw it: a foot sticking out from the turf."

I gasped. "A foot?"

Miss Lewes nodded, an expectant look on her face. No doubt she'd heard the story many times before.

"Yes, a foot," her mother went on, "clad in a leather shoe. Mr Lewes approached it hesitantly, thinking perhaps it was someone recently buried, a victim of a heinous crime."

"And was it?" I turned in some surprise to see Quin standing next to my chair. I hadn't heard him come up beside me, so engrossed in the story had I been.

Mrs Lewes shook her head. "My husband managed to free the rest of the body, but the density of the peat covering it made him think it couldn't have been a recent grave. And the body was buried several feet underground, in a bog that had been cut up for decades, meaning it must have been well below the surface for all those years before."

"But who was it?"

Mrs Lewes gave me a conspiratorial look. "Well, that was the strange part, you see. For the more of the body my husband unearthed, the more he realised it was old, much older than he'd initially thought. There were bits of clothing beneath the turf, unlike any he'd ever seen before. Even the shoe was of a kind not seen for centuries."

"Do you mean to say, this body had been in the bog for hundreds of years?" Quin asked. "And it hadn't decayed?" His eyes met mine briefly, revealing a deep scepticism of Mrs Lewes' story—if not her sanity.

She nodded, though, looking earnestly from one observer to the next. I saw that Anne and Ollie were also there, listening intently.

"Hard as it is to believe that was precisely the case.—At least that's what the naturalist said, whom my husband consulted. With it being evident that the grave was not the scene of a recent crime he saw no need to call the police and instead decided to learn all he could about the strange body he'd stumbled upon. My husband was not a very influential man, or a rich one, but he'd always been interested in the natural world and had made a few likeminded friends, you see." Mrs Lewes sighed. "It was this interest that saw him frequently visit Dublin, which is where we met." A faraway look appeared on her lined face as she stopped speaking.

When she remained quiet her daughter picked up the tale. "My father had collected several scraps of fabric from the bog and had these investigated, enabling him to come up with a theory about the man's origins."

"And?" Anne looked at Miss Lewes with big eyes, hanging on her every word.

"He believed the body to have been that of a man who lived hundreds of years ago, even several centuries before Christ. But"—Miss Lewes lifted a finger to still her audience—"my mother has not yet told you the most intriguing part."

"What?" I demanded, forgetting my manners entirely.

"Besides the strangeness of the body being so well preserved after all this time, with even tufts of reddish hair still clinging to the skull, it also had a gaping wound running from ear to ear across its neck, which my father believed to show that the man was killed as a human sacrifice."

There were several gasps around me, and I felt goosebumps spring up on my arms. I recalled Emmett's light-hearted comments about having a human sacrifice at the Bealtaine festival in the way of the ancient Celts. The Leweses' story made the grisly practice seem far too real, and it gave me an eerie feeling to think of its victims buried beneath our feet.

"Several such bodies have been found in bogs across Ireland, and elsewhere," Mrs Lewes said, causing further consternation. "The idea quite intrigued my husband, and he spent every free moment traipsing through boglands, examining sites and hoping to come across another find."

"Did he?" Ollie asked.

Mrs Lewes shook her head, a small smile on her lips. "Something like that is unlikely to happen more than once in a lifetime."

"But why bogs?"

I looked toward Ham, who was standing at the edge of the group next to Archie, with the Cartwrights alongside.

"My father said the ancient Celts may have believed boglands to have supernatural qualities," Miss Lewes said, "being neither solid nor liquid, their strange terrain linking dry land with water, like a space between two worlds—the perfect place for a human sacrifice, I suppose."

We were all quiet for a moment.

Suddenly, Colleen scoffed. "Supernatural bogs? Human sacrifices left buried for centuries that don't decay?" She wrinkled her delicate nose in distaste. "It sounds like humbug to me."

"My father saw it with his own eyes," Miss Lewes said sharply, a frown appearing on her face.

Colleen sniffed. "It simply doesn't make sense."

"It doesn't make sense only because we don't understand it," I said. "Perhaps there's a peculiarity in the bog itself that prevents decay, something nobody has yet discovered."

Mrs Lewes nodded. "That's just what my husband and his friends concluded." She gave me an approving look. "I think he would have enjoyed talking to you about this topic."

Colleen emitted an unladylike snort. "Well, I *don't* enjoy talking about this topic! Disgusting bodies found in filthy bogs? The entire conversation is utterly repulsive!—Even if it is just a hoax." She glared around the assembly, daring anyone to bring it up again.

I exchanged a glance with Quin, coming just short of rolling my eyes. He grinned at me before offering to refill my glass. The gesture caused the rest of the party to suddenly remember their desperate thirst, making a bustle of activity ensue as normal chatter resumed.

"Was it not peculiar how Cousin George disappeared in the middle of dinner?" Miss Lewes observed as she handed her mother a drink.

With the rest of the party having dispersed the three of us found ourselves temporarily alone.

Mrs Lewes shrugged, turning her attention to her lemonade. "It was a bit, but Cousin George is a peculiar man."

"What do you mean?" I asked.

"We don't see much of him and when we do, he reveals very little of himself.—But I suppose that's just his way."

"I suppose it is," I agreed.

I hadn't gotten much of an impression of George Cartwright, either, during our brief acquaintance. He had mentioned several times that he liked to play cards, but what man didn't?

"What about the rest of the Cartwrights? Do you see much of them?"

"Not much, no." The older woman shook her head. "We don't spend much time in Dublin, you see."

"Unlike the Cartwrights we much prefer the country," her daughter said, waving a hand toward the luscious landscape surrounding us.

I smiled at her, enjoying the gentle breeze blowing off the lake and the chatter of birds nearby.

"Not that the country is as peaceful as it once was." Mrs Lewes' aged eyes took on a melancholy look. "What with desperate folk turning up at one's doorstep at every turn.—One can scarcely go anywhere without seeing the ravages of the famine."

"And yet many choose not to see it," I said, the gaunt-looking faces of the beggars we'd encountered earlier flashing across my mind.

"That is a sad truth, my dear.—And with the passing of Daniel O'Connell and Lord Lieutenant Bessborough, there will likely be many more who choose not to see it."

I nodded. Both politicians had appealed tirelessly for greater aid for Ireland from Britain but had died within days of each other in May, their efforts having been in vain. Whether anyone would step into their shoes and achieve greater success remained to be seen.

"I dare say, though, as much as the British have been vilified for their half-hearted actions"—Mrs Lewes threw a quick glance at Quin and his friends—"I doubt the famine could have been prevented even had they done more, what with the Irish people's utter dependence on the potato and the far-reaching consequences of the blight."

"I would think a few thousand people might have been spared, at least," I said rather brusquely.

Mrs Lewes sighed. "Perhaps. I doubt any Irishman alive or yet unborn will ever forget the Black '47."

My throat felt tight at the name by which the year's horrors were likely to be remembered. Following the second consecutive failed harvest, disease and death were everywhere, with no part of Ireland being spared the famine's ghastly effects.

"Did you know that Ireland was once able to boast having one of the finest networks of medical facilities in Europe?" Mrs Lewes said, a distant look on her face. "But that was before the famine, of course, when the numerous hospitals and dispensaries provided relief across the land. Even if the supplies themselves were rudimentary at times, at least people had somewhere to go when they needed help. But now...there is far too much sickness for anyone to hope to deal with."

"Even with Bessborough's fever hospitals and his attempts to enlist more doctors," I agreed, my heart feeling heavy. The Lord Lieutenant's valiant efforts had achieved next to nothing in the face of the enormous burden of disease

Ireland faced, and with the limited remedies available for the deadly ailments that afflicted those already malnourished and weak.

Perhaps Mrs Lewes was right, I thought. Perhaps no power on this earth was great enough to have prevented all the horrors that had ensued once the blight had struck the land.

Silence descended around us as we were each lost in our own thoughts.

Finally, Mrs Lewes took a deep breath and briskly shook her head. "But we must all remember to reap what pleasures we can from life," she said, "for making ourselves miserable will do little to help anyone."

I held her eyes briefly, feeling her words keenly, aware as I'd been throughout my life of the injustices that prevailed in Ireland, even before the famine—never able to ignore the plight of the less fortunate but never able to help all of them either.

But at least I could use my own prosperity to help those living on our estate, I thought for the thousandth time.

When Quin, Archie and Ham joined us a few minutes later the conversation quickly turned to lighter matters. We spent the rest of the afternoon in pleasant companionship, enjoying the fine weather and the green rolling hills surrounding the lake.

The setting was imminently peaceful—and made more so by the fact that the Cartwrights stayed amongst themselves at a safe distance from the rest of us.

I suppressed a laugh at the uncharitable thought, catching Quin's eye. He lifted one brow, making me smile wryly. I darted a quick glance at the Cartwrights before looking back at him, and Quin gave me a knowing grin.

I did feel a little sorry for Ollie and Anne, who were sitting with the Cartwright trio, looking none too comfortable. Knowing what I did about the strained relationship between several of the parties I imagined the conversation to be rather stilted and, indeed, it looked like long minutes were spent in silence. When Mrs Cartwright declared it was time to head back to the house, Ollie and Anne practically leapt from the picnic blanket in their eagerness for better company.

Both of them seemed relieved to be able to converse with the guests at dinner, rather than their family members. Miraculously, all three Cartwrights were on their best behaviour throughout and so the meal passed pleasantly enough. I did struggle to stay awake, though, and was in danger of collapsing onto my plate until Quin finally announced he was escorting me to our rooms.

I held onto his arm as he led me through the house, my eyes feeling heavy. I barely noticed as he put me to bed and fell asleep instantly, his kiss on my cheek the last thing I remembered.

"KEEP IT DOWN!"

Quin grinned at Ham as he admonished Ollie in loud tones.

"I am keeping it down," Ollie countered just as noisily.

"If this is their idea of keeping it down, I don't want to be around when they start yelling," Archie said drily, making Quin chuckle.

"Besides," Ollie continued at high volume, oblivious to Archie and Quin, "the Cartwrights are hardly in a position to complain to me." He snorted with mirth as he trudged through the house, the others close behind.

It was well past midnight and everyone else had gone to bed. Having played a few rounds of billiards and a hand of cards—all in the company of yet another good bottle of whiskey—the friends had decided to head back to the lake for a swim.

"This was all your idea," Quin said to Archie, watching Ollie and Ham sway along the hallway. "If one of them is about to drown you're the one who's going to rescue him."

"You underestimate the reviving potential of a cold Irish lake, Quinton."

"Hmph." Quin eyed his friends sceptically, making Archie sigh dramatically.

"Do not fear, I am more than capable of saving their hides. I am not nearly as foxed as the two of them, after all."

That was undoubtedly true. While Archie and Quin had held back on the whiskey after the recent night's excesses, Ollie and Ham had shown no such restraint.

By now they'd reached the large double doors that led to the lawn. Ollie opened them with a flourish and started marching across the greenery, ignoring the path that ran alongside.

The cool night air hit Quin's face as he stepped outside, and he breathed in the fresh scent.

He followed the others until he had to stop suddenly, barely avoiding crashing into Ham.

Ollie was standing stock-still in the middle of the lawn, staring down at the grass at his feet, a look of bewilderment on his face.

"We didn't finish the game," he said, his eyes wandering from one man to the other. "We didn't finish the cricket game."

"No, we didn't," Quin agreed slowly.

Between George's abrupt departure and the Cartwrights' argument at dinner that night the game had been quite forgotten.

"But how do we know who's won?" Ollie looked around wildly.

"How about we call it a draw?" Archie suggested, placing an arm across Ollie's shoulders.

"But…but…"

"I think that's fair, don't you?" Archie insisted, trying to lead Ollie away.

"Perhaps we could…" Ollie waved vaguely toward the house. No doubt he was about to suggest fetching the equipment so they could finish the game that instant.

"I think it'll be a bit difficult to see the ball at night." Archie pointed up at the sky and the half-moon that shed only a little light onto the grounds.

"I suppose so." Finally relenting, Ollie let himself be steered toward the edge of the lake, which shone in the pale moonlight, looking still and peaceful.

Ollie perked up at the sight. "A swim! Didn't we want to have a swim?" Not waiting for an answer, he quickly tore off his clothes, leaving them strewn haphazardly on the grass as he rushed toward the water wearing only his drawers, followed by Ham. They splashed into the shallows before diving under, emerging spluttering and hooting like loons.

Quin grinned at Archie, who lifted his shoulders and started stripping down himself. Quin followed suit and soon the four of them were immersed in the freezing water. After the initial shock over the temperature had worn off, they started splashing each other like children and making a hellish racket.

"Didn't you want to spend time with your wife this evening?" Ham asked Ollie during a brief lull, digging an elbow into his friend's side.

They'd all seen the renewed affection between the Penhales that day and wouldn't have been surprised if Ollie had made his excuses after dinner.

"Or did you have your *fill* last night?" Ham roared with laughter at his own joke, clearly still a little addled from the whiskey.

Ollie gave him a sly look. "As a matter of fact, I did," he said, "but that doesn't mean I don't want to have it again tonight."

Ham howled once more, soon joined by Archie and Quin.

"Well, then I'm very honoured you chose our humble company tonight," Ham managed at last, inclining his head regally, making Ollie shovel a handful of water into his face.

"If you must know, it was a close thing. If it weren't for the fact that you're all leaving tomorrow afternoon I might have chosen otherwise. Besides"—Ollie's smile widened—"the night isn't over yet."

Archie snorted. "Anne won't thank you for coming to her bed half frozen and wet."

"Nor would your half-frozen parts be much use to her either," Ham added mirthfully.

Ollie rolled his eyes. "I'm glad my matrimonial escapades are such a source of amusement for you," he said dryly.

"We're happy for you," Quin said, clapping him on the back. "Happy the two of you have reconciled."

"Well...thank you." Ollie looked around at his friends, before dropping his gaze and clearing his throat in embarrassment. "If only I could rid myself of her family!"

They all laughed, which started them splashing each other with water again until they finally emerged from the lake, dripping and shivering. With their fingers stiff from cold and no towels to dry themselves with, they struggled to get back into their clothes.

Waging battle on his own trousers Quin chuckled at the spectacle, sorry he didn't have a few more days to spend with his friends.

# 10.

"AND SO, THE Tuatha Dé Danann were defeated by the Milesians and driven underground, where they are said to live to this day."

I looked at the wide-eyed faces in front of me and smiled.

We'd arrived back at Glaslearg the day before. Although I'd been more than happy to bid the Cartwrights farewell it had been surprisingly difficult to part from Anne. In the few days we'd spent together at Cornac House we'd grown quite close, and I wished we didn't live so far apart.

I had nevertheless been looking forward to coming home, of course, and had been especially eager to see Glaslearg's children. They'd come a long way since I'd started teaching them some months before and most of them eagerly awaited their twice weekly lessons. Seeing reactions like they were showing today also gave me immense joy. While they all knew the ancient Irish legends, hearing them told in English was causing no little excitement among them.

"Those are the Sidhe," Alfie Garvey burst out, forgetting to raise his hand in his eagerness. Realising his mistake, he hunched his shoulders.

I lifted my chin but answered, nonetheless. "That's correct, Alfie. In fact, the name for Ireland's old folk comes from the Gaelic word for burial ground, which is where the Sidhe are said to live.—Yes, Emmett?"

"Is that why the Sidhe can do magic? Because they come from the old gods?" Emmett was sitting on the edge of his seat, fascinated as always by the topic of fairies and folklore. Although he didn't need to learn English—which had been the main purpose behind me teaching the tenants' children—he never missed a lesson. And for the same reason, neither did Benjamin. Aware that most children had a similar thirst for knowledge I made a point of discussing a variety of topics with them. Keeping their interest meant they learnt English without having to put in too much effort, and many of them were almost fluent by now.

"I imagine so," I said.

Emmett's hand shot back into the air, and I nodded at him to continue. "You said the Tuatha Dé Danann was magical creatures what landed in Ireland in a cloud o' mist after they was thrown out o' heaven.—But if they could do magic, how'd they get defeated by humans in the first place?"

"I dare say it was no easy feat. Some say they were outwitted, others that they were outnumbered, but in the end, the Sons of Mil were able to claim Ireland as their own."

Emmett didn't seem particularly satisfied with this answer but didn't argue when one of the other children asked another question instead.

"Are we all Milesians then?"

"Perhaps. It is said the Milesians were the forefathers of the ancient Celts, whose descendants include Niall of the Nine Hostages who founded the clan of O'Neill, which is my own family clan. But who's to say that all of us aren't descended from the Milesians?"

"Well, I'm not, anyway," Emmett grumbled under his breath, clearly frustrated about hailing from as boring a place as England.

A few of the children laughed, while Benjamin and Conor on either side of Emmett elbowed him in the ribs. Seeing one of the younger ones trying to suppress a yawn, though, I decided we'd done enough for the day. While the children were eager to learn, their lessons didn't excuse them from the chores they were expected to do at home. Even before coming to class in the morning most children had already tended livestock or fields, and their work was far from over when they returned to their cottages.

I clapped my hands. "That's it for today. Please take the benches outside and replace the table and chairs."

Chattering among themselves the children got to work. With no proper classroom on the estate Mr Connell had kindly agreed to let me use his cottage for my lessons. Quin had provided benches for the children to sit on, since there were too many to fit around the Connell's table. Although the arrangement required a bit of effort to organise every day, it meant the children didn't have to walk all the way to the manor house on the other end of the estate, where we might otherwise have set up.

Within a few minutes the Connell's cottage was returned to normal, and the children skipped off as I went to retrieve my mare, Emmett and Benjamin trailing behind me.

"Good lesson, was it?"

I turned in surprise at hearing Quin's voice. I smiled but was forestalled from answering by Emmett.

"Oh, it was, sir!" he said as Quin dismounted from his horse. "Mrs Williams told us all about the folk what used t' live in Ireland."

"Like the Tuatha Dé Danann with their four great treasures," Benjamin added, looking as enthralled as Emmett.

"Four great treasures, hm? That does sound most intriguing."

"It is, sir!" Emmett assured Quin, who gave me an amused look.

"They 'ad a cauldron that could feed a whole army," Benjamin burst out, "and a stone that could pronounce a man king." Emmett gave his friend an annoyed look. Clearly, he'd wanted to be the one to list the Tuatha Dé Danann's famed possessions. Unperturbed, Benjamin went on, "The greatest treasures was a sword and a spear. But not just any sword and spear. Ones that no enemy could escape from!"

"Ye see, it just don't make sense." Emmett narrowed his eyes at Benjamin as if the whole thing were his fault. "If the Tuatha Dé Danann was so powerful, how'd they lose t' the Milesians, who was only mortals?"

"Even gods can be defeated," Benjamin insisted.

"Not by humans!"

"If there was enough o' them."

"Hmph."

"And if they was clever enough t' trick the Tuatha Dé Danann."

"Ye can't trick the gods!"

"Ye can!"

"No, ye can't!"

"Yes, ye can!"

"No, ye can't!"

"I see Mrs Williams has given you much to think about," Quin interrupted the pair, who stood nose to nose, glaring at each other. "Do try not to come to blows about it." Quin gave the boys a stern look.

"Hmph." Emmett stalked off toward the pony standing patiently at the side of the cottage next to my mare. He started untethering the beast but stopped suddenly, turning to give Benjamin a dark look as he evidently remembered he'd have to share his mount with his erstwhile friend.

I looked down at the ground, pressing my lips together to stop myself from laughing out loud. Only once the boys had gotten reluctantly underway—their heads turned in opposite directions and sitting as far apart as was possible on the back of a horse—did I dare to meet Quin's eyes.

He grinned at me. "Do you think they'll make it back to the house in one piece?"

"I hope so," I said. "I hadn't realised Irish folklore was such a contestable subject matter."

"For most people it probably isn't. For boys though…"

"In that case I rather hope we're having a girl!" I patted the growing bulge of my stomach.

"And girls are less prone to arguing?"

I laughed, remembering my own stubborn streak. "Perhaps not."

Wearing an amused expression, Quin helped me onto my mare before mounting Gambit in one smooth movement.

"Were you visiting one of the tenants?" I asked as we started ambling along the path back to the manor house.

Quin nodded. "The McAndrews' hut is showing further signs of damage. The whole thing really ought to be pulled down. Who knows how long it's been standing there?"

"Is it still safe to live in?"

"I think so. I don't expect it to collapse, at any rate, not unless there were an earthquake."

"Which is virtually unheard of in Ireland."

"Thank God for that! Still, the walls will probably continue to crumble, the door is warped and barely closes, and now the roof has sprung a leak. It hardly seems worth the effort to replace the thatch under the circumstances.—But they insist on staying in the old mud hut so what am I to do?" Quin shrugged. "At least their hut is situated on higher ground, so the floor doesn't turn into a swamp every time it rains."

He glanced up at the sky, where thick clouds were billowing, the threat of rain never far away in Ireland.

"I imagine that's one of the reasons the McAndrews are content to stay where they are," I said. "As long as they can sleep dry, they don't care too much what their home looks like, as they don't spend much time there, being busy on the fields most of the day."

"I suppose." Quin frowned as the first drops started to fall. "Can you imagine working in the rain all day only to come home in your soaked clothing to a wet floor, a wet bed and wet turf with which to attempt to light your fire?"

We were both quiet for a moment, contemplating such an existence, which was an unfortunate reality for many people across the land.

Quin shook his head and breathed in heavily. "I shall ensure the McAndrews' thatch is replaced forthwith and that the walls are supported with wooden binders to prevent them from giving in. And they'll get a new door and proper flooring too, I'll insist upon it!"

I smiled at him, and he gave me a sheepish look.

"Ah, and how was your morning?" he asked.

"Good," I said. "The children are eager to learn. The old stories kept them riveted today, even though they've probably heard them countless times. I suppose it was the novelty of hearing them told in English, rather than Gaelic."

"You've done a wonderful job with them. Their English has improved tenfold, and their general knowledge besides."

"It has. How much difference it will make to their future, I can't say, but at least I've given them that." I compressed my lips briefly. Despite the small amount of education I was able to provide—which was nevertheless more than they'd likely have received otherwise, being of the lower class—it would be exceedingly difficult for any of Glaslearg's children to escape the circle of poverty they'd been born into.

I pushed away the thought but then remembered something else that had been bothering me.

"The Murphys' children haven't been attending class," I said, throwing Quin a sideways glance.

"Hm. Since my last…conversation with their father, I suppose?"

"Yes."

"There's not much I can do about it. Although it is a shame, of course."

"It is a shame," I agreed. "Especially Bridget was showing such promise." The Murphys' eldest, ten-year-old Bridget, seemed to absorb knowledge like a sponge, her eyes lighting up every time she set foot in the classroom.

"So you've said. Still, I can't force Robert Murphy to send his children to your lessons." Quin's face took on a look of regret.

"But…"

"Alannah," he said before I could continue, "nothing good would come of me raising the subject with the man."

"But if…"

"He never liked me to begin with and already resents me for interfering with his private affairs once before. I shall not discuss with him what he should or should not be doing with his children—not again."

"So you'll rob them of their future?"

"That's not fair and you know it. It's because of his children that the family still has a home to live in. What they make of that opportunity is up to them."

"Opportunity? Without an education the children have no opportunity!"

"That's hardly *my* fault! I've done everything I could to make the lives of my tenants better."

"But…"

"The fact that they have no chance in this God-forsaken land has nothing to do with *me*!"

"God-forsaken?" I snarled, bristling at the insult to my home. "If that's what you think of Ireland, why are you still here?"

"There are times when I haven't the faintest idea!" he growled, his own eyes narrowed in anger.

I made a sound of disgust as I urged Milly into a canter. Quin swore under his breath behind me, but I didn't slow down, speeding the rest of the way to the stables without looking back. When I got there, I handed the horse to one of the grooms and stomped toward the house.

Quin caught up with me in the courtyard. Easily able to outpace me he grabbed me by the arm and turned me to face him.

"Alannah, please be reasonable."

"I am being reasonable. Whereas you've obviously tired of *God-forsaken* Ireland and want to go back to England, where everything is easier."

"I never said that!"

"You could have fooled me!"

Quin's nostrils flared as he loomed over me, his face only inches from mine. "Aren't you the one always telling everyone to be kind to others?" he demanded.

I shook off his hand and took a step back, crossing my arms in front of my chest. "That does not apply when speaking to one's pig-headed husband!"

"I see. And is that an apt description of me then?"

"Well," I said, lifting my chin in defiance, "since I'm not a bigamist I suppose it must be, mustn't it?"

We stared at each other in silence, until at last, the corner of Quin's mouth twitched. It took another moment but finally, we both broke into a reluctant smile.

He shook his head as he pulled me close. "I am not pig-headed."

I snorted. "If you say so."

"I do say so. And I wish you'd listen to me...at least occasionally." He paused briefly before leaning back a little so he could look at me. "Nothing good will come of me speaking to Mr Murphy, you know that as well as I do. It won't change anything...and probably only make things worse."

"You're right, I know you are." Even speaking to Mary would achieve nothing, cowed as she was by her husband. I knew she appreciated everything we'd done for her family and would have wanted the children to continue their education, but she would never defy his wishes, no matter what it cost her. I sighed. "It's just...it all seems so unfair and makes me feel so powerless." I leaned against Quin's chest, not caring which servants might be around to see us. "The one thing that might give the children the chance to make a better life for themselves is denied them because of their father's bitterness. How can he not see what he's taking from them?"

"He doesn't want to see it," Quin said. "He's so wrapped up in his own sense of injustice that he can't spare a thought for anyone else, even his own family."

"I suppose you're right. If he cared about them in the first place, he wouldn't be laying into them with his fists at every opportunity."

"I'm sure he justifies his actions, telling himself they've defied him, that he's the victim. He's only performing his duties as the head of the family, after all, disciplining his wife and children."

I narrowed my eyes at this statement, making Quin raise one brow. Indeed, it was true that physical punishment was within the realm of a husband's and father's expected duties. Duties nobody would question unless they resulted in serious injury—which Mr Murphy had thus far avoided.

Quin squeezed my hand. "He's a weak creature who convinces himself the abuse he's meting out is simply well-deserved punishment." He shook his head slowly, a look of resignation on his face. "I've met men like him before—they don't much listen to reason."

"But then what can we do?"

Quin was silent for a moment before answering. "Support the rest of the family the best we can. And hope.—Hope the children somehow defy the odds."

This wasn't a very satisfactory answer to me, but I knew Quin was right.

There wasn't anything else we could do.

# 11.

THE CARTWRIGHT'S HOUSE party soon felt like a distant memory as they settled back into their daily routine.

Glaslearg's livestock was thriving and the fields were blooming, and Quin remained hopeful of a bountiful harvest. Alannah, too, was blooming with the life she carried, and Quin watched her growing belly in wonder and fascination.

It was only a few more months until he could hold their baby in his arms, and he smiled in anticipation, lost in thought.

Finally recalling himself to the present some minutes later he turned toward his desk, where several letters were waiting for his attention. He found one from his father, which he turned to first. It was a brief note ensuring Quin all was well in London and asking after their welfare. Peculiarly, the baron's envelope contained another sealed letter, this one addressed to Alannah. Quin wondered about the contents and was tempted to open it himself. He did no such thing, of course, only putting it aside to show Alannah later, eying it with interest for a moment. Aside from the letter to Alannah, his father had also included a piece of newspaper, which Quin unfolded next. It was an article from the *Illustrated London News*, dated 8 May 1847, entitled *Loss of an Emigrant Ship, and Two Hundred and Forty Passengers*. Quin's heart sank as he continued reading, his eyes scanning over the page as he picked out phrases here and there.

*We are sorry to have to record the loss of the ship* **Exmouth**, *under very painful circumstances, the loss of life being very great.*

*According to the statement of three sailors, the sole survivors of the wreck...the* **Exmouth** *sailed from Londonderry for Quebec between three and four o'clock on the morning of Sunday, the 25$^{th}$ ult., with a light south west breeze. She had a crew of 11 men (inclusive of the captain), and about 240* *emigrants, consisting principally of small farmers and tradesmen, with their families. Many were females and children going out to join their fathers and protectors, who had already settled in Canada.*

*The vessel was registered for 165½ passengers; but, as two children count as one adult, and as a very large proportion were under age–there being only about 60 men amongst the passengers–the survivors of the wreck think that the total number of these ill-fated emigrants must have amounted to 240.*

Quin inhaled sharply though his nose. Two-hundred-and-forty souls lost. He had to swallow heavily before going on.

*The ship lost sight of land about four o'clock on Sunday afternoon. The breeze, which had been light in the morning, increased to a gale during the day, and about eleven p.m. it came in terrific squalls, accompanied by heavy torrents of rain.*

*About eleven o'clock on Tuesday night (the 27th ult.), land, and a light, were seen on the starboard quarter, which Captain Booth, at first, took to be the light on the Island of Tory, off the north west coast of Ireland, and, in the belief that he thus had ample sea-room in the course he was steering, he bore along. As he drifted near the land, however, and observed that the light was a flashing, instead of a stationary one, he became conscious of his error and dangerous position, and made every effort to repair it, by bringing the ship farther to the northward and westward; and, with the view of "clawing" her off the land, the maintopsail and the foretopmast stay sail were set, and the jib half hoisted. The effort, however, was an ineffectual one; the ship soon got amongst the broken water, and, at half-past twelve on Wednesday morning, was dashed amongst the rocks. If the above be a correct version of the impression on the captain's mind as to his position–and it is distinctly spoken to by two of the survivors–the result shows that he must have been fully a hundred miles out of his reckoning; but, perhaps, it could not well be otherwise. The sun was obscured all the time by black clouds; the moon was only seen through a heavy haze at intervals, and from these causes it was impossible that any observation could be taken. The light seen was in reality that of Oransa or Oversay, on the point of the Rhinns or Runs of Islay, to the north-west of the entrance of Lochindaul; and the land seen, and on which the brig eventually struck, was the western part of the iron-bound coast of the island. She went ashore, and after striking once was dashed broadside on alongside the rocks, which rose to the height of the mast-head. She struck violently against the rocks three times, and at the fourth stroke the mainmast went by the board, and fell into a chasm of the rock.*

*A quarter of an hour elapsed from the time of the brig first striking until the three survivors got upon the rock.*

*There was no cry from the multitude cooped up within the hull of the ill-fated brig; or at least it was unheard, for the commotion of the elements was so furious that the men on the top could scarcely hear each other at the top of their voices. The emigrants, therefore, must have perished in their births, as the rocks rapidly thumped the bottom out of the vessel.*

Quin sighed and ran a hand across his face, imagining the horror of perishing upon the rocks of Islay, so close to home and yet so far from safety. He sat silently for a moment before finally shaking himself and turning toward the rest of his correspondence.

He spotted a letter from Glaslearg's former overseer, Mr Dunne, and managed a smile as his heart lifted. The man had left Ireland several months ago to search for the woman he loved—the daughter of his former employer who'd been sent away by her father as punishment for her affections for the overseer. Having finally tracked her to America Dunne had wasted no time in taking ship and following her.

Quin quickly slit open the envelope, eager to read what Mr Dunne had found.

*Boston, Mass., June 29th, 1847.*

*Mr Quinton Williams,*
*The estate of Glaslearg,*
*County Tyrone, Ulster P.*

Sir,—I write to you in a state of deep gratitude for having survived the journey from Ireland to America. You may think this opening declaration to be overly dramatic, yet I assure you it is anything but. Naturally, I had heard something of the dangers of seafaring voyages, but my wildest imaginings could not have prepared me for the perils that awaited me aboard the Alberta on its way to Boston. While heavy storms battered the ship most alarmingly for several days, this was no more a danger than awaited me elsewhere on my voyage.

With so many of my countrymen leaving Irish shores voluntarily or by force, the crowds descending on the lodging houses of Liverpool where they sought passage were such as I have never seen. Many seemed to have no inkling of the length of journey they were embarking upon and were thoroughly unprepared, while others succumbed to disease in their crowded quarters before even setting foot aboard ship. Those able to embark may have thought themselves fortunate were it not for the appalling conditions that prevailed on board many of the numerous ships taking emigrants to British North America. Treated little better than cargo, hundreds of men, women and children were bundled belowdecks, where I'm told they spent most of the six-week journey without the benefit of light or air, wallowing in filth in vessels that could scarcely be deemed seaworthy, desperately hoping to survive the journey.

Conditions on the Alberta may well be described as luxurious in comparison, and I count myself fortunate for having the means of purchasing the more expensive passage upon this better-equipped ship. Better-equipped being a relative term, though, with a large number of poorer souls nevertheless crammed into steerage, and food and water for their journey being in limited supply. Within three weeks of our departure a fever had broken out in the hold, and I spent most of the remaining voyage in my meagre cabin praying I might avoid the contagion as it spread throughout the rest of the ship. By the time we reached Boston, nineteen of my fellow travellers had found a watery grave, while many of the remaining passengers looked little better than corpses themselves. One can only hope their luck improves in their new home.

*As for myself, I was pleased to locate Miss Thompson's name on one of the passenger lists at the port upon my arrival. I had discovered in Liverpool that she had taken passage upon a ship heading for Boston, which was the reason for me doing the same. Having undertaken the journey myself I was most relieved to learn she had survived it! Indeed, I felt a brief sense of gratitude towards her father for having placed her upon a seaworthy vessel rather than one of the floating coffins heading further north—although, with her departure preceding the onset of the famine and the ensuing exodus by several months, her journey no doubt would have been far removed from the horrors of these deeply troubled times. The blank and gaunt faces crowding the docks haunt me daily with their suffering and I find myself anxiously praying for their deliverance in this new world.*

*But I digress with my maudlin thoughts.*

*I have taken a room at an inn whilst I make enquiries about Miss Thompson's whereabouts. Though I entertain the hope that she may have settled in Boston, I have no inkling of her circumstances and no notion of the state in which I may find her. And while I may wish for her father to have provided her with the means to see herself settled, knowing the man makes me fear for the worst.*

*I do hope most fervently I am wrong.*

*Please send my warmest regards to your wife, and all at the estate.*

*Your most obedient servant,*
*Lachlan Dunne.*

Quin folded the letter and replaced it in the envelope. He wondered how long it would take Dunne to find Miss Thompson—or if he ever would. Any number of things might have happened to her since her arrival in the city several months before. In fact, Quin suddenly realised, it wasn't only months before but years. Mr Dunne had meant to start working at Glaslearg at the end of 1843, the year Quin himself had arrived in Ireland. Instead, the overseer had found himself imprisoned for allegedly assaulting his former employer after

Thompson had told Dunne he'd sent his daughter away. Which meant Miss Thompson would have been in America for almost four years by now.

There was no telling how or where—or if—she lived.

Quin set aside the letter, intending to show it to Alannah later. He had to admit Dunne had exhibited remarkable industry in locating Miss Thompson on the ship's register. With her voyage occurring some years earlier, it would have been a considerable challenge to hunt down the correct records, whether in Liverpool or in Boston. And yet Dunne had found her, twice.

Perhaps he would find her a third time and they would be reunited at last.

Quin hoped so. Lord knew good news was in short supply. His mind flitted to the thousands of Irish people crossing the Atlantic. Whether choosing to seek a better life for themselves across the ocean or being forced upon a ship by their former landlords who wanted them off their hands, Dunne's letter—and the disaster of the Exmouth—had brought to light the dangers of their passage.

The fate of those remaining in Ireland was no less precarious, though.

As they had been for months now, the Irish people were desperate for food. So much so that riots had become commonplace, with crowds attacking bakeries and shops, governmental depots and anywhere else they might be able to snatch a life-saving morsel for themselves or their families. Imprisonment for theft, and even transportation or hanging, had long since stopped being a deterrent for the enormous number of men, women and children who continued to starve across the land each day.

The death toll was horrific, despite the soup kitchens that had already doled out millions of rations to those in need, despite the enormous quantities of food sent from America—arriving in warships to the agitation of the British and Irish populace, the ships' white flags with a shamrock wreath and thistle the only indication of their peaceful intentions—and despite the hundreds of thousands of dollars donated by Irish immigrants in America to help suffering relatives and friends back home. Even all of this was proving insufficient, coming too late for scores of people who succumbed to disease.

And the future continued to look bleak.

For while the summer had been warm and dry, giving hope of a good harvest, the potato acreage planted in the spring had been vastly reduced. With so few seed potatoes available following two disastrous seasons, there was little hope of the peasants finally reaping enough bounty to once more feed their families.

Knowing this, many labourers had started demanding monetary payment for working Ireland's grain fields, when in the past they might have been given a potato garden to grow their own crops. But with little work available in the first place and few means for the poor to plant anything other than cheap potatoes, an entire system was threatening to collapse.

There was a knock at the door and Quin lifted his head, glad of the distraction to take his mind off Ireland's troubles.

"Are you coming in to eat?" Alannah asked as she came to stand in front of the desk.

Quin glanced at the small clock in front of him, surprised when he realised it was past suppertime.

"I must have lost track of time," he said, waving at the letters.

"I see." Alannah looked down at the paperwork strewn across the tabletop. "Is that from Mr Dunne?" Her voice was tinged with excitement as she pointed toward one of the envelopes.

"It is." Quin smiled and slid the letter over to her.

She took a seat opposite him and eagerly started reading. When she was done, she sighed. "I do hope he finds her."

"So do I."

They were both quiet for a moment. After a while Alannah cocked her head toward the door. "Shall we?"

He started to nod but then suddenly remembered the letter from his father. "I almost forgot," he said, handing her the envelope.

Recognising the seal, Alannah's eyes went wide. "From your father? Addressed to me?"

Quin shrugged and passed her the letter opener. She quickly slit open the envelope and removed the pages within. Unfolding them, she gasped.

"What is it?" Quin asked, leaning forward on his chair.

Alannah didn't answer, though. Scanning the writing intently, her eyes suddenly filled with tears.

"Alannah?" Quin came around the desk and placed a hand on her back.

"It's Niall. It's…it's mine." She swallowed heavily and a tear rolled down her cheek as she handed one of the papers to Quin.

It was a deed to the neighbouring estate, Talamh na Niall, called Niall for short by the O'Neills who'd once lived there—until the last O'Neill, Alannah's brother Kieran, had been blackmailed out of his land some years before.

Quin sat back against the desk, feeling stunned.

"It was your father. He remembered."

The baron had known about Herbert Andrews, who'd taken the estate from Kieran, and had helped see the man convicted of his numerous crimes.

"Andrews' assets were confiscated after his conviction. But because of the nature of his…acquisition of Talamh na Niall, nobody even knew it existed. Until recently."

Alannah handed Quin a second page, which was a note from his father accompanying the deed.

"He convinced the courts to give the estate back to you, as your father's sole surviving heir." Quin gave a breath of a laugh, imagining the baron throwing his weight around to get his way.

It would have been no easy feat. With the laws of land ownership being what they were very few women ever inherited property. Some land was historically entailed to male heirs only, leaving even well-meaning fathers with their hands legally tied. And once married, any property a woman did own, automatically passed to her husband.

"It's yours now." Alannah's voice was soft as she stared into the distance. "Even though my name is on the deed."

"You know I would never take it from you."

She gave Quin a brief smile and he offered her his hand, pulling her to her feet. He held her close for a moment before leading her out the door. In the entrance hall she stopped, turning toward the staircase.

"I'm feeling rather tired. I think I'll go to bed."

Quin wrinkled his brow in concern. "Are you alright?"

"Yes. You go on ahead."

She squeezed his hand and started up the stairs.

"What about dinner?" he called after her. "Are you not hungry?"

She turned back and shook her head. "Just tired." She held Quin's eyes for a moment before heading back upstairs, Quin watching her until she disappeared.

THE GHOSTS OF my past did not let me sleep.

What I'd told Quin was true. I was tired. Exhausted, in fact. But my exhaustion stemmed from the mental, not the physical.

Holding the deed to Talamh na Niall in my hands had been a shock.

I had been so angry when I'd found out Kieran had lost the estate, and unutterably sad to learn he'd been blackmailed out of his land because of the poor choices he'd made in the past. But I'd long since resigned myself to the fact and managed, for the most part, to think only of the happy memories we'd shared in our childhood home.

I'd never imagined Niall might one day be returned to me, not even when Herbert Andrews met his well-deserved end in a London prison cell.

Being given back the land my family had held for generations in the face of English persecution and hatred, had brought with it an immense rush of joy—followed almost immediately by an equally immense rush of sadness at all that had been lost.

Looking at the crisp black pen strokes on the single page had made me long for things to be as they once were.

I wished for my father to still be alive, and my mother—and dear, deluded Kieran. How I wished Kieran had made a life for himself, started a family of his own and lived at Niall still, carrying on the O'Neill family legacy.

As I lay in bed thinking about the past, I found myself wishing for so many things to have been different, not only in my own life but for those around me—for the Irish people to have been treated differently, their voices to have been heard, their customs to have been upheld, and for their lives to have mattered to the English who'd conquered them, then and now.

The irony of my family's estate being returned to me under the circumstances had not escaped me. For although I'd been declared the legal owner of Talamh na Niall I could neither sell the estate, rent it to someone else or do anything at all with it without Quin's consent. Which meant the property was now firmly in the hands of an Englishman—my husband, who was lord and master over me as far as the law was concerned (and perhaps the reason why the English courts had granted the baron's request in the first place).

I knew Quin would never act the part and yet, at that moment, I resented him for the fact. It was not logical or even rational and it certainly was not fair, as it was the fault of the men who'd made the laws not Quin himself, but the thought of any more Irish land going to the English deeply upset me. After my ancestors had held onto the estate against all odds and my brother had lost it because of his foolishness, it was returned to me only to now effectively belong to my English husband because women were not thought capable of complex reasoning and dealing with anything more difficult than running the household and raising children.

It was the same belief that excluded women from higher education, sitting in parliament and any number of things that might actually make a difference in their and other people's lives.

I sighed, rolling onto my side.

I'd thought about all of this many times before, of course. In fact, there was a time when I'd thought about little else—when Kieran had dashed my hopes of attending university by informing me that women weren't allowed to go.

Thoughts of Kieran made tears come to my eyes once more as I contemplated for the thousandth time the life he might have lived if he'd made different choices.

Immersed in my own misery I was only vaguely aware of the door opening some time later. Quin slid into bed behind me and cautiously laid a hand on my hip. I patted his fingers, and he came closer, draping an arm around me and hugging me against his chest.

"Are you alright?"

The concern in his voice made me feel instantly guilty for my earlier resentment of him for something that wasn't his fault.

"Yes," I said, pulling him closer. "Just a little overwhelmed."

"I understand. It's all very unexpected."

"It certainly is that."

Quin kissed the back of my head. "What will you do?"

I was quiet for a moment, contemplating my options. "I don't know."

"We could live at Niall if that's what you want."

I thought about my family home and living there with Quin, bringing our child into the world at the small estate where I'd grown up. For an instant it was a future I desperately wanted, to go back to the house I'd shared with my parents and brother, where I held so many fond memories of loved ones who were no longer with us. And yet, I knew I could never reconcile those fond memories with the realities of the here and now. The house and estate should have belonged to Kieran. He should be living there still with a wife and children, dear neighbours who would visit us at Glaslearg for tea.

I shook my head in some regret. "Glaslearg is my home now."

"You need only say the word if you change your mind," Quin said, stroking the swell of my abdomen with one hand.

Although the words were kindly meant I felt suddenly irritated at the reminder that it was not my choice at all. "So you can grant your permission for me to do what I want with the house that belongs to me?"

Quin shifted behind me and rolled me gently onto my back so he could look at me. "You don't need my permission."

"According to the law, I do."

The light from the lamp on the nightstand flickered across Quin's face, reflecting in the shiny surfaces of his eyes. "I cannot change the law, Alannah. But I am telling you, you can do with Niall what you wish. It is yours. I do not believe myself to have any claim on the estate that rightfully belongs to your family."

At the mention of my family, my throat felt tight, and a trickle of tears ran down my cheek. Quin wiped them away with one thumb, before cupping my face in his palm.

"Take some time to think about it. There's no need to rush into anything."

I nodded and Quin kissed me softly on the lips. When I wrapped my arms around his neck, he rolled with me, so we lay on our sides, facing each other.

"I know this came as a shock to you," he said, stroking my cheek. "And that you'll be thinking of Kieran and what might have been." He smiled at the surprise that must have shown on my face. "I know you quite well, Alannah." He became serious once more before continuing, "I also know you still miss him every day."

The tears that had just dried started flowing again. I could do nothing to stop them as Quin pulled me against his chest.

"It's going to be alright," he whispered into my hair, while he ran one hand up and down my back.

He held me as I shook with emotion, overwhelmed with the day's revelations, until at last, I drifted off to sleep.

## 12.

WHILE MY SHOCK at having been given the deed to Talamh na Niall soon abated, I remained undecided about what to do with the land. Quin didn't press me, though, and so, for now, all remained as before, with Niall's tenants living in the farmhouse the way they'd done since Kieran had lost the estate to Herbert Andrews a few years earlier.

I did wonder who had been collecting the tenants' rent following the man's arrest and subsequent death. No doubt a former steward of Andrews was enjoying keeping the money for himself, I thought, remembering Mr Brennan, the overseer employed by the baron before Quin had arrived at Glaslearg. Quite content to be in control of the estate in the absence of the landlord Brennan had not only managed to dupe incoming tenants into paying more rent for less land but had also been happy to pocket the surplus earnings without telling Quin or his father about it. Fear of retribution had made the man turn tail and disappear before Quin's arrival at Glaslearg, the money gone with him.

It was this thought that finally decided me.

Michaelmas was soon approaching, one of the four quarter days on which rent was typically collected. I wouldn't give a dishonest man another chance at lining his pockets.

It was thus that I found myself standing in front of the door to my childhood home with Quin close beside me. He caught my eyes and his lips quirked, no doubt recalling the first time we'd met, when he'd come here to speak to Kieran and had instead encountered me. I smiled at him, feeling my pounding heart begin to slow.

Although we'd briefly met the family that lived at Niall when they'd first arrived I hadn't been back inside the house since Kieran's eviction by Andrews. I vividly recalled that last day, when Quin and I had come upon the chaos of Kieran attempting to move Niall's furnishings. With him having no idea where to go or what to do, the courtyard had been strewn with tables, chairs and sundry items, all of which had eventually found their way into Glaslearg's manor house—to my brother's mortification—where they remained to this day.

Looking around now at the neat courtyard made me think of happier times I'd spent here, and a sudden feeling of gratitude came over me at owning this land once more. While none of my family members currently lived here that may well change in the future. Perhaps our son or daughter would make Niall their home, I thought, laying a hand on my abdomen. The baby kicked as if in agreement, just as the door was opened by a woman I recognised as the tenant's wife, Mrs Lynch.

She looked surprised to see us at her threshold but greeted us courteously and bid us to enter.

It gave me a strange feeling following her to the drawing room, seeing the familiar space filled with other people's things.

Three young children suddenly came barrelling down the passageway, screeching when they spotted their mother. Mrs Lynch tried to quieten them, looking toward the back of the house as if searching for someone. Before long a portly, elderly woman in smock and mobcap appeared. She gave us a brief, wide-eyed curtsy before gathering the children and bustling them out the drawing room door.

Mrs Lynch looked fondly after them for a moment before turning toward Quin and me. "How may I assist you, Mr and Mrs Williams?" She looked from Quin to me and back again, clearly wondering what we were doing there. Aside from exchanging occasional pleasantries at chance meetings we'd had no contact with the Lynches since they'd moved to Niall.

"Mrs Lynch," Quin said, "we were hoping to speak to you and your husband. Is he here, perhaps?"

"I'm afraid he's out on the fields. Although"—Mrs Lynch glanced at a small clock on the mantel—"he should be returning shortly for his tea. Would you like to wait for him?" She blinked at Quin, seeming torn between wanting us to wait and wanting us to leave.

"Yes, thank you," I said, trying to put her at ease.

She nodded. "Then I shall arrange for some tea and biscuits."

Once the tray arrived we waited in an awkward silence for several minutes. "How old are your children, Mrs Lynch?" I asked at last, as much to have something to say as because I wanted to know.

The woman's features softened. "Rory has just turned ten, Donal is eight and our Erin will be six next month."

"They're lovely," I said.

"Thank you." Mrs Lynch smiled. Her gaze dropped briefly to my abdomen before returning to my face. Although she could clearly tell I was pregnant the topic was not one to be broached in polite company, certainly not by someone who was barely an acquaintance, and absolutely not by a tenant to a landowner.

"How have you enjoyed living at Talamh na Niall?" I asked.

"Very much so."

"Yes, we're very happy here."

The voice coming from the doorway made me look up, to where Mr Lynch was just entering the drawing room. Although he'd evidently made an effort to scrub the day's dirt off his hands and face he was still dressed in his work clothes. He lifted his head high, though, ignoring the contrast between his grubby attire and Quin's pristine wardrobe. Coming closer he gave his wife a brief, curious look before turning toward Quin and me.

"Mr Lynch," Quin greeted the man, extending his hand.

"Mr Williams."

When the niceties had been concluded everyone settled down and the Lynches looked expectantly at Quin.

He cleared his throat. "Mr and Mrs Lynch, you may not be aware that Talamh na Niall belonged to my wife's family for generations."

The couple exchanged a startled glance as Quin took the folded deed out of his jacket pocket.

"And while ownership changed hands a few years ago the estate has recently come into my wife's possession once more."

Mr Lynch perused the piece of paper, his jaws tensed. Next to him his wife leaned closer, her eyes flitting across the black ink. When she looked back up her eyes were wide with apprehension.

"We have no intention of evicting you," Quin assured them quickly, seeing the looks on their faces. While the Lynches were clearly doing well for themselves, having the means of farming a sizeable estate and supporting their family in the midst of a famine, as tenant farmers they were nevertheless at the mercy of their landlord.

And having an unknown landlord appear on their doorstep unexpectedly was obviously making them think the worst.

"But…" Mr Lynch shook his head in confusion, waving the deed in the air.

"Mr Andrews obtained the estate illegally," Quin explained, causing the other man to raise his brows. "Upon his death the deed reverted back to my wife, the rightful owner.—Which means she is your landlord now."

Mr Lynch nodded mechanically as he tried to make sense of this new information.

"We have no intention of evicting you," I repeated Quin's earlier assurance. "But we would like to discuss with you your tenancy and draw up a new contract."

As I began to lay out the terms of their contract and the amount of rent we expected them to pay each quarter the Lynches began to visibly relax. In fact, they seemed pleased at the changes we proposed and admitted they'd thus far been tenants-at-will, with Andrews' agents having informed them they could be evicted without notice.

"And so we had no choice but to pay what he asked for last quarter," Mr Lynch said, shaking his head. "Which was far more than we'd agreed."

I frowned. By the previous quarter Andrews was already dead, confirming what I'd suspected, that his steward had used the opportunity to make himself rich.

"It's lucky all the land isn't planted in potatoes, for the grain harvest has seen us through many dark times. But we haven't got much in the way of money to spare." Mr Lynch glanced at his wife, who was looking down at her lap.

"You won't have to worry about that anymore," Quin said and removed another document from his jacket. "If the man shows up at the estate expecting to be paid again, show him this." He handed Mr Lynch the paper. "It's a copy of the deed I had drawn up for you.—And if he should not be satisfied with that then send him to me. I shall be delighted to receive him and list the crimes he has committed."

Mr Lynch chuckled, seeming entirely comfortable for the first time that afternoon. "Thank you, Mr Williams, Mrs Williams."

Quin inclined his head and I smiled, catching Mrs Lynch's eye.

"Would you like another cup of tea?" she asked.

I accepted, finding that the strangeness I'd first experienced at being in my old home had disappeared and that I was quite enjoying the Lynches' company. Although they'd been reserved at first, they started chatting more easily now that our business had been concluded.

When Quin and I left an hour later I felt that I'd made a new friend, Mrs Lynch and I seeing eye to eye on a number of topics. How close we might become in the future remained to be seen, though, the perceived difference between tenant and landowner being what it was.

But at least we'd settled the matter of Talamh na Niall, and I returned to Glaslearg knowing my family's land was in good hands once more.

# 13.

WHILE THE QUESTION of Alannah's inheritance had been settled to everyone's satisfaction there was still plenty to think about over the next few weeks. Besides being preoccupied with the rapidly approaching birth of their child Quin was also much concerned about the tenants' upcoming potato harvest. The plants themselves appeared healthy enough, it was true, but revealing what lay beneath the soil would be the ultimate test. And with the blight having wreaked havoc over the past two seasons, neither Quin nor his tenants could help approaching this year's harvest with nervous caution.

And so it was that Quin found himself holding his breath as Mr Garvey drove a spade into the ground between the sprawling vines of his small plot of land one day at the beginning of autumn. It gave way with an earthy pop, and several plump brown globes emerged, clinging onto sturdy roots. Mr Garvey grinned at Quin and the audience gave a collective sigh as Garvey quickly dug up a few more healthy plants.

Garvey's neighbours soon set off to dig up their own fields, while Quin launched himself into Gambit's saddle to visit the other tenants. Relief spread over him like a blanket as he took in the piles of potatoes Glaslearg had yielded, which would soon be carefully stored in pits. Although the harvest was not nearly as substantial as before the start of the famine Quin hoped the absence of blight this season meant Ireland was finally on its way to recovery, making him feel cautiously optimistic about the future—for the first time in a long time.

NEWS OF THE year's healthy potato harvest spread rapidly and England herself soon declared the famine to have come to an end, calling on the Irish people to act now to rebuild their land—as if it were nothing but a simple matter of discipline to achieve results.

Quin stared down at the newspaper clipping in front of him, sent by his father from London. It depicted a caricature of a healthy potato holding the hand of a cheap loaf of bread. Clearly, the British Government had no further concerns about the Irish populace, believing them to be well supplied with food by the season's potato harvest and the increase in grain yields across Ireland, as well as the continuous imports coming from America.

But while all these factors had indeed improved matters, especially in eastern and northern parts of Ireland, there were any number of people whose situation remained dire. For as expected, with so few seed potatoes planted in the spring the overall potato yield was dismal despite the successful harvest, being no better than the disastrous year before. This, despite the fact that the government had been urged to purchase seed and distribute it to the poor to prevent exactly what had now occurred. Even on Quin's own estate, most families would still have to supplement with other foods, while elsewhere in Ireland, those who had no alternative to their inadequate harvest would continue to starve—with no help coming from the soup kitchens that had fed hundreds of thousands of people in the months before, as these "temporary relief measures" had all been closed by September.

The horrors of the famine were far from over—which the British would have known had they bothered to look a little closer.

Instead, caught up in their own concerns and yielding to the demands of a population denouncing high taxation, many in Britain—and even the wealthier parts of Ireland—condemned any further attempts at charity. They believed enough British resources had been drained by the multitude of Ireland's poor and that it was time the land became self-reliant in what was believed to be the wake of the famine. Just so had the government refused to provide the desperately needed seed in the spring, for the entirely foolhardy reason that doing so would discourage the Irish people from preserving their own seed potatoes, as they had always done before.

How exactly the Irish were supposed to achieve any semblance of self-reliance, Quin had no idea. With virtually no resources, crowds of poor people continued seeking help at workhouses across Ireland, many of them already at death's door. But the workhouses were packed to bursting, and with insufficient work and provisions available, conditions were reportedly appalling. Diseases spread rapidly, resulting in dozens of deaths per day, including among the thousands of abandoned or orphaned children who lived there.

Quin swallowed heavily, thinking of the short and wretched lives those poor children had lived.

How different the life of his own child would be, born into the lap of luxury, with little likelihood of ever having to experience hunger or great hardships. As he'd done so many times before Quin contemplated the fairness of it all. Through no fault of their own—a mere accident of birth—thousands of people were doomed to suffer, virtually from the moment they entered this earth.

Although he wasn't much of a believer, Quin found himself thanking God for his own lot in life and the opportunities his station would afford his son or daughter—even as he felt a sense of guilt for all he'd been given when others had so little.

"You're looking rather glum."

Quin glanced up at the sound of Alannah's voice.

He shrugged. "It's difficult to be cheerful when surrounded by so much misery." He waved a hand toward a copy of the Freeman's Journal, an Irish publication that did a far better job of portraying things how they really were.

Alannah was silent for a moment before patting her protruding belly. "We have something to look forward to, at least."

Quin got up from behind the desk. He pulled Alannah close and kissed her forehead. "That is undoubtedly true." He leaned back a little so he could look her in the eyes. "How much longer?"

"Mrs Hogan says about three weeks."

Mrs Hogan, the midwife, had visited Alannah that afternoon. A cousin of Mrs O'Sullivan, Quin had been instantly reassured by the woman's firm and self-assured demeanour.

Still, he couldn't help but worry.

"Did she seem…optimistic?" Quin tried not to show his unease but couldn't help thinking of the many things that could go wrong.

"She didn't have any immediate concerns," Alannah said, before urging Quin's head down to hers so their foreheads were touching. "Everything is going to be alright."

Quin only nodded, finding himself unable to speak. He tightened his arms around Alannah, the child cradled safely between them.

"How are you feeling?" he finally asked, trying for a more positive air. It would do Alannah no good for him to worsen her own worries.

"Big…and awkward. Ready to burst."

Quin smiled, running a hand along her cheek. "I think you're beautiful."

"Oh yes, there's nothing more beautiful than a woman having to relieve herself every five minutes."

Quin laughed but Alannah gave him a stern look. "I'll have you know it's no laughing matter to have someone pummelling your bladder all day long."

As if in demonstration the baby gave a strong kick, which Quin felt through the layers of clothing between them. He looked down to see the top of Alannah's belly bulging alarmingly. With the palm of one hand, she gave the bulge a firm push and it disappeared.

"Or any of your other innards for that matter." Alannah rubbed a hand under her ribs, before pressing her knuckles into the small of her back. "I'll be glad once the baby is born."

Quin pulled Alannah closer once more so he could dig his palms into the muscles of her back. She gave a low moan, her breath tickling his ear.

He caught her lips with his mouth, holding her to him for a long, lingering kiss.

"As long as you don't forget about me once the baby is here," he murmured, running his lips along her neck as he continued rubbing her back.

"I won't," she said, sounding a little breathless. "Besides"—her hands slid down his sides before coming to rest on his buttocks—"we have a little time to ourselves yet."

Quin looked at her in silent question. Alannah's lips quirked in wry amusement as she gave a particular part of his anatomy a light squeeze.

Quin inhaled sharply. "I dare say there probably aren't many wives who would proposition their husbands this close to their confinement."

"Lucky for you I'm one of the exceptions." She tilted her head toward the door.

Quin glanced at the clock on the desk. There was still time until dinner. Any matters requiring his attention before then would simply have to wait.

Grinning, Quin took Alannah by the hand and started leading her up the stairs. As soon as the bedroom door closed behind them, she turned into his arms. His every touch seemed to inflame her, and she pressed herself against him, as close as her belly would allow. Rather surprised by her ardour—but thoroughly pleased to be its recipient—he let her take the lead. He soon found himself lying on the bed, sighing in contentment while she floated above him, her skirts billowing around his hips, thinking how fortunate he was to be able to call Alannah his wife.

# 14.

A FEW DAYS later Quin was sitting in the drawing room with the newspaper when he became aware of a commotion in the entrance hall. He glanced up to the ceiling and the bedroom above, where Alannah was lying down for a nap, feeling much exhausted these past few days. It wasn't his wife's voice he was hearing, though, but rather a child's—and an angry one at that.

"Ye can't just come in here!"

Quin got up and poked his head through the door, spotting Emmett standing with his legs splayed and his arms crossed, barring the way into the house.

"But I have t' speak t' Mr Williams!" a breathy voice came from the front door, accompanied by a head bobbing up and down, trying to look around Emmett's immobile form.

"I said ye can't!"

Emmett raised a menacing hand and waved it in front of his adversary, who raised both of his own hands and gave Emmett a shove, sending him stumbling backward. Emmett sputtered before rushing forward once more.

"Why you…"

Quin quickly snatched up the boy by the back of his shirt, making him squawk and wriggle as he attempted to escape.

"Emmett." Quin's softly spoken voice made his quarry still instantly, although it didn't stop him from voicing his outrage.

"He wanted t' come right int' the house," he huffed, twisting his head around to look at Quin, "without even knockin'! Luckily I was just walkin' by t' stop 'im!"

"I had t' speak t' ye, sir!"

Quin turned toward the distressed-sounding voice, which belonged to a young, skinny boy standing on the threshold, his face bright red with exertion. Quin recognised the Lynches' eldest son, Rory. He let go of Emmett's shirt and gave him a quelling look before turning to his visitor.

"What is it, Rory?" Quin waved a hand, beckoning him inside but the boy shook his head.

"Ye must come, sir." He reached into his shirt and withdrew a small, crumpled piece of paper. "Ye must come now."

Quin quickly unfolded the piece of paper. It had the words *Please come* scrawled across the top, giving him no further indication of what had so distressed the neighbours' child—although he could hazard a guess.

"He's come for the rent," the boy's words confirmed Quin's suspicions. "Only we 'aven't got it." Rory looked like he was about to burst into tears as he stepped closer to Quin. "Please come, sir."

"Of course." Quin gave the boy a reassuring smile before turning toward the study. "I'll be there in a moment," he called over his shoulder as he rushed past a scowling Emmett and through the study door. Yanking open one of the desk drawers he pulled out a pistol, which he quickly loaded and shoved into his waistband.

He hurried back through the entrance hall and toward the stable, where he was happy to see John leading one of the horses outside.

"I need that horse," he announced before taking the reins out of the groom's hands.

John's eyes grew wide as Quin swung up onto the horse's bare back.

"A saddle, sir?"

"No time," Quin yelled, spurring the animal toward the courtyard, where he spotted Rory running in the direction of the road. Quin pulled up next to him, picked him up under the arms—grateful he didn't weigh very much—and deposited the boy in front of him before setting off again.

It took them only a few minutes to reach the Lynches' front yard. As soon as they'd come to a stop Quin slid off the horse and reached up to help Rory down. The boy's eyes were wide with excitement at their mad dash from the neighbouring estate and Quin grinned at him briefly before turning toward the house, where the sound of yelling was coming through the window. A sudden crash and ensuing screech made Quin rush through the front door. He looked back and forth for a moment before dashing to the drawing room.

A hulking figure was leaning menacingly over Mrs Lynch, who was cowering in one of the chairs.

Quin pulled out his pistol and cocked it, the sound making the brute straighten up suddenly. He turned around slowly, his face filled with fury.

"Well, I didn't think I'd ever see *you* again," Quin said, levelling the gun at the man's chest. "In fact, I'd rather hoped our acquaintance had come to an end." Quin wrinkled his nose as he perused the intruder, who was none other than Herbert Andrews' former guard, a man Quin had clashed with on a few previous occasions, none of them pleasant.

The man growled deep in his throat, evidently as unimpressed by the current encounter as Quin himself. "This don't concern you, Williams." He took a step closer, his eyes flashing briefly to the gun, clearly wondering whether he could disarm Quin before the weapon went off.

"Now that's where you're wrong," Quin said, bracing himself for an impending attack. "This estate no longer concerns *you*. I, on the other hand, am the rightful owner, or rather my wife."

The guard's lips pulled into a snarl. He darted a quick glance toward the floor by his feet, where several pieces of torn-up paper were scattered across the rug—the Lynches' copy of the deed to the house, Quin assumed.

Quin nodded toward the paper. "So you see, you no longer have the right to come here and demand rent.—Not that you did before."

Out of the corner of his eye Quin could see Rory hovering in the doorway. He hoped the boy would stay there until the guard had been subdued.

"But I suppose you fell on hard times after your employer was arrested," Quin continued while he tried to think of a way for all of them to get out of there unscathed. As much as he wanted to, Quin could hardly discharge the gun in the drawing room, with Mrs Lynch sitting right behind her assailant and her son close by. "Collecting moneys on an illegally obtained property must have seemed just the thing."

"Mr Andrews won the estate in a *business transaction*."

By the slow way the guard said the last two words it was clear this was something he and Andrews had been in the habit of saying to convince themselves of the fact.

"If you say so." Quin waved the hand holding the gun. "But either way, as I said, you no longer have any right to demand rent from Talamh na Niall's tenants—legally or otherwise. So I'd suggest you make yourself scarce and never show your face here again."

The man's eyes darted back and forth as he weighed his options. "I'll take what's owed t' me first," he snarled before lunging suddenly backward and grasping Mrs Lynch by the arm.

She shrieked as he dragged her off the chair, her knees hitting the floor as she lost her balance.

"Mama!" With a shriek of his own Rory raced past Quin and threw himself at the guard, pummelling his back with both fists.

Grunting, the man let go of Mrs Lynch and turned toward this latest nuisance, snarling as he picked Rory up bodily and started shaking him so that his teeth chattered together.

"Stop!"

"Rory!"

Quin's and Mrs Lynch's cries collided as he rushed forward, the pistol useless in his fingers, being unable to fire it for fear of hitting Rory. Thinking it would make a formidable weapon even so Quin drew back his hand, intending to strike the man on the head with it. Before he could reach the hulking form, though, the man's arms suddenly went slack and Rory slipped out of his grasp. The guard's eyes rolled up in his head and he slid to the floor, landing with a thump that shook the floorboards.

Quin looked down in some surprise and then back up at Mrs Lynch, who was standing next to the guard, the remains of a large pottery vase grasped in one hand, her face awash with shock.

"He already ruined the other one," she said, waving toward the wall, where bits of broken pottery were strewn over the floor. "They were part of a matching set."

Quin barked a surprised laugh, making her lips twitch.

"Mama!" Rory rushed into his mother's arms and she dropped the rim of the ruined vase and pulled him to her.

"Mama!"

"Mama!"

Two more children's voices echoed through the drawing room, which was suddenly filled with people.

"Are you alright, Joan?" Mr Lynch asked his wife as he inspected her for damage. "I came as soon as Donal and Erin found me."

"I'm alright," Mrs Lynch said as her children clung to her and her husband hovered nearby. "Mr Williams here was a great help."

Quin waved away her thanks. "You very ably took take care of the situation yourself, Mrs Lynch," he said, bending down beside the guard and scrutinising the growing lump on his head.

"Oh?" Mr Lynch looked around in some confusion, making Rory launch into a recitation of the afternoon's events—embellished only slightly—while Quin used his cravat to tie the intruder's hands behind his back.

When the man's eyes fluttered open a moment later Quin hunkered down next to him.

"We really must stop meeting like this," Quin said. "I'm not sure how many more bumps to the head you can withstand—vases and crates and such are unlikely to be good for the constitution, no matter how thick your skull may be."

The man growled and started spewing profanities, which had the Lynches attempting to cover their children's ears with their hands while the youngsters themselves looked rather fascinated at the expansion of their vocabulary they were being subjected to.

Finally, Mr Lynch stuffed his handkerchief into the guard's mouth while the latter continued to thrash back and forth, kept from scrambling to his feet by Quin's knee in his gut.

"What do we do with him now?" Mr Lynch asked, running a hand across his sweaty forehead, his face red with exertion.

"I believe your uninvited guest will find he has a room waiting for him at the Constabulary Police Force in Ballygawley." Quin grinned at his adversary, whose eyes were brimming with hatred. "Although he may find the accommodations to be a little sparse and confining for his liking."

"I DON'T SUPPOSE we'll see him again."

Quin shook his head, running a hand over my protruding belly. The occupant heaved, making him smile, showing the dimple in his cheek.

"No, I suppose not." He shifted next to me on the chaise longue and I made to get up, being currently sprawled along the length of the couch. He stilled me with his hand, though, and I shrugged, glad to be off my feet at the end of the day, even if it meant taking up most of the available space. "He'll be facing counts of unlawful entry into the Lynches' home, destruction of property and blackmail, not to mention assault. I also made sure to tell the constable about his association with Herbert Andrews, so the courts will find plenty of crimes to charge him with, no doubt. With any luck he'll be transported and out of our hair for good."

There was a distinct note of satisfaction in Quin's voice—hardly surprising when the man had tried on more than one occasion to do Quin serious bodily harm.

"It does make one wonder how many more of Andrews' thugs are hulking around the countryside," I said, arching my back to ease the discomfort of late pregnancy.

"None that have any interest in us, I'm sure." Quin leaned forward and kissed me lightly on the lips.

"I suppose not," I agreed, thinking that was a good thing, too, with everything else there was to worry about. "At least we don't have any particular enemies to contend with." I blinked owlishly up at Quin as I suddenly had to suppress a yawn. I'd had a lie-down that afternoon and yet I was dreadfully tired once more, as if the baby were sapping me of my energy, my body solely focused on giving it life.

"Come, let me take you to bed."

Quin helped me gently to my feet, making me groan. "I can hardly wait for the baby to be born. These last few days have felt interminable."

Quin chuckled. "It won't be long now."

"I hope so! My body feels ready to burst at the seams."

Quin dug his knuckles into my lower back and I sighed. He ran his hands up and down my arms and pulled me against his chest, his fingers splaying across my swollen middle. I closed my eyes and leaned into him, and we stood together for a moment, not speaking, just swaying gently in unison as the seconds ticked past, drawing us ever closer to that life-altering event that would bring our unborn child into the world.

# 15.

QUIN PACED UP and down the corridor, a frown plastered to his face.

Alannah's pains had come on that morning, and she'd been confined to the bedroom ever since. Mrs O'Sullivan had promptly taken over and banished him from her side, insisting the birthing room was no place for a husband. Mary Murphy had stood next to her, nodding her agreement while avoiding Quin's eye. Ever since his confrontation with Mr Murphy after the Bealtaine festival the maid seemed to shrink in on herself whenever she was around Quin, clearly finding the entire situation deeply uncomfortable, her loyalties obviously torn between her husband and her employer.

Quin had no time to think about that now, though, as he anxiously awaited the birth of his first child.

Mrs Hogan, the midwife who'd arrived at the manor house around midday, had agreed that Quin's presence by his labouring wife's bedside was entirely unsuitable, and so Quin had been left twiddling his thumbs as the women went about their business. Mrs Hogan had emerged once or twice to ensure Quin all was well but as the afternoon dragged on he found himself unable to sit idly waiting.

It was well into evening by now and Quin was trying unsuccessfully to remain calm. It seemed to him the birthing was taking an inordinately long time.

He clenched his jaws as he continued his pacing. If this went on any longer, he'd wear a path right through the runner to the wooden floor.

He stopped abruptly when he heard Alannah let out a low moan. The sound ended on a sharp cry and a sliver of fear crept down Quin's back. What if something was wrong? What if…? He swallowed heavily, leaning against the wall as a cold sweat broke out on his skin. He'd heard any number of terrifying stories of women dying in childbirth, mother and baby locked forever in an agonised battle that saw them consigned to an early grave.

He bunched his hands into fists. He had never before felt so helpless.

Another tortured wail filtered through the door and Quin reached for the handle, wanting desperately to do something. Anything. He was stopped short by a hand on his arm. Looking back in irritation he met the large, anxious eyes of Rupert.

"Come sir." The valet gently tried to turn him away from the door.

"But..." Quin stammered, resisting his efforts.

"You should leave the womenfolk to their work, sir. There is nothing you can do."

Quin glowered, making Rupert hunch his shoulders. He continued to coax him down the passage, though, unperturbed. Reaching the staircase he ushered him toward the study, where he saw Quin deposited behind the desk, equipped with a generous portion of whiskey. Quin gulped down most of it to drown out the ongoing sounds of Alannah's suffering, muted though they were.

"They'll be alright, sir."

Quin looked sceptically up at Rupert, who was hovering on the other side of the desk.

"Really, sir," the valet said, bobbing his head vigorously up and down. "My mum screamed much louder than this when she birthed my brothers and sisters. And they all came out of it right as rain."

Quin did, in fact, feel a little reassured by this. With numerous siblings, Rupert would have been quite familiar with childbirth growing up. Perhaps what Alannah was going through was normal after all.

He sincerely hoped so as another dampened wail filled the air.

Rupert himself seemed little bothered. "When Emmett was born my mother screamed so loudly all the neighbours came looking," he said. "It was the middle of the night, too, and the house filled with folk as she screamed and screamed upstairs. When she stopped suddenly, we all thought she'd died. The midwife did tell us later that she almost did.—Emmett was lying sideways, you see."

Catching sight of Quin's face Rupert quickly added, "But she came through fine, sir, and my brother did too...and all my other siblings besides."

"I see," Quin managed, now filled with brand new horrors to contemplate. As an only child—not to mention a male of the species—he was completely out of his depth.

He downed the rest of his whiskey in large gulps, making his eyes water. The drink did at least have the effect of dulling his senses a little so that a degree of detachment settled over him.

Rupert topped up his glass and Quin gave him a silent nod of thanks before taking a few more sips. Holding the glass in front of him, he swirled the amber liquid around the sides. He stared into its depths as the minutes passed by, moments of silence broken by the muffled sounds coming from upstairs.

Quin had no idea how long he'd been sitting there when he slowly became aware that the nature of the noises had changed. Alannah's low moans rang out almost continuously, interspersed with the barking of a harsh voice. Quin couldn't make out the words but thought it sounded like a general issuing commands during battle.

And a battle it most certainly was, he realised, swallowing heavily.

A sudden cry made him leap up from his chair. Without conscious thought he flew out the door and up the stairs, taking two at a time. He didn't care that he was meant to stay away. He simply had to see his wife.

*It might be the last chance*, a small voice whispered at the back of his mind as all his earlier fears returned. Heart pounding, he raced down the passageway and through the sitting room, dimly aware that Rupert was following him, feebly attempting to hold him back.

Quin burst through the bedroom door but came to an abrupt stop, making his valet crash into his back. The midwife was at the foot of the bed, between Alannah's legs, where a pink, blood-streaked form was emerging, slithering into a pair of large and capable hands. As it was lifted free of its mother, the bundle squawked briefly before launching into a healthy yowl of protest at its abrupt entrance into the world. Frozen to the spot, Quin watched as the midwife—ignoring his entrance entirely—tied and clamped the cord with brisk efficiency, quickly looked over the tiny body and wrapped it in a soft blanket.

Seeing Alannah's arms settle around the small parcel as Mrs Hogan placed it gently onto her chest, Quin finally came back to himself. He was standing in the middle of the doorway, still holding the handle. Rupert seemed to have disappeared. Quietly closing the door behind him he walked slowly toward the bed. The sight of the tiny head cradled against Alannah's breast made his throat feel tight with emotion. He caught her eyes, which were filled with tears in a face marked with exhaustion but glowing with elation.

He dropped to his knees beside her. Unable to speak he kissed her cheek and stroked her hair with one hand. She smiled at him, even as her tears overflowed, mingling with his own as they bent their heads over the tiny creature between them. Quin carefully laid a hand on the small back, almost afraid to touch it for fear of breaking it.

"It's a girl," Mrs Hogan said from the foot of the bed, looking sternly across at Quin. Clearly, she wasn't best pleased with his premature appearance in the birthing room.

Quin didn't care. He felt his lips break into a wide smile as he looked back down at the baby.

"A girl," Alannah said, placing a tender kiss onto the small, fuzzy head as a few more tears ran down her cheeks.

"As beautiful as her mother," Quin said, running a hand gently over the soft wisps of black hair. He traced one finger along a tiny cheek, creased with the rigours of birth, the eyes closed in the exhaustion of the newly born. Marvelling at the miniscule size of nose and ear, he barely noticed the midwife or Mrs O'Sullivan and Mary as they continued to bustle about.

The midwife now urged him aside, though, and he obediently got up. To his surprise, she took the baby from Alannah and placed it in his arms, raising her chin as if expecting him to protest. He didn't, although he stared at the small form in fascination, afraid to move. He carefully cradled the head in one hand, a surge of emotions accosting him at sight of the tiny, fragile skull that rested in his palm. He had never felt this way before—an overwhelming tenderness and the need to protect at all costs this small being that was his daughter.

"My daughter." His throat constricted at the words, and he pulled the bundle closer until a sound from the midwife made him look up.

She had been tending to Alannah—doing things Quin didn't want to know too much about, he had to admit—but was now looking down at the bed, the fingers of one hand tapping rhythmically against her leg. Noticing Quin watching her she attempted to rearrange her features but couldn't quite erase the expression of concern on her face. Quin raised his brows, questioning.

She pursed her lips, evidently trying to decide what to tell him. "The bleeding is heavier than it should be," she said at last, making Quin's heart lurch in his chest.

He glanced anxiously at Alannah, who was lying back against the propped-up pillows with her eyes closed, looking pale and exhausted. He opened his mouth, but no sound came out.

Mrs Hogan came up next to him and placed a hand on his arm. "It will usually slow down on its own," she said. "Let the baby start suckling first."

Quin had no idea what that had to do with anything but as if on cue, the baby's nose scrunched up and its lips puckered as it moved its head from side to side, emitting small snuffling sounds.

Alannah opened her eyes and reached out her hands. "Is she hungry?"

"Let's give it a try," Mrs Hogan said and, taking the baby from Quin, laid it carefully in Alannah's arms and showed her how to put it to her breast.

Alannah's eyes popped open in surprise as the small mouth latched onto her nipple. Quin watched in fascination as the soft body moulded itself to its mother, round cheeks working mindlessly in search of nourishment.

Alannah smiled, but stopped suddenly, gasping in pain.

"What is it?" Quin hovered over her, eyes flicking back and forth between her and the baby.

"It feels like…"

"It's nought but the womb contracting," the midwife interjected. "It's just what we want." She nodded to herself as she turned away and started packing up some of her things.

Quin sat down on the edge of the bed and stroked Alannah's hair. It was sweat-soaked and bedraggled from her efforts. "What can I do?" he asked, suddenly feeling entirely superfluous.

She patted the bed beside her. "Come lie down next to us."

Though he was a little surprised Quin complied. With a glance toward Mrs Hogan, he kicked off his shoes and crawled slowly across the mattress, careful not to jostle the baby. He thought she was asleep, but the eyes popped open suddenly, regarding him with what looked like intense curiosity.

"Hello," he said softly, mesmerised by the dark blue gaze. She continued to look at him as he stroked her downy hair and the soft skin of her cheek.

A sharp intake of breath from Alannah made him tear his eyes away from his daughter and look at his wife.

"It feels like I'm about to give birth again," she said, suppressing a moan.

Mrs Hogan seeming pleased, though. Having inspected Alannah once more, she helped her swaddle the baby, who'd fallen asleep, small mouth gone slack. She placed her gently in the cradle before picking up her basket. "I'll come see you in the morning, Mrs Williams. Try to get some rest."

Realising belatedly that the midwife was about to depart, Quin pushed himself up on the bed, intending to see her out.

She waved a hand, though, making him pause. "Don't trouble yourself, sir. I'll see myself out." And with a nod and a twitch of the lips that almost passed for a smile, she did just that, followed by a smiling Mrs O'Sullivan and Mary.

Quin lay back down and turned toward Alannah.

"How do you feel?" he asked, taking her hand.

"Tired.—And not a little bit tender." She winced slightly as she settled herself more comfortably, closing her eyes.

"I'm sorry."

Quin kissed Alannah's forehead and she opened her eyes a slit, glancing first at him and then the baby. "It was worth it," she said, squeezing his fingers, before her hand went slack and she drifted off to sleep.

Quin felt rather tired himself, worn out with emotion and the hours of worrying. He tried to push his fatigue aside and get up for form's sake, it still being relatively early at night. Looking around the room, though, he decided that form could go hang.

He wanted to stay with his wife and child.

He quickly changed into his nightshirt, confident that his staff was entirely capable of putting the house to bed without him. He closed his eyes, seeing again the delicate contours of his daughter's face, making him contemplate the novel thought of being a father. Until today it had been something of a vague concept, even when stroking Alannah's bulging belly as the occupant rolled to and fro. But holding the tiny, warm body in his arms had been startlingly real.

He smiled to himself, thinking his heart might burst with the joy of it—and the healthy dose of pride that accompanied it.

Nestling closer to Alannah's slumbering form he ran a hand gently over her head, feeling immensely grateful for his blessings. Holding her close he drifted peacefully off to sleep.

I WOKE UP suddenly, instantly aware that I had to do something, although it took me a moment to realise what that was. I turned toward the noise that had awakened me but winced as I got up. Walking the few steps to the cradle felt like dredging painfully through thick molasses, and my brain felt like it was filled with the same substance. Exhaustion, I supposed as I leaned over the fussing baby.

She was making small mewling sounds and moving her head from side to side. I picked her up and brought her back to the bed, where I changed her clout the way the midwife had shown me. Finished, I propped up the pillows and gingerly sat down, putting the baby to my breast. Feeling exhausted from this small action, I leaned back and closed my eyes.

"What shall we name her?"

I open my eyes a slit to look at Quin. "I thought you were asleep."

He only smiled in response, lifting a hand to cradle the baby's head.

"How does that feel?" he asked, tilting his chin toward my breast.

"A little strange at first. But good," I said, stroking a tiny fist. As I did so it opened and the miniscule fingers wrapped around my thumb, the nails so small and soft as to be scarcely visible.

"In England, most upper-class women wouldn't dream of suckling their own babe," Quin said. "Is it any different here?"

"No, it's much the same in Ireland."

"What made you decide to go against the grain, then?"

I frowned a little at the question but heard no reproach, only interest. I paused before answering as I moved the baby to my other breast.

"For one thing, the midwife, Mrs O'Sullivan and Mary all insisted it was the best thing for the baby. For another..." I had to stop suddenly as my throat thickened in remembrance. "Margaret," I went on softly, looking down at the fuzzy head in my arms. I pulled the baby closer, making her emit a soft snort. "Margaret," I repeated with a sigh. "Seeing her feed little Quinnie so, holding him close. It just seemed...natural. And she did tell me it was the most wonderful thing in the world being able to nurture your own child at your breast."

We were both quiet for a moment, remembering the maid and her young son, taken from us too soon.

"My own mother felt much like Queen Victoria," I said at last, "that nursing a baby was a most sordid practice.—She was wrong." I looked up at Quin, who wrapped his arms around the two of us.

"I think it's beautiful," he said, kissing the top of my head. "*You're* beautiful. And I'm so proud of you." He gave us a final squeeze before leaning back with a grin. "Although I can't say I'm not just a little bit jealous." He looked pointedly at the baby's mouth clamped around my nipple, making me laugh.

"I suspect you'll have to wait a while until marital relations can be resumed." The thought alone made me wince.

"All in good time," he said, patting my hand. "Now, shall we give this little girl a name, or will she go through life known only as *baby Williams*?"

"We could name her Baby, to make it easier," I suggested wryly.

We had, of course, discussed possible names in the months leading up to the birth, but hadn't been able to reach an agreement.

Quin gave me a stern look. "I think not.—Elizabeth, that's a good, traditional English name."

"A little too regal for my liking," I said, suppressing a yawn.

"But she will be treated like a queen." Quin laid a hand on the baby's rounded back, a tender look on his face.

I smiled but shook my head. "Too much expectation."

"Hmph. What about Mary?"

"I think there are quite enough Marys in the world, don't you?"

He looked up briefly at the ceiling but went on gamely. "Eleanor?"

"Oh no. There was a girl called Eleanor I knew as a child. All she ever did was pull my hair and wail incessantly when I returned the favour."

Quin laughed. "Alright, not Eleanor then.—What about Amelia? Harriet? Clementine?"

I closed my eyes, feeling as though I were drifting underwater.

"Eveline?"

I cracked open one eyelid and looked down at my daughter's face, which was now blissful in sleep, the mouth slack in a perfect little O.

"Eveline," I said, running a finger down her cheek, making her lips twitch in response.

I glanced at Quin, who looked at me expectantly.

"Eveline," I repeated, carefully tucking the baby back into her swaddling clothes. "Yes, I think…" The rest of the sentence went under in a jaw-cracking yawn that made my eyes water before they fell closed once more.

I felt the rustling of the mattress next to me, followed a moment later by the lifting of the baby's small weight from my arms.

"Eveline," I mumbled as I gratefully sank down into the surrounding fog.

# 16.

THE NEXT FEW days went by in a blur. Still exhausted from the birth I fed and changed the baby without conscious thought, going through the motions that were becoming increasingly familiar to me, even as the rest of the world seemed to be turning at a great distance.

"Are you alright?"

I looked up at Quin, who was eying me with an expression of concern on his face. I was sitting in our bedroom, having put Eveline down for a nap.

I nodded but Quin didn't seem convinced.

"You look exhausted," he said, coming to stand next to the settee.

I lifted one shoulder, the movement feeling like a great effort in the thick sludge that seemed always to be surrounding me since the birth. "A good night's sleep seems rather unlikely."

"How many times were you up last night?"

"Three or four. I'm not sure. Everything seems…rather hazy. I feel like…I'm not really there." For some reason I felt myself close to tears and lowered my face to hide it from Quin.

He kneeled in front of me and tilted up my chin. "Is there anything I can do to help?"

I shook my head. "Mrs O'Sullivan says it will pass. That I will soon feel like my old self again."

That possibility seemed even more unlikely than getting a good night's sleep. Despite the midwife assuring me I was recovering as expected it felt like I'd been irrevocably changed by Eveline's birth. The thought made a tear trickle down my cheek.

Quin wiped it away and gave me a worried look. "Are you sure there's nothing I can do?"

I sighed. "You can hardly feed the baby for me."

Quin's lips twitched and he kissed my forehead. "No, that isn't something I can do."

With an expression of regret on his face he disappeared, leaving me to nod off for a few minutes, until Eveline's cry woke me with a start.

I was sitting with her in the nursery when Quin came in.

"What would you say to getting a little help with the baby?"

I gave him a questioning look.

"I thought we could ask Geraldine O'Hagan to assist you." I recognised the name of the young woman whom Rupert had been pining after for some time. "Rupert told me she's had the care of several younger siblings from the time they were infants.—And her family could well use the money I would pay her."

Quin's eyes flickered between mine as he assessed my reaction. I was quiet for a moment, contemplating the suggestion. Finally, I nodded.

Quin smiled. "There's a small room next to the nursery. We could set it up for her if she agrees."

"I'm sure Rupert will be delighted," I said with a laugh.

IN FACT, RUPERT was so flustered that he not only went bright red but stammered incoherently for several minutes after Quin informed him that Geraldine would be coming to live in the manor house with us.

I wondered if he would ever work up the courage to tell her how he felt. Based on Geraldine's behaviour at the Bealtaine festival I was quite sure his feelings were returned and yet, neither seemed willing to take the next step. I shrugged, deciding that the two of them living under one roof was likely to bring things to a head sooner or later.

I for one was happy to have Geraldine's company. She was friendly, thoughtful and competent, a combination that proved more than useful as I navigated the early stages of motherhood without any female relatives to assist me.

"Here, I'll take her," she said to me after she'd been with us for about a week.

I had fallen asleep in the nursing chair with Eveline on my arm, only to jerk up suddenly, feeling as though we were both about to fall.

"She's full as a drum." Geraldine smiled at the baby. "I'll lay her down in her cradle. You should get some rest." She handed me a woollen blanket, which I laid over my legs before drifting off again.

When I woke up about an hour later, I felt much restored, with my head clearer than it had been in days.

"Mrs O'Sullivan may have been right," I said to myself, thinking that perhaps I was starting to recognise myself again after all.

My body was healing, and I was getting used to the constant demands of motherhood. While I was still dreadfully tired most of the time, the feeling of detachment that had plagued me for the first few days had finally disappeared.

"You're awake."

Quin's voice made me turn toward the door. He opened it all the way and came into the room. Seeing Eveline still asleep in her cradle his eyes softened. I got up and came to stand next to him.

"She's so beautiful," he said quietly, taking hold of my hand. "And so small."

I squeezed his fingers, my throat feeling tight at the overwhelming emotions I felt looking at my daughter. We were silent for a moment until Quin turned to face me.

"How are you feeling?"

"Better," I said.

"Good." He pulled me to him, and I closed my eyes briefly.

"I've missed you," I said, running one hand up and down his back.

"I've been here the whole time."

"I know but...everything's changed..."

"Not between us."

He lowered his head and gently pressed his lips to mine. I pulled him closer, wrapping my arms around his neck and deepening the kiss.

He chuckled. "Everything will be alright," he murmured, his breath tickling my ear.

I nodded, laying my cheek against his chest. I felt a deep sense of contentment coming over me as I stood there in Quin's embrace, with our daughter sleeping peacefully beside us.

A daughter who'd been born healthy and whole despite all my fears.

A daughter who grew closer to my heart with each passing day, so that I could scarcely recall a time before her arrival in our lives—a time before night-time awakenings and bone-deep exhaustion, but also a time of unutterable joy.

AS WINTER ARRIVED at Glaslearg I cherished each moment I could spend with Eveline, embracing my role as her mother. I got to know her a little better each day, and we soon settled into a routine.

In the evenings, after I'd put her to bed, I would sit with Quin in the drawing room before turning in myself. I came to look forward to this time we could spend together, just the two of us, even if it was sometimes spent in companionable silence.

"I believe Rupert is working up the courage to speak to Geraldine's father," Quin said to me on one such occasion, when Eveline was about four weeks old.

"Oh?"

"He wants his permission to court her." Seeing the surprise on my face Quin smiled. "It's rather old-fashioned, I know, but I believe he's concerned anything else might seem improper, with the two of them living under the same roof."

"I suppose it would be," I said in some amusement, recalling the temptation that had come with being in close proximity to Quin before we were married.

Quin's smile widened as he clearly read my mind.

"Do you think they'll marry?" I asked, suppressing a yawn. I would be heading to bed soon, hoping to catch a few hours of sleep before Eveline was hungry again.

Quin nodded slowly. "I expect so. He certainly is enamoured of her, and I believe…"

A sudden pounding at the front door made him pause, and we looked at each other in confusion. The sound came again, this time even more forcefully.

Quin frowned as he got up to investigate, heading into the entrance hall with brisk steps.

Our elderly butler had already retired for the night as we hadn't expected anyone, and it was getting rather late for a formal caller. I felt a stab of apprehension, following Quin toward the door.

When I got there, he was standing on the threshold with a young man who looked dishevelled and exhausted. Without waiting for the door to close behind him he handed Quin a piece of paper.

Quin's jaws clenched as he took it, clearly expecting bad news. Unfolding the note and scanning its contents, his eyes flew open, and he inhaled sharply through his nose.

"What is it?" I asked, placing a hand on his arm.

"Anne's father has been murdered.—And Ollie's being accused of the crime."

# 17.

"WHERE IS OLIVER Penhale?"

Quin scowled at the constable manning the front desk of the Dublin Metropolitan Police station, his whole body vibrating with tension.

"Who?" the man asked in a bored voice, not raising his eyes.

"Oliver Penhale," Quin repeated through his teeth. "You're holding him for murder."

The constable paused, wrinkling his forehead in thought. "Ah, yes," he said slowly as he finally looked up at Quin. "He's no longer here."

Quin's heart lurched in his chest. "What do you mean he's no longer here? Has he been...?"

"Oh no." The constable waved a casual hand. "He simply isn't *here*. It seems your...friend"—he lifted one brow in query, making Quin give a jerky nod—"has what we call *connections*. He's been allowed to stay at his residence, watched of course"—the constable gave Quin a stern look—"until the...um...matter has been resolved."

Quin breathed out heavily in relief. He bid the constable a brief farewell before staggering out onto the street, which was already dark on this late winter afternoon. His knees shook alarmingly as he walked to the hitching post where he'd left Gambit soon after he'd arrived in Dublin. Taking a deep breath, he swung up into the saddle and made his way to Ollie's townhouse.

When he got there, he flew up the steps and banged on the door, which was opened by a bewildered-looking butler. Quin barely made it through a civilised greeting before demanding to see the master of the house.

The butler rushed off toward the drawing room and a moment later Ollie himself appeared in the hallway. Quin clasped his friend by the shoulders before embracing him and thumping him heartily on the back. Stepping away he eyed Ollie closely, taking note of his dishevelled appearance and the dark rings under his eyes. Clearly, the man was under some strain—and who could blame him? It wasn't everyday one was accused of murder.

"I'm glad you came," Ollie said solemnly, leading Quin into the drawing room.

"Quin!"

He looked up at the sound of Anne's voice. "Don't get up," he said, crossing the room in a few strides to greet her.

Anne's face was blotched with tears, and a few more escaped when Quin offered his condolences on the loss of her father. She nodded silently and pressed a crumpled handkerchief to her eyes. Ollie waved toward one of the armchairs before sitting down next to his wife.

Quin looked between the two of them as he took his own seat, feeling a little uncertain. "What happened?" he asked gently, watching Anne for signs of distress at the question.

She shook her head, swallowing heavily as Ollie took her hand.

"We don't know," Ollie said. "We had come to dinner at the Cartwright's house. With the weather turning ghastly, we were invited to stay the night in the guest room. Anne's father retreated to his study after dinner, intending to deal with a few matters before bed, while her mother and sister went up to their rooms."

"One of the maids found him the next morning," Anne said softly.

Quin waited for her to say more but she clamped her lips together as fresh tears ran down her cheeks.

Ollie gave her a concerned look before turning back to Quin. "He was shot with a crossbow."

"He was what?" Quin's eyes bulged as he sat forward in his chair, while Anne seemed to fold in on herself.

"He was a collector of weapons," Ollie said, squeezing Anne's hand, "oriental swords, rare artifacts and the like. The crossbow was hanging on the wall of his study."

"And it was not only loaded but functional?"

"He took great pride in his collection, regularly polishing and inspecting each item. I suppose having the bolt in place ensured its authenticity."

Quin tried to picture the inside of the Cartwright's house as it had looked during the Penhale's engagement and wedding celebrations. He recalled seeing several decorative swords, much like those adorning the walls of Cornac House, which affirmed Ollie's account of Mr Cartwright's interest in military matters—an interest the man himself had revealed at the house party on more than one occasion, of course.

Coming back to the present Quin looked from Ollie to Anne and back again. "But why would anyone think *you* killed him?"

"Because of the inheritance."

"I don't understand," Quin said.

"Unfortunately, I seem to be too smart for my own good." Ollie rubbed a hand over his face before continuing. "You see, when I was...coerced"—he glanced briefly at Anne, who looked down at her lap—"into paying Mr Cartwright's debts, thus preventing him from having to sell Cornac House, I insisted that he change his will. Since the man had no title and the estate wasn't entailed, I had him name his eldest daughter as primary heir."

"Ah." Quin nodded his understanding. With Anne inheriting the bulk of her father's fortune upon his death, the estate would effectually belong to her husband, in the same way that control over Niall now belonged to Quin. "You meant to keep your investment."

"I'm not a complete dunderhead.—Still, I probably wouldn't be in this predicament if I were."

"But is there any actual evidence against you?"

"Aside from the change in the will you mean?" Ollie gave a brief snort before sobering up. "With the murder weapon being what it is, the police are convinced the perpetrator must be a man.—And I was at the residence at the time of the crime. Other than that, though, they have nothing, but who knows what they might find...or fabricate."

"You don't really believe that do you? I would hope you'd get a fair trial."

At mention of the court case Anne buried her face in her hands.

"Um...not that it will get that far, of course," Quin amended quickly, throwing her a guilty look. "We'll simply have to do a little investigating ourselves."

They all fell quiet, the only sound the longcase clock ticking in the corner. The silence was broken some time later by the appearance of a footman bearing a tea tray.

Once he'd left Quin asked, "Were your movements unaccounted for at all around the time of the murder?"

Ollie cleared his throat uncomfortably as he reached for the teapot. "Something I ate at dinner didn't agree with me and I had to...ah...excuse myself for a time after the port had been served, before retiring for the night."

"And did you leave before or after Mr Cartwright announced he was going to his study?"

"Shortly after."

"Hm." Quin accepted a steaming cup as he contemplated what he'd learnt. The timing of Ollie's departure was less than optimal and could easily be construed as a clear indication of his guilt, with no way to prove he hadn't in fact followed Mr Cartwright to the study and performed the dastardly act. It wasn't a rare event for a suspect's word to mean very little in the eyes of the law. Still, Quin hoped Ollie's standing in society would count for something.

"Who else would have reason to harm Mr Cartwright?" Quin asked, watching Anne's reaction, thinking it might be better for the two men to have this conversation in private. She showed no indication of leaving, though, and seemed no more distressed than before, so Quin shrugged, looking expectantly at Ollie.

It was Anne who answered, however. "A few people, most likely." She gave a deep sigh. "As much as I loved my father, he...well he'd gotten himself into a bit of a bind...even after Ollie had paid his debts." Her voice broke and she took a moment to collect herself. "He liked to gamble and spent money he didn't have on things he didn't need..."

"So he owed people money?"

She nodded. "I don't know the particulars but I overhead him and his steward talking about his financial situation, which appeared to be rather bleak once more. I..." She stopped, glancing briefly at Ollie before lowering her gaze.

Ollie compressed his lips. "Anne told me what she'd overheard and asked me to intervene but...well I said it was time her father took responsibility for his own actions. I refused to give him another penny.—So I suppose his death must be on my conscience after all."

"Absolutely not!" Quin insisted, while Anne patted Ollie's hand mechanically. "Whatever trouble the man got himself into, it had nothing to do with you.—Besides, we don't even know who killed him."

Ollie gave him a sceptical look but didn't argue.

"Are you sure you can't recall a name, Anne? Anyone your father might have mentioned even in passing."

"No, I'm sorry. I...well I tried not to listen too closely to his grievances, aware of how he handled his affairs. But for all I know it might have been his steward or any of his servants who..." She swallowed heavily before continuing. "Who knows when any of his staff last got paid?"

"Hm." Quin thought for a moment. "Was anything stolen...when he was killed, that is?"

Anne shook her head. "Not that anyone's noticed."

"In that case it seems unlikely the culprit is anyone who was owed money...or wages. For what would killing Mr Cartwright achieve then? Unless something of value was taken after the act."

"Vengeance seems a nice motive," Ollie said drily, "by someone who can afford to lose a little blunt.—Although it does seem rather unlikely."

"So what does that leave us with?" Quin asked.

Ollie took a deep breath. "It leaves us with me looking at a gibbet."

"Pish posh!"

The booming voice from the doorway made them all look up. Archie strode into the room followed by Ham, with the butler hot on their heels as they went to pay their respects to Anne. The butler looked anxiously toward his master, but Ollie only thanked him for showing his guests inside. With Archie and Ham likely regular features in the household, Ollie clearly didn't require his staff to stand on ceremony.

"What's this about a gibbet?" Archie demanded as he thumped Ollie on the back before turning to Quin.

Ollie sighed. "If the courts want to see me hang for the crime, then I will."

Archie glowered at his friend. "I've never known you to be such a pessimist, Oliver Penhale. It doesn't behove you to start now!"

"Why in the world would the courts *want* you to hang for the crime?" Ham asked, having dispensed his own greetings. "Mr Cartwright was no-one of great importance—begging your pardon, Anne—and you are of a higher social standing. There is no benefit to anyone to see you convicted."

"Except the appearance of having solved a murder—to the satisfaction of the populace."

Archie pointed a menacing forefinger at Ollie. "That's quite enough out of you! While you stew in your self-pity the rest of us shall construct your defence.—Now, Quinton, tell me your thoughts. Where shall we begin?"

Quin couldn't help grinning at the sight of bearlike Archie looming over slight Ollie, feeling suddenly as though, of course, between the four of them they'd find the evidence to see Ollie released and the true culprit arrested.

"We've just been discussing possible suspects," Quin said as they all sat down once more. "With Anne being named her father's heir the police have convinced themselves of Ollie's guilt. Since Mr Cartwright was rather free with his money, though, and likely had numerous debts, there might be any number of people who would want to do him harm.—But since nothing was stolen it's also conceivable that the murder had nothing to do with money at all."

"A slight avenged? A disagreement settled?" Ham nodded slowly. "It's been known to happen."

"Or perhaps a business deal that went awry?" Archie suggested. "Did he have any particular business partners?" he asked Anne.

She shook her head. "I'm not sure. His steward would know." She gave a deep sigh, looking suddenly forlorn.

"Are you alright?" Ollie asked, concern etched across his face.

"I will be. But I think I'd like to go to bed."

"Of course."

Ollie got up to oblige her, despite the fact that it was only early evening. She leaned into him as he walked her to the door, where she turned briefly to bid the others goodnight. She was about to step into the hallway when she stopped suddenly and whirled back into the room, a distraught expression on her face as she looked at Quin.

"I didn't congratulate you on the birth of your daughter," she said, her eyes flashing back and forth between his. "I'm so sorry, Quin. How selfish of me."

"Nonsense," Quin said, coming to stand in front of her as the others, too, offered their belated well-wishes, having learned of Eveline's birth in Quin's letters. "You've had much on your mind of late."

"I did send a note," she said, clearly still distressed, "but I'd meant to congratulate you in person. But…" She waved a hand weakly to encompass all that had happened in the last few days.

Quin patted her lightly on the arm. "I know you sent a note, Anne, and Alannah was delighted when she received it. As was I."

He smiled at her and she nodded absently. Next to her, Ollie clenched his jaws as he looked at his wife. His eyes met Quin's over the top of her head and Quin felt keenly the burden his friend carried.

"Come, Anne, I'll take you up to bed." Ollie placed an arm gently around her shoulders and turned her back into the hallway.

A distinct sense of sadness settled over Quin as he watched Anne being led away. Not only had her father been brutally murdered but her husband was the prime suspect—a husband who seemed dear to her despite the difficulties they'd faced early on in their marriage. And even though her father hadn't quite been the paragon of decent behaviour one might have hoped for, he'd been her father, nonetheless, and there had been definite affection between them.

Behind him, he heard the clinking of glasses as Archie filled a few tumblers with whiskey. He placed one in Quin's hand and the three men toasted his recent fatherhood. Under the circumstances, though, the celebration was short-lived and they soon settled into silence, Quin wishing he hadn't had to leave his newborn daughter so soon.

"The police suspect Ollie because they found a copy of Mr Cartwright's will among his things."

Quin pulled his attention away from his ever-gloomier thoughts and back into the room, where Ham was wearing a contemplative look.

Seeing everyone watching him Ham continued, "And with Ollie unquestionably inside the house at the time of the murder he could easily have done the deed, thus availing himself of the man's fortune.—It's a neat theory."

"It's complete ballocks, is what it is," Archie muttered.

Ham waved a hand. "Of course it is. My point is, if it weren't for the will, the police likely wouldn't have suspected him."

"And?" Archie gave him an impatient look.

"Ollie told us he'd forced Mr Cartwright to change his will before he would settle his debts. *Change* it." Ham looked meaningfully from Archie to Quin and back again.

Quin nodded slowly. "Cartwright had named someone else as his heir before being forced by Ollie to recant."

"Precisely," Ham agreed. "We only found out about the will because of this wretched business.—Who's to say the initial inheritor knew anything about it being changed?"

"Of course!" Archie jumped up from his seat. "Who was supposed to inherit the Cartwright estate?" he demanded from Ollie, who was just coming back into the drawing room.

"Ah...a cousin." Ollie gave his friends a confused look before heading to the whiskey decanter and pouring a generous portion for himself and topping up the other glasses.

"Why would Cartwright name a cousin as his heir instead of one of his daughters?" Quin asked as he accepted his second glass. "You said the estate wasn't entailed."

"He believed the Cartwright name would live on illustriously after his death if he'd abide by the time-honoured tradition of male-preference inheritance, regretting, of course, that he didn't have a son of his own." Ollie gave a brief snort. "At least that's what he told me. In actuality I suspect he was afraid if he left the estate to his daughters, their husbands would get their grubby hands on it in the end.—Rather ironic, isn't it?"

"I see now why the man didn't appear terribly fond of you," Ham said drily, making Ollie lift one shoulder.

"But what about his daughters?" Quin asked.

With a daughter of his own now he couldn't imagine being so callous as to leave her with virtually nothing. Thinking of Eveline once more made his heart squeeze painfully in his chest. He'd felt awful leaving her and Alannah so soon after the birth and had been terribly torn about going. It was only when Alannah had insisted his friend needed him that he'd agreed—after she'd promised him they would be alright in his absence.

He could only hope Ollie's name would soon be cleared so he could return home.

"He did care for them, I believe," Ollie said, recalling Quin to the present, "and intended to see them well provided for. Having settled Anne with a wealthy husband"—he snorted in irritation—"he was sure the same could be arranged for her sister. This, in his mind, was the perfect solution, ensuring his daughters were taken care of while his name would live on after his death."

"He did a miserable job safeguarding his estate if that was his intention," Ham said. "What a pleasure to inherit nothing but debt!"

"He wasn't a bad man," Ollie said, "just...disillusioned and perhaps...well..."

"Not the *most* intelligent of men?" Ham suggested.

"No, not that, which is why he was so terribly upset about the will. Instead of seeing the benefit to his own daughters he was enraged at the thought of his so-called legacy being lost for lack of a male successor."

Ham opened his mouth to say something, but Archie growled suddenly, leaning forward in his chair. "As much as I'm enjoying hearing intimate details about a dead man, you still haven't told us who Cartwright named as his heir!" He narrowed his eyes at Ollie before casually waving his hand. "But by all means, do keep that information to yourself if you have no objections to meeting the hangman!"

Ollie cleared his throat. "Um...yes. It was a cousin, as I said. A distant one.—In fact, you all met him at the house party."

"George? George Cartwright?" Quin glanced at Ollie, who gave a brief nod. "Do you think he might have...?"

Archie clapped him on the back. "We'll go and ask him, shall we?"

"I DIDN'T THINK we'd go ask him immediately."

Archie turned toward the window he'd just closed, making as if to open it once more. "If you'd rather wait until your eyes are bulging from the noose around your neck, then please climb back inside."

Ollie huffed. "I've already snuck out of the house. I'm not staying behind now."

"If the two of you don't stop your bickering," Quin hissed, "we'll alert the constable standing by the front door.—Which is something we are trying to avoid." He glared at Ollie, who narrowed his own eyes, but at least lowered his voice when he spoke again.

"Because escaping my own home will make me look even more guilty than the police already believe me to be?"

"Because escaping your own home will make them lock you in a cell."

Quin knew Ollie was fully aware of the minutiae of his situation, but his friend was obviously feeling a streak of rebelliousness at the rotten treatment he'd received—which might make him do something stupid.

"Come now." He put his hand on Ollie's shoulder and propelled him past the mews. As they reached the lane at the back of the property Ham trotted up to them from the other side.

"He didn't notice a thing," he said with a grin. "With constables like that on your case you'll be a free man in no time."

"I'd rather be a free man because I was proven innocent," Ollie muttered, "not because those wishing to see me hanged are incompetent."

"Then let's go prove your innocence, shall we?" Quin cocked his head toward the main street, where they intended to hail a hack to get them to George Cartwright's house.

Ollie gave a grim nod as he led the way.

"Do you think Cousin George even knows you've been arrested?" Ham asked.

"He may have called on Anne's mother and sister at her aunt's house. The murder *was* mentioned in the papers, after all. How much they might have told him, I can't say."

"And the press haven't gotten wind of your…um…circumstances?" Quin asked.

"I believe I am simply being referred to as a *suspect* at this time."

"Well, that's something at least," Archie said.

"Hmph."

Quin's lips twitched in amusement. While Ollie was obviously outraged at being accused of murder, he was also clearly insulted at not being mentioned by name—even though his anonymity was by far the preferable option as far as his reputation and privacy were concerned.

Quin wondered who had prevented the newspapers from printing Ollie's name. He didn't get a chance to ask, though, as they'd reached the handful of public conveyances waiting for customers. Ollie waved down the nearest one and gave the driver the address.

"He lives near the docks?" Archie asked in surprise as he climbed into the cab.

"In a reasonably respectable neighbourhood, but yes."

"A clear sign of his guilt," Ham said.

"He's not very well off and has fallen on hard times," Archie speculated with a nod, "so he killed Mr Cartwright to acquire what he thought he was inheriting."

"Precisely."

"Possibly," Ollie countered. "I'm not sure he even knew he'd been named Cartwright's heir in the first place. Anne was terribly upset to find out about it herself...from me. It's entirely possible her father made the will at his solicitor's and told no-one about it, simply leaving things to sort themselves out after his death."

Archie scowled. "Not the confrontational sort, I suppose?"

Ollie shook his head.

"How well do you know George Cartwright?" Quin asked.

"Not very. We would see each other only at the occasional social event and didn't have too much to talk about when we did.—You saw what he was like at the house party. Reasonably pleasant and all but...well..."

Quin understood immediately what Ollie meant. While the man had seemed agreeable enough, he'd never really revealed anything personal about himself over the course of the two days he'd been at Cornac House. The only thing Quin could say for certain was that George Cartwright liked to play cards—which was perhaps an important consideration under the circumstances. It was entirely possible he'd gotten himself into gambling debt, which might have made him desperate enough to seek out his cousin.

"He's definitely our killer," Archie declared, making Quin chuckle.

"Because he doesn't especially get on with Ollie?"

"Yes," Ham said while at the same time Archie exclaimed, "Of course!"

Ollie's cheeks went pink, and he gave a small cough. "I thank you for your ardent belief in the wholesomeness of my character, but we need a little more evidence than the man's disinterest in my person."

"And that's precisely what we're going to find," Archie insisted.

"Assuming he did it."

Archie rolled his eyes. "One more word out of you, Penhale, and I'm going to deposit you at the Dublin Metropolitan Police station myself!"

"Are we just going to march into Cartwright's house and demand to know whether he killed his cousin?" Ham asked Quin, ignoring the other two.

Quin shrugged. "I suppose it depends on how he reacts to finding us on his doorstep."

"I doubt we'll get a particularly warm reception either way," Ollie said. "It is rather late in the day, after all, especially for an unannounced visit from someone who's not much more than a passing acquaintance."

"That does mean he'll be immediately on his guard," Archie said, evidently contemplating the possibility of goading the man into a quick confession.

The other three nodded before lapsing into silence as the carriage rattled through the streets.

Quin wondered what they would find at Cartwright's home. With little knowledge of the man's character, he had no idea how the intended heir might have reacted to finding himself in a desperate bind with what he believed to be a potential fortune within his grasp—or to learning the potential fortune was no longer within his grasp after all. Either situation might have led the man into a murderous rage—assuming he'd known about the will in the first place.

While Quin's thoughts were wandering the carriage came to a stop at the entrance to a narrow street. He followed the others onto the pavement, looking around surreptitiously. Reasonably respectable the area might be, but at this moment it seemed rather dark and foreboding.

"Did anyone think to come armed?" Quin narrowed his eyes at a partly concealed doorway, wondering how many cutthroats might be lurking in the shadows. The row of houses was built in the one-floor, over-basement style that was becoming popular for the city's lower middle classes, with their semi-subterranean lower levels largely hidden from view.

"I have a knife in each boot," Archie said as he bent down to his footwear.

"And I have a pair of pistols in my waistband," Ham announced, withdrawing the firearms with a flourish.

Quin gaped at his friends. "What exactly were you expecting to encounter while visiting Ollie at his townhouse this evening?"

Archie lifted one shoulder. "Until this whole mess is resolved we decided to be prepared for anything."

"I see." Quin took the sizeable blade Archie handed him—which made a far more formidable weapon than his small pocketknife—and slid it into his trousers.

Having accepted a pistol from Ham Ollie led the way down the street, coming to a stop in front of one of the numerous doors in the dark brick facade. While he hesitated, Archie marched up the steps and knocked. When no answer came, he knocked again before trying the handle, to no avail.

"Perhaps we should come back in the morning," Ollie suggested, glancing back toward the hack, which was waiting for them at the end of the street.

"Some of us have duties to attend to in the morning, Penhale," Archie said drily as he lifted onto his toes to try and look through the fanlight window over the door.

"Even so, if the man is not home…"

"Wait a moment. There's a light in the lower level." Quin pointed toward the small window below the banister, which was glowing dimly.

Taking this as a clear indication of Cartwright's presence in the house Archie started hammering on the door. "Open up, Cartwright. We know you're there," he boomed when no-one answered.

A noise to his right made Quin look up. Several children in nightgowns were watching them curiously, crowded into the adjoining doorway and spilling out onto the landing. Quin looked back at them in some surprise, wondering how many people were crammed into the small house.

There was a sharp command and the lined face of a harried-looking woman appeared. When she spotted Quin and his friends a look of alarm flashed across her features, and she quickly urged the children back into the house before firmly shutting the door behind them.

"There must be at least a dozen people living next door," Quin said.

Ollie gave them a dismissive look. "They'll be better off here than in the tenements."

Quin compressed his lips, knowing Ollie was right. However cramped Cartwright's neighbours might find their home it was likely luxurious compared to the Dublin slums. Large townhouses crudely divided to lodge multiple families, the tenements were well known for the poverty and squalor that abounded there—conditions that had only worsened since the start of the famine, with hundreds of desperate people flocking to the city from the surrounding countryside, looking for work and a place to live.

Engrossed in his thoughts Quin hadn't noticed the lightening of the window above George Cartwright's door but turned toward the entryway now as it swung open, revealing a dishevelled-looking man bearing a half-burnt candle in a crude holder. Quin recognised George but couldn't believe the change in him since they'd met a few months before. While Cartwright's appearance had been amiable enough at Cornac House he now had dark rings under his eyes, which flicked nervously back and forth.

Ham glanced Quin's way, clearly thinking as he was that the man appeared deeply troubled. Guilt over murdering his cousin, perhaps?

"Hullo, George," Ollie said, stepping out from behind Archie.

Cartwright's eyes went wide and his mouth fell open before he collected himself. "Oliver, I thought you were...um...that is...what a surprise to see you here." His gaze flitted from Ollie to the street behind him and back again, never quite coming to rest.

"Might we come in for a moment?" Ollie asked, taking a step forward.

"Come in?" Cartwright swallowed as his hand tightened on the door. "Um..."

"It will only take a moment."

"I...well...I suppose..." He reluctantly opened the door wide enough for them to enter, sluggishly waving a hand toward the hallway.

As they all filed into the house Quin looked around, surprised to see the inside was larger than he would have expected, the building extending further from the street than it seemed from the outside.

Cartwright led them to a sitting room at the front of the house, which was sparsely furnished. There was no fire in the grate and the room was cold, but Cartwright made no move to light one—perhaps because there was no firewood in the basket standing alongside. He did light a pair of lamps, which at least brightened up the dark space, before offering them a seat. Since there were only three chairs, though, they all declined.

An awkward silence descended on the group, which was finally broken by Ollie. "You remember my friends, Archie, Quin and Ham? You met them at the house party Anne's father held in June."

A muscle in George's cheek twitched but he gave a curt nod.

"It's a terrible thing that's happened, isn't it?" Ollie continued.

George shifted his feet as a puzzled look appeared on his face. "Ah…"

"Anne's father.—His murder." Ollie placed a hand on the other man's arm, making him jump.

"Yes! Yes! A terrible thing!" George swallowed heavily and took a step back, wringing his hands. "Simply terrible." He glanced sideways at Ollie before looking back down.

"We've come to see how you're taking the news," Ollie said, stepping closer once more.

"How I'm taking…? Oh, yes, yes, of course. I am…ah…well…I'm devastated of course." He shook his head, his shoulders drooping. "It was a terrible shock." He looked forlornly from Ollie to Ham, Quin and Archie. "A terrible, terrible shock."

"Yes, it was." Ollie patted his arm. "Do you have any idea what happened?"

George gasped. "Me? Why would I…why would *I* know what happened?"

"Because he was your cousin."

"Well, yes, but…you know we weren't all that close. In fact…in fact I hadn't seen him since the house party." He bobbed his head up and down a few times as if trying to convince himself. "Yes, that's right, I hadn't seen my cousin since the house party."

"Hm…so you have no idea what might have happened to him?" Ollie leaned toward George, narrowing his eyes.

"No, no. None at all, none at all," George sputtered before suddenly glaring at the shorter man. "If anyone should know what happened to him, it would be you!"

"Me?"

"Yes, you!" George fidgeted with the frayed cuff of his sleeve, not meeting Ollie's eyes. "For certainly, you would have visited with him more frequently, being married to his daughter.—In fact, weren't you...?"

"Wasn't I what?"

George cleared his throat and waved his hand. "Nothing. I simply meant that...um...you were closer to the family than I, by virtue of your wife."

"Perhaps."

"Um...if that is all?" George looked toward the sitting room door, a hopeful expression appearing on his face.

Quin exchanged glances with his friends. Archie grimaced while Ollie inclined his chin toward the hallway.

"We shall bid you goodnight, then," he said, extending his hand.

George looked at it for a moment before clasping it in a brief shake. "Thank you for your concern," he said, accepting the others' condolences and leave-takings, before showing them briskly to the door.

"He's as guilty as sin," Archie said once they were well away from the house.

Quin nodded. "Did you see his shock when he recognised Ollie?"

"He must have thought he'd be locked away by now," Ham said. "Which means he's fully aware Ollie's been accused of Cartwright's murder."

"And the fact that he said nothing must surely mean he did it himself." Ollie looked back over his shoulder and glowered toward the house, while Archie growled.

"Oh, he did it, alright. All that fidgeting and mumbling and stuttering, and then trying to insist he barely knew the man, even though they were related..."

"How do we prove it, though?" Ham asked.

Archie emitted a snort. "If the police took one look at his house, they'd know he was guilty. He's got hardly any furnishings, nor firewood to keep himself warm. Clearly, he's desperate, and we all know what they say about desperate men."

"Unfortunately, there's no-one to place him at the Cartwright's house that day," Quin pointed out, "whereas Ollie was not only present at the dinner party that evening but also stayed the night."

Ham sighed. "Rotten luck."

"I assume you are simply listing the challenges of proving our Ollie's innocence, not the impossibility thereof?" Archie gave Quin and Ham a stern look.

"Of course!" both confirmed without hesitation.

"I shall go to the station tomorrow," Quin said as they reached the carriage, "and talk with the constable in charge. I'm sure I can induce him to do a little more investigating."

# 18.

AS IT TURNED out the following day, though, it was rather difficult to induce the constable to do a little more investigating.

"We've got the will," the man said, his formidable moustache quivering as he shook his head. "It proves Penhale did it.—Unless you believe it was his wife?" He raised one mocking brow.

"The will proves nothing," Quin said through clenched teeth. "As I've told you the will was *changed*. The man we believe actually murdered Mr Cartwright is his cousin, Mr George Cartwright, who expected to inherit."

The constable sighed, running a hand over his face. With the city overflowing with desperate citizens and revolts threatening daily the Dublin Metropolitan Police had plenty to keep them busy. Still, Quin had no intention of seeing his friend hang simply because of a lack of resources.

"If you could just send someone to talk to him, I'm sure…"

"Hmph."

The constable swung his head slowly from side to side, like a stubborn bull refusing to be moved. Quin pulled himself up to his full height and squared his shoulders, ready to wait it out as long as necessary. He leaned a little forward, all the better to look the constable in the eye. A minute of silence ensued, neither man willing to give in.

At long last, the constable lifted his hands in surrender. "Alright, alright. I shall send one of my men to interview the victim's cousin."

Quin breathed out heavily in relief, but the constable stabbed a finger in his direction. "Just know that it's likely to come to nought, Mr Williams. Your friend was at the residence on the night of the murder, with much of his time unaccounted for. And with him standing to inherit the bulk of the estate through the deceased's daughter, it's as clear a case as I've seen without the perpetrator being found with the murder weapon in his hand. Which, incidentally, was a weapon of war—rather suitable for a former member of the British Army, don't you think?"

Quin's nostrils flared as he bit back the cutting response that sprang to his mind. "Thank you, constable," he said instead, inclining his head before making his way to the door. Behind him he could hear the man muttering about pompous aristocrats and the resources required to deal with them, even when they were clearly guilty of murder.

Quin paused in his stride, seething with anger, but forced himself to keep walking. Getting into a fistfight with the constable in charge wasn't going to do Ollie's case any good.

Outside, Quin started aimlessly wandering the streets, waiting for his irritation to subside. It didn't much but he eventually decided to do something more useful with his time and visit the solicitor who'd drawn up Cartwright's will.

This exercise also proved pointless, though, as the man refused to divulge any information about his clients, alive or dead. While Quin applauded the solicitor's sense of discretion the encounter did nothing to improve his mood—nor did the sleet that blasted him in the face the moment he left the man's office.

It was thus that he arrived back at Ollie's townhouse dripping and spewing curses shortly after noon.

"The constable isn't interested in our theory, then?" Ollie asked as soon as he saw him, the hopeful look on his face vanishing.

Quin sighed. "Not particularly, no."

Before he could say anything else, Ollie nodded. "It's because we're only telling him about the will *now*, isn't it? How convenient for a murderer to accuse a disgruntled family member after the fact."

"You're not a murderer."

"Why didn't it occur to me earlier that George might have had something to do with this?" he demanded, ignoring Quin's comment as he started pacing the entrance hall. "I knew he was meant to inherit the estate, after all."

"You said yourself, you didn't know whether *he* knew he was meant to inherit the estate. Besides"—Quin placed a hand on Ollie's arm, making him pause—"you've been under an enormous amount of strain over the last few days. It's hardly surprising you didn't think of it."

Ollie shook off Quin's hand. "That will be of very little comfort to me or to Anne once the rope tightens around my neck."

"Ollie!"

"He'll just deny it anyway. He'll tell the police he knew nothing of the intended inheritance, and they'll believe him."

"Ollie."

"And even if he admits he *did* know about it, he'll go along with everyone's assumption that he must therefore also have known about the changes to the will—which, of course, would make Cartwright's murder an entirely useless exercise as far as his disinherited cousin is concerned."

"Ollie."

"For what other reason might the man have had to pick up the crossbow? A murderous rage over no longer being named the heir? Ha! Unlikely, when I present a much better candidate for the crime!"

"Ollie, for God's sake!" Quin took his friend by the arms and gave him a shake. "Try to calm down."

"Calm down? I…"

Quin growled. "The constable agreed to send a man to interview George."

"I told you, he'll simply tell them…"

Quin took a step forward, so he loomed over the shorter man. "The police will interview him, I said."

Ollie's mouth snapped shut and he was silent for a moment. "I suppose that *is* something," he said at last. He breathed in heavily before taking a closer look at Quin. "Did you get caught in the rain?"

"Whatever gave you that idea?" Quin snarled, realising suddenly how much his own nerves were frayed from the entire sordid affair. He ran a hand over his wet hair, making droplets splatter onto the floor.

Ollie cleared his throat, looking embarrassed. "I shall have one of the maids draw a bath for you."

"Thank you," Quin said, forcing himself to smile.

Ollie returned the gesture, although weakly. "Thank *you*.—For trying."

"You're not giving up, are you?" Quin asked softly. "We're going to prove George did it," Quin insisted, "even if the police turn out to be of little help." And based on what the constable had muttered in Quin's hearing he wasn't expecting the man to be of much help at all.

"But what if…?" Ollie swallowed and placed a hand across his throat.

"None of that! We're going to prove your innocence and that's all there is to it." Quin clasped his friend's upper arms once more, even as a sliver of fear speared through him.

What if they *couldn't* prove Ollie's innocence and he was condemned by the courts to hang?

"We're going to prove your innocence," he repeated, as much for himself as for Ollie.

The two of them looked at each other for a long moment. Finally, Ollie nodded. "I shall send for that bath," he said, taking a deep breath before turning away.

# 19.

"MY DEEPEST CONDOLENCES, Mrs Cartwright, Miss Cartwright."

Quin bowed over the women's hands, which were wreathed in black lace gloves. He'd come to see Anne's mother and sister the following afternoon, compelled to do so out of courtesy, even though he could hardly claim much of an acquaintance with either of them.

Straightening up he was at a loss for words and an awkward silence fell around the drawing room. It was broken at last by Mrs Walsh, Mrs Cartwright's sister whose house the two women were staying at, who suggested they send for some tea. Quin had no idea what they would talk about but agreed with thanks.

"Please, take a seat, Mr Williams," Mrs Walsh continued, indicating a chair across from mother and daughter.

Sitting down Quin noticed that the Cartwrights seemed less than thrilled at his continued presence, their red-rimmed eyes and downturned mouths emphasising the similarities in their appearance. With her red hair, Mrs Walsh looked more like Anne, although she was taller than her niece.

"I hardly think that's appropriate."

"I beg your pardon, Miss Cartwright," Quin said, quickly getting up again, "I shall leave you to your grief."

"That's not what I mean." The young woman's face was masked in an expression of disgust. "How dare you come here? You, who's friends with that…that monster."

Quin frowned. "If you're talking about Mr Penhale…"

"He killed my father!" Miss Cartwright's nostrils flared as she glowered at Quin.

"There is no evidence…"

"He was there!" Colleen got to her feet and balled her hands into fists, her eyes continuing to bore into Quin's. "He was there at the house, and I know he did it! I always knew he was a bad apple."

"Miss Cartwright, I have known Oliver Penhale for years and…"

"He has left me without a father and my mother without a husband." She glanced at Mrs Cartwright, who was sitting stiffly on the settee, her mouth pinched in stony silence. "What are we to do?" Before Quin could answer she went on, viciously spitting the words out, "He and my wretched sister deserve each other! I am only glad that I haven't been saddled with the likes of him!"

Quin breathed out heavily and bit his tongue, reminding himself that, whatever else she might be, Miss Cartwright was a daughter grieving for the loss of her father. That she'd forgotten how much Ollie had done for her family was irrelevant at this moment.

"I should go," he said to Mrs Walsh.

The poor woman looked distraught, wringing her hands as she glanced back and forth between the two of them. Finally, she nodded, getting up to see him out.

"The noose will be too good for him!"

Quin turned slowly back toward Miss Cartwright, narrowing his eyes. "Ollie is innocent," he managed to grind out between his teeth. "And I will prove it.— No matter what it takes!"

"AT LEAST THEY didn't have you arrested."

Quin snorted at Ollie's dry remark.

"Although it might have been entertaining to share a cell."

"Hmph." Following his disastrous visit with the Cartwright women Quin had returned to his friend's townhouse in almost as foul a mood as the day before. Knowing where he'd been headed it had taken Ollie little time to guess the reason for Quin's testiness. Quin was only surprised Ollie wasn't more upset about the encounter himself.

"Don't concern yourself with them," he said, handing Quin a glass of whiskey. "They're not very nice people."

"Yes, I'd gathered as much," Quin muttered and took a long drink.

"They haven't called on Anne once, haven't so much as sent a note. As if they were the only ones affected by Mr Cartwright's death.—Although I shouldn't be surprised, really. They were never what one might call a close family. And as soon as I was suspected of Cartwright's murder they condemned Anne alongside me."

Ollie glanced up at the ceiling, to the upper floor where Anne was resting in the sitting room, before giving a dismissive shrug. Quin could see, though, that the harsh treatment of his wife by her own mother and sister bothered Ollie more than he wanted to admit.

"You really ought to stop looking so glum, Oliver, else people will think you're old before your time."

Quin turned toward the doorway where Archie was strutting into the drawing room with purpose, evidently intent on fortifying himself.

"And you ought to stop barging into my house unannounced, Archibald," Ollie said, the corners of his mouth turning up at the sight.

Archie waved a large hand. "I think we've known each other long enough to forego any formalities. Besides, you wouldn't begrudge a man a drink, would you?"

"Certainly not. Please help yourself."

Having already done so Archie grinned. "Ah, that's better," he said after taking a healthy gulp and collapsing into one of the armchairs.

"Trying day?" Quin asked.

Archie gave him a long-suffering look. "Don't ask. I'm already regretting not following Ham's example and going straight to bed."

Quin and Ollie exchanged amused glances while Archie lay back and closed his eyes. After a minute or two he opened them and ran a hand vigorously across his face.

"So, George Cartwright," he said abruptly, seeming once more fully alert.

Ollie leaned forward, looking bewildered. "What about him?"

"You see, I have connections. People who know people, who know other people…"

"I know what connections are," Ollie interrupted, "and I know all about yours. What did you find out?"

"Well, as soon as I saw Cartwright's miserable excuse for a home I was sure he must be in some difficulty. Being convinced it was of a financial nature—as we had, of course, surmised already—I decided I'd ask an acquaintance who…let's just say…has his ears to the ground when it comes to such affairs, the proprietors of many an establishment appreciating his intimate knowledge of their patrons—lest they be unable to foot the bill, you understand."

Ollie gave him an impatient look. "Yes, yes. And?"

Archie wouldn't be rushed, though. "Having to fulfil my military duties during the day I was required to accost the man at an ungodly hour yester morn, there being little time to lose." He glanced briefly at Ollie's neck. "The promise of a healthy sum in return for his expertise did speed him from his bed, though, and he assured me he'd look into George Cartwright's affairs forthwith."

"And I assume he did so or are you simply enjoying telling us about your day?"

Archie sniffed at Ollie's outburst but otherwise ignored it as he continued, "Besides being acquainted with many influential people in Dublin society my man is also familiar with a number of less than savoury characters, including those who lend money at great—and potentially dangerous—costs."

"And one such character is after George?" Quin guessed.

Archie gave a curt nod. "Indeed. And, in fact, likely more than one. George seems to have made a habit of approaching money lenders for funds, probably in large part to pay off previous ones he owed. And as his need for blunt grew his choice of usurer became ever more dangerous to his health."

"Hmph." Ollie's face was pinched with a growing rage.

"I wonder if that had anything to do with him leaving the house party so suddenly," Quin said, remembering George's strained expression as he made his abrupt departure from Cornac House.

"Most likely," Archie said. "He may have been given an ultimatum—pay up in the next three days or bid your kneecaps farewell."

Quin cringed at the thought but Archie was probably right. "And I'd guess that's when he sold almost everything he owned."

"And perhaps approached yet another unsavoury character for a loan, one who wouldn't be satisfied with shattered kneecaps if there was still money that was owed."

"But how is any of this going to help us?" Ollie snarled suddenly, jumping up from his seat. "It's all very well and good knowing the man was in debt but how will that prove he killed Anne's father?"

"It does provide him with a motive," Quin said calmly but Ollie threw him a disgusted look.

"About as much of a motive as I have myself. Less, actually, since I am the one who *does* inherit the bulk of Mr Cartwright's estate now that he's dead. Except I won't, of course, because I'll soon be swinging from a gibbet!"

"It will make the police take a closer look at him, for a start." Quin tried to sound confident in his assumption although he had his doubts, the constable in charge having been unable to hide his scepticism at Quin's tale.

"Hmph."

"I'll keep an eye on George myself," Quin said, "report anything suspicious to the police." Perhaps George's nervousness—or his guilty conscience?—would cause him to slip up.

Quin came to stand in front of Ollie and clasped his shoulders. "You're not alone in this, Ollie. We will fight for you, to the end."

# 20.

"MRS LYNCH, PLEASE come in."

I got up from my chair as Mrs Lynch hesitantly took a step into the drawing room while Denis performed a brief bow and tottered off.

"Mrs Williams, I hope I'm not disturbing you."

I waved away her concern. "Not at all. I'm happy to see you again." In fact, with Quin's absence from the estate and having no way of knowing how he was faring I was glad of the distraction a visit from my neighbour afforded me. Aside from dealing with the challenges of new motherhood without my husband by my side I'd spent countless hours since Quin had left worrying about his welfare and Ollie's fate. Would Ollie be tried and found guilty of murder or would his friends be able to clear his name?

"Have a seat," I invited my visitor, trying to shake off my concerns and focus on the here and now.

Mrs Lynch inclined her head in thanks and we both sat down. She looked around a little uncertainly, though, seeming unsure what to say.

"How are you faring at Talamh na Niall?" I asked into the awkward silence.

"Oh, very well, thank you. We are most relieved not to have to worry about uninvited guests." She gave me a shy smile that I returned.

"Yes, I'm sure. It must be a great weight off your shoulders knowing Herbert Andrews' agent will no longer be coming around demanding payment."

"It certainly is." She held my eyes, radiating a genuine warmth. "I wanted to congratulate you on the birth of your daughter, Mrs Williams."

"Thank you, Mrs Lynch, that's very kind of you."

"I would have come sooner but I know how difficult the early weeks can be and…well…I didn't know…"

She trailed off and I thought I understood her hesitation. The Lynches were our tenants. Despite the fact that we'd gotten on well at our last meeting, that may be enough reason for some to keep their distance.

"I am very glad you came," I assured her. "Would you like some tea?" I smiled at Mary who'd just come into the drawing room bearing a tray, but she set it down without meeting my eyes.

"Yes, thank you, I would."

"How did you know I'd had a daughter?" I asked once the tea had been served.

A soft blush crept up Mrs Lynch's neck. "Oh…well…the servants talk…"

She gave me a sideways glance but I laughed. "Yes, they do."

We spent some time talking about our children, exchanging anecdotes, and I found I was enjoying her company very much—mostly for herself but also for keeping thoughts of Quin's adventures in Dublin at bay.

"How you manage with *three* children I'll never know," I said, having just recounted my frustration at a recent sleepless night and restless day that Eveline had spent fussing endlessly.

"It does get easier as they get older. And fortunately they were born one at a time. Now, having to deal with three *babies* at once?" She shook her head, imagining the horror, making us both laugh.

A sound at the door made me look up and I beckoned to Geraldine, who was hovering at the threshold with Eveline in her arms.

"Mrs Lynch, this is Geraldine, who's been helping me with the baby."

I took the bundle from her arms as the two women greeted each other.

"She's beautiful, Mrs Williams," Mrs Lynch said after Geraldine had left, gazing down at the tiny being I held.

As her mother I could hardly disagree. "Thank you, Mrs Lynch.—But please, you must call me Alannah."

Mrs Lynch looked at me in some surprise as a blush returned to her cheeks. "That's very kind of you…Alannah," she said, sounding undeniably pleased. "And you must call me Joan."

With the use of our Christian names the last bit of restraint between us disappeared and we chatted amiably for several more minutes until Eveline started fussing.

"I'm sure she's hungry," I said, getting up.

Joan followed suit. "I should go, leave you to your daughter. My own children will probably be wondering where I've gotten to." She smiled as I accompanied her to the door.

After I bid Joan farewell I went up to the nursery, where I put the baby to my breast. Leaning back in the nursing chair I thought fondly of the afternoon, hoping I would see more of Joan in the future. Unfortunately, though, thoughts of the future inevitably led to thoughts of Quin and I wished fervently—for the umpteenth time—that I knew what he was doing.

The note that had arrived on our doorstep only a few days ago had shocked me deeply—as it had shocked Quin. But he, at least, must have some answers by now, whereas I was left brooding about the same questions over and over again. Why had Mr Cartwright been murdered? And why was Ollie being accused of the crime? And, most importantly, what could Quin and his friends hope to do about it if Ollie was found guilty and condemned to die?

A cold sweat broke out on my skin thinking of shy Ollie facing his death on the scaffold. It was simply not possible that he could have killed Anne's father in cold blood, I was sure.

And what about Anne herself? What must she be feeling? What must she be thinking? Not only had she lost her father in the most brutal of ways, she may very well also lose her husband in the coming days.

A squawk interrupted my rampant thoughts and I looked down at Eveline, who was making small grunting noises as she moved her head irritably from side to side. I stroked her cheek and moved her to my other breast, where she latched on eagerly. The rhythmic motion of her feeding soothed me as much as her until, finally, I felt myself relax.

I could help neither Anne nor Ollie from afar, and nor could I help Quin.

The best I could do was to take care of his family while he was away and pray he found a way to save his friend.

# 21.

"WHY IS IT, that whenever you come to Dublin, I find myself lurking in strange alleyways after dark?"

Quin grinned at Archie, who was eying his surroundings with a dubious expression on his face, his breath steaming in the cold night air.

"Because I know you have a penchant for adventure."

"That may be true...although it doesn't feel like much of an adventure just yet."

Quin nodded. Archie was right. There was nothing to suggest that tonight would be any more exciting than the last three uneventful nights had been.

"I was sure the visit from the constable would cause George to panic," Quin said irritably.

Rather to his surprise the police officer in charge of the investigation into Mr Cartwright's murder had, in fact, sent his colleague to interview George Cartwright two days earlier, as promised. As Ollie had suspected, though, George had denied all knowledge of the will and his possible role as inheritor, insisting he was devastated by his cousin's death.

"George must have a better penchant for playacting than we gave him credit for," Archie said.

"If that's the case he was in poor form when the four of us showed up on his doorstep unannounced." Quin scowled. Although the constable had assured him brusquely they'd continue looking into George as a potential suspect, the man's poorly veiled insinuations had made Quin think the noose was already descending over Ollie's head. Even Archie's discovery of George's sizeable debts hadn't swayed the policeman in his opinions, as it didn't change the fact that Ollie would be the one inheriting the murdered man's estate.

"Our appearance probably alerted him to a likely visit from the police," Archie said, pulling Quin from his thoughts, "so he was prepared. But that doesn't mean he won't still panic…especially if nobody's been officially charged."

"And how much longer is that likely to take?"

With no apparent evidence against George despite his monetary ills, Ollie's presence in the Cartwright house at the time of the murder and the fact of the blasted will would likely see their friend condemned in a matter of days.

"Hmph." Archie's hands formed into sizable fists. "We have to confront him."

"I tried that. He didn't so much as open the door."

With the constable's efforts proving less than satisfactory Quin had decided to knock on George Cartwright's door the morning after the interview. Receiving no response to his civilised knocking he'd hammered on the door for several minutes, calling for the man to talk to him. But besides a horde of curious faces appearing at the neighbour's window, nothing had happened. Either George truly hadn't been home, or he'd simply ignored Quin and waited for him to disappear.

"We have to give him no choice about it."

"Challenge him on the street, you mean?" Quin asked sceptically.

As he'd promised Ollie he'd been watching the man's house for much of the day and night—no pleasant feat in early winter—hoping he would do something to incriminate himself. But so far, George had yet to show himself at all. Quin was sure he was hiding—whether from Ollie and his friends, the police or the creditors likely to appear on his doorstep with cudgels, he didn't know, although it was likely to be all three. In either case, Quin was quite certain the man hadn't fled the city as he'd seen the occasional, dim light in the window. That knowledge would do them little good, though, if they couldn't get him to confess.

Archie was unperturbed. "He has to leave the house eventually. Even if he's intent on ignoring you every time you knock, he must go out occasionally, if for no other reason than to get something to eat."

"No doubt you're right. And yet I've seen neither hide nor hair of him these past three days." Although Quin hadn't been able to keep up a constant surveillance, and Ham and Archie had only been able to assist him intermittently between their duties, he would have expected to see a few glimpses of the man even so.

"He's making himself scarce. A clear sign of his guilt if we'd needed any more. He's lying low, waiting for Ollie to be convicted, upon which time he'll feel himself safe.—At least from the police." Archie waved a dismissive hand at the man's numerous concerns.

"Well, we can't wait that long, can we?" Quin said irritably. "We'll have to draw him out."

"That's precisely what I was thinking."

Quin looked back toward George Cartwright's door. They were crouched in front of the house across the street, behind a convenient bush at the top of the staircase leading down to the lower level. Although the occupants of that house may well have seen them through the basement window, Quin felt himself relatively safe on account of the outer shutters being firmly closed—which they had been for the past three days.

A rustling to his left made him lift his head. Two dark figures materialised beside him, and his heart leapt into his throat.

"What the devil are you doing here?" he hissed when he recognised the two men.

"Ollie insisted on joining the party. He'd had enough of sitting around at home."

Ham grinned but Quin grimaced. He was about to say something when Ollie took a step forward. "I'm going to clear my name. Tonight." He looked defiantly from Quin to Archie and back again, daring them to object.

"What's your plan then?" Archie asked. "Hold a knife to the man's throat until he gives himself up?"

"If I must." Ollie pulled a blade out of his waistband with a flourish.

"Well, there's something to it. Except for the fact that Cartwright's not been seen these past three days, as we've just been discussing."

"But he's here." It was less a question than a statement and Ollie's lips lifted in a snarl. "I know he is."

"We could break into the house," Ham suggested, looking contemplatively toward George's front door.

"And wake the neighbours?" Quin gave Ham a sceptical look.

"Why would we do that? We didn't bring a battering ram.—I do, however, have one of these." With the air of a magician Ham withdrew a long, thin metal device from his pocket.

The other three crowded around him to get a closer look.

"You can pick locks?" Archie asked, a note of admiration in his voice.

Ham smirked. "You can't?"

"Nothing above a simple padlock." Archie waved his hand. "And you think you can get us into Cartwright's house without alerting him to our presence?"

"I do."

After a little discussion it was decided that Ham would attempt to break into the basement door, as that would make him less visible from the street. Ollie would accompany him while Quin and Archie kept an eye on the front door, lest the man attempt to escape.

"What about the back of the house?" Ollie asked. "There may be another door if there's a yard."

"You're right," Quin said. "I'll go around and keep an eye on the back." Having watched the house mostly by himself he'd had no choice but to stay at the front. He wondered suddenly whether George had been coming and going out the backdoor all this time but dismissed the thought. There was nothing he could do about it now, in any case.

Once they'd agreed on how to proceed Quin set off, walking past several houses before turning into a small alley leading to the neighbouring street. As Ollie had suspected there was indeed a small yard attached to each of the houses, including those on the street next to Cartwright's. Unfortunately, though, there was no path between the backs of the two rows of properties, meaning Quin would have to go through the adjoining yards to reach George's house.

With a brief look at the dark windows on either side of him he stepped into the first yard. Moving as quickly as he could he climbed over fences and skirted piles of rubbish, glad of the pale moonlight on what would otherwise have been a gloomy night. Not wanting to lose his bearings he paused after a moment to count chimneys. It would do the others no good if he stopped at the wrong house. But nor would it help if he arrived too late and so he quickly set off again, sweating freely.

"This must be the longest row of houses in all of Ireland," he muttered as he shoved aside several half-rotten crates barring his way, having quite given up on stealth in his efforts to reach his target.

He glanced quickly at his pocket watch. Ham must have started working on the lock by now, he thought.

A movement up ahead caught his eye.

A dark figure was scrambling over a fence, turning his head to look behind him before rushing away.

Sure it must be Cartwright attempting to escape, Quin redoubled his efforts. *So much for getting into the house without alerting the man...*

Quin growled in annoyance as he launched himself over obstacles to finally reach what he assumed to be George's yard.

"He's out here!" Quin yelled through the open door at the back of the house as he raced past.

George was still two houses ahead of him when he abruptly turned right and disappeared. When Quin arrived at the spot, he found himself standing on another narrow pathway connecting the neighbouring streets. Cursing himself for not having realised there was a faster way of getting to Cartwright's backyard he pounded along the track, just in time to see George turning left onto the main road.

Hearing footsteps behind him Quin waved his arm but didn't slow down. "He's gone that way!"

With his heart pounding Quin followed George through the streets, Ollie, Ham and Archie hot on his heels as he somehow managed to keep their quarry in his sights.

"He's heading to the docks," Archie's voice came from behind him.

As if the words had been a catalyst the smell of the docklands started creeping up Quin's nostrils, with its heady miasma of stenches from the gasworks, the fertiliser plants and the River Liffey's sewage-swollen waters.

Trying not to breathe through his nose Quin glanced ahead, to where George was running toward a sizeable building with numerous chimneys. Several large shapes loomed through the multi-paned windows, making Quin think it was some kind of factory, in what looked to be an industrial area. Reaching the double doors George tried to yank open one side. When it didn't budge, he started frantically rattling both handles. Realising his way was barred he gave up and rushed toward the edge of the building.

Quin pumped his arms and legs even faster in an effort to catch up with the man before he could round the corner and disappear. Reaching out a hand he managed to grasp George by the scruff of his neck. Wasting no time Quin pulled him back viciously, eliciting a high-pitched squeal in return. Quin spun him around and put his fist to good use, making George cry out and slump against the wall.

"I've done nothing!" George wailed, holding his hand against one cheek and breathing heavily.

"You killed Anne's father!" Ollie snarled as he came up behind Quin.

"No." George shook his head but lowered his eyes.

"Why did you run then?" Archie demanded, looming over Cartwright, puffing like a steam engine. "Hoping to lose us in there?" Archie lifted his chin toward the factory, a look of disgust on his face.

"I…"

"You'd have done better to head to the shipyard if you wanted to disappear."

"I didn't…I mean…I thought…"

"You thought we were the money lenders coming to collect," Quin said, "didn't you? The time for repayment must surely have come."

George's eyes rolled back and forth in panic, confirming Quin's suspicions.

"We know you did it!" Ollie interrupted, his hands fisted at his sides as he dismissed George's monetary woes. "We know you killed Mr Cartwright!"

"No...no..." George looked between the four men surrounding him and swallowed heavily, his chest still heaving. "You must believe me...I didn't...I didn't kill anyone."

"You thought you would inherit the Cartwright estate, is that it?" Ollie demanded.

"No...no...of course not."

Ollie took a step closer. "You killed him because you found out you were getting nothing?"

A muscle in George's cheek twitched. "I... No, no!"

"Just admit it! When you found out you weren't getting a penny you killed him!" Ollie raised one fist, holding it menacingly in front of George. "Admit it!"

George was moving his head stubbornly from side to side, his jaws clenched and his eyes lowered.

"Admit it, George! You did it! You killed your cousin because he was leaving you nothing."

Ollie's fist struck George's temple, making the man's head bang against the wall. He cried out and blood started trickling past his eye. When he looked up at his assailant his face was suffused with hatred.

"He wouldn't even give me a penny while he was alive," George growled out between his teeth.

"He didn't *have* a penny to give," Ollie snarled, leaning into the man with his face only inches away.

"Lies, lies! He had an entire estate to his name!"

"An estate that was so heavily in debt he would have had to sell it all if I hadn't come along to save his skin."

George shook his head stubbornly, sending droplets of blood flying as he stared daggers at Ollie. "That's not true! It's not true! He just didn't want to help me...his own cousin."

"That's why you were at the house that night, isn't it?" Ollie said, ignoring George's mutterings. "You came to ask him for money. You asked him for money and when he couldn't give you any, you killed him."

George's lips twisted into a snarl. "I only needed a small loan!"

Archie snorted. "A small loan? It's highly doubtful that a small loan would have saved you from your troubles."

"What would *you* know about it?"

Archie gave him a pointed look. "More than you might think, Cartwright. And you forget, I've been inside your house."

"You mean, you *broke into* my house."

Archie shrugged, unbothered by the accusation. "Only the second time.—Besides, that doesn't change the fact that you killed a man in cold blood."

George started shaking his head again and opened his mouth to say something, but Ollie cut him off. "It's over, George. We know you did it."

George shrank back, his eyes flitting between the four men, looking like a caged animal. Suddenly, though, he launched himself at Ollie with a roar.

"All I needed was a little money to tide me over," he shrieked, straining against Archie and Ham, who'd quickly grasped his arms to restrain him and were pressing him into the wall. "And he wouldn't even grant me that! I thought the crossbow would loosen his pockets, make him realise that we're family…but he still wouldn't help me. So I told him I would take my inheritance.—Do you know what he did?" His eyes rolled madly back and forth in his head as they flashed from one man to the other. "He laughed at me!"

"He knew you would get nothing," Archie said.

"He'd told me I would inherit! He'd told me!"

"Things change," Ollie said, his face tight.

"This is all your fault!" George screeched, the cords of his neck standing out as he tried to pull away from his captors. "This is…"

His voice cut off as Ollie's hand closed around his throat. "If it wasn't for me there would have been no estate to inherit in the first place," Ollie hissed. His nostrils flaring, he leaned closer to George. "How nicely it would have worked out for you if you *had* been the heir, with me condemned for murder.—And you not lifting a finger to save me!"

George made a gurgling noise as Ollie tightened his grip.

"Ollie!" Quin laid a hand on Ollie's arm and shook his head. Ollie's eyes locked with Quin's until at last, he let go.

George slid down to the ground, clutching his neck and gasping for air. "You have no proof," he wheezed, "no proof of anything."

"You just confessed in front of four witnesses," Archie scoffed. "I think you'll find that's proof enough."

"As is this," Ham said, dipping a hand into his pocket. "I believe it's Mr Cartwright's signet ring. I recognised it from the house party. I found it on the mantelpiece in your bedroom before you made a run for it."

George's shoulders slumped as he put his head in his hands. "It's a monogram. GC.—We have the same initials." His body started to shake, and a cry escaped his lips. "I didn't mean to kill him," he whispered. "I didn't mean it." He looked up at Ollie, tears streaming down his face. "I didn't mean it! I didn't mean it!"

Ollie compressed his lips but extended a hand to help George to his feet. "Come man. If you carry on like this, perhaps you'll escape the noose and end up in a lunatic asylum instead.—It's the best you can hope for," he added under his breath before leading the sobbing man away.

## 22.

"HE WAS ARRESTED immediately."

Quin gently patted Eveline's back, holding her against his shoulder. He'd arrived at Glaslearg that afternoon, exhausted but happy to be home.

"Archie was right. George's confession to the four of us was sufficient for the police, even after their initial scepticism about the man's guilt. Once we'd made our statements he was taken into custody and we were sent on our way, including Ollie, who was cleared of all charges and received a grudging apology for what he'd been forced to endure."

Eveline gave a small belch, making Quin smile. Alannah's eyes softened as she looked at the two of them.

"So George Cartwright was in debt?"

"Yes, most terribly.—Something of a family trait, it seems." Quin snorted, thinking of all the lives that had been ruined for the sake of a few bets on a hand of cards.

"And when Mr Cartwright wouldn't lend him any money, he thought he'd take his inheritance instead. Or what he thought he was inheriting."

Quin nodded. "I think he regretted it in the end. It's why he took the ring, a sentimental token.—Which will put the final nail in his coffin I suppose."

"Do you think he'll hang?"

"Probably. Aside from the murder itself there's not much to suggest he's insane, which would have been his only defence."

Quin turned his face toward Eveline, who'd fallen asleep against him, trusting utterly that she was safe in his arms. For a moment he wished that he, too, could feel such contentment instead of being worn down by the knowledge that the world was filled with wretchedness.

"Why did nobody see him that night at the Cartwright's townhouse?"

Quin looked back at Alannah, who was wearing a quizzical expression.

"It seems he'd been hovering around the house for some time, waiting for Ollie and Anne to leave so he could talk to Mr Cartwright in private." Once George had realised he'd been caught the truth had spewed out of him like a fountain, as if the telling would somehow save him from his doomed fate. "When the storm came, and it became clear the two of them would stay the night he contemplated leaving. But he was desperate. He'd already sold everything he could sell, and his creditors were coming to collect."

"He was trying to avoid debtors' prison."

"He was trying to avoid ending up at the bottom of the River Liffey."

Alannah's eyes widened.

"He didn't make the best choices," Quin said, recalling George's blubbering form as they escorted him to the station, admitting to one bad decision after the next. Quin sighed, suddenly longing for his bed. "In any case, when he saw Mr Cartwright alone in his study through the window later that night, he thought he'd take a chance and snuck into the house. He knew his way around and everyone else had gone to bed. He thought he could persuade his cousin to help him."

"Except his cousin was in debt himself." Alannah's face became suffused with sadness. "Poor Anne. As much as she admitted that he often disappointed her, she loved him even so. He was her father, after all. And to lose him like that…and by his cousin's hand…"

Quin pressed his lips to Eveline's soft temple, inhaling her sweet scent and closing his eyes, praying he'd be a better father to her than Mr Cartwright had been to Anne.

"Come."

Alannah's voice near his head and her hand on his arm made him open his eyes again.

"You're tired. Come up to bed."

She took Eveline's slumbering form into her arms and cocked her head toward the door. He followed her up the stairs and into the nursery, where Alannah gently laid the baby into the cradle.

"I've been away for less than two weeks, and I'd swear she's changed," Quin said softly.

Alannah smiled. "She's changing daily. You can almost see it happening when you watch her."

They stood side by side for a moment, looking down at their daughter. Quin took Alannah's hand, squeezing her fingers lightly. She turned toward him, her eyes locking with his in silent understanding.

He led her to the bedroom, where he drew her into his arms. Her mouth met his, softly at first but with increasing urgency as she wrapped her arms around his neck. He undressed her slowly, savouring her touch as she undid his cravat and removed his waistcoat and shirt.

"It's been too long," he whispered, running his hand down her naked back and pulling her toward the bed.

She nodded, even as a look of apprehension flitted across her features.

"It will be alright."

Quin kissed her mouth, her neck, her breasts, as if touching her for the first time, until she quivered beneath him, longing for more. He moved slowly, letting her take the lead, holding her eyes as she looked up at him, her face awash with emotion. When she gasped, he lowered his mouth to hers, swallowing her cry even as he lost himself in the tide that came crashing over him.

# 23.

EVELINE AND I were delighted to have Quin back at home—the estate simply wasn't the same without him. Naturally, I was also relieved that he, Archie and Ham had managed to save their friend from the gallows but I often found myself thinking about the Cartwrights, Anne and Ollie, and the way in which their lives had been irrevocably altered in a matter of minutes. I was glad, therefore, to receive a letter from Anne about a week after Quin's return and eagerly tore open the envelope to start reading the single page.

*Dear Alannah,*

*I have been looking at this blank piece of paper wondering how to summarise all that's happened over the past few weeks. Seeing as you will probably have heard all the details from Quin I shall say only this: we are managing.*

*Since Ollie's release we have been trying to continue with our daily lives and yet, everything seems to have changed. Every morning it feels like a great effort to get out of bed and each afternoon I feel as though the weight of the world were upon my shoulders. I had thought I might find some comfort from my grief by sharing it with my mother and sister despite the difficulties we've had in the past. Alas, it was not to be. Even with George having confessed to the crime, Colleen continued to attack Ollie ruthlessly, blaming him for the situation that precipitated my father's murder, while my mother threw me accusing looks as I was called selfish, uncaring and grasping.*

*I do not know what came over me to do what I did, but when Colleen went on to viciously debase Ollie's character I could listen to her no more. As if I were watching myself from a distance I saw my arm swing back in a great arc, only for my hand to come hurtling forward and land on Colleen's cheek with a resounding crack. Such was the force of the blow that my hand—which was devoid of its glove in my relative's home—left a dark mark on my sister's skin, shocking her into silence. My poor aunt could only sputter incoherently while my mother's mouth fell open in disbelief at what she had just witnessed.*

*Feeling in equal parts astonished and deeply vindicated at my own actions I made a hasty exist, leaving the three women gaping after me. Although the incident was, of course, upsetting even to me I must admit with some shame that the sight of Colleen's stunned and reddened face is one I shall likely think fondly of in the coming months. Having thus alienated myself completely from my immediate family I am more grateful than ever for Ollie's comforting presence in my life. It is he who is helping me make it through each day and supporting me in my darkest moments as I try to move past the devastating events of the last few weeks.*

*I only wish I lived closer to you, dearest Alannah, for I feel sure seeing you would further brighten my days.*

*And I do so wish to meet your daughter!*

*I hope all of you at the estate are well and send my warmest regards.*

*Yours most fondly,
Anne*

I looked down at Anne's letter for a minute, wishing as she did that we could see each other more frequently.

I also wished most fervently that I could have seen Anne silence her wretched sister as effectively as she had.

I laughed, picturing Colleen's shocked face. I wondered whether her behaviour might now change for the better. Probably not, I decided. A woman like Colleen Cartwright may well respond to such a humiliating encounter by lashing out to others even more. Besides, she was simply a selfish, judgmental and odious person and nothing was likely to change that.

With an ease that would no doubt infuriate her I put the woman out of my mind and turned back to my own affairs, glad Anne had experienced the satisfaction of putting her in her place at last.

# 24.

OVER THE FOLLOWING few days we settled into a routine once more. Since Eveline's birth much of my time was, of course, spent taking care of her, which meant I was less involved in the estate's business than I had been before. But I would often chat to Quin about the tenants, the fields and the livestock, keeping myself informed. Geraldine was still a great help to me, although she started taking on more of the household chores as I needed less assistance with the baby than I had at first.

The young woman and Quin's valet continued to skirt around each other, throwing each other furtive glances but taking things no further, making me wonder whether Rupert would ever work up the courage to tell her how he felt. He evidently had not worked up the courage to speak to her father as he'd planned, else he would surely have behaved differently toward her by now. As it was, though, their peculiar antics provided the household with much amusement, with some of our staff members placing bets on how long it would take for the two of them to finally move past the stalemate they found themselves in.

During the relative respite of winter, Quin and I enjoyed our time together, watching Evie—as we'd started affectionately calling Eveline for short—grow and learn, entirely content in only each other's company. We spent a quiet Christmas at the house and soon after, rang in the new year filled with hope for our family and the estate, and for Ireland as a whole as she tried to drag herself out of the misery of the past few years.

Days turned into months, and the dreary fields began to fill with life once more as the busy spring season of planting began and the landscape was touched with splashes of green. By the time Glaslearg's hills were blooming with fresh new growth Evie was starting to sit up on her own and trying solid food, making me marvel at how much she'd already learned.

I looked at her sometimes, amazed at how quickly she was changing before my eyes. It was true what they said, I decided, about noticing the passage of time more clearly in the company of children. Already, Evie was far from the tiny, helpless baby we'd welcomed into the world only a few months before.

I smiled as Quin sat her down on a blanket in the drawing room one sunny but cold afternoon in May. She wobbled precariously for a moment, Quin hovering close by until she settled down. He made a face at her and she giggled, a high-pitched sound that warmed my heart.

Emmett and Benjamin stormed through the doorway a moment later. The sudden noise startled Evie and she turned her head a little too far and tilted backward. Quin caught her with an outstretched hand and picked her up. Not sure if she ought to be distressed or not, she placed her thumb into her mouth, a habit she'd lately adopted.

Oblivious to the effects of their tumultuous entrance, the two boys continued their chatter—which was not quite an argument yet—before turning to Quin for his expert opinion. As he began speaking Emmett started nodding enthusiastically. Looking at him I suddenly realised that the young boy I'd first met in London was showing signs of morphing into that awkward phase between boy and man, his gangly limbs starting to fill out and the pudgy features of his face beginning to harden. A little older, the changes in Benjamin were even more pronounced, his childhood almost at an end.

The days were indeed hurtling on at an inexorable speed.

The thought made me feel a moment of panic and I quickly looked at Eveline, who was observing the boys with big eyes. I suddenly wished desperately that I could pause the inevitable onslaught of time, that I could hold onto this moment forever and keep my family safe and whole by my side, constant and unchanging evermore.

Quin caught my eyes, making me take a deep breath, reminding myself to focus on the present. Even as the days passed by and we all changed as we got older, there were many more moments of joy lying ahead.

Whatever else was going on around us, I had to believe in that.

# 25.

"SIR! SIR!"

Quin lifted his head from the list of numbers he'd been perusing, to meet the anxious faces of Benjamin and Conor as they rushed into the study. Both boys were panting as if they'd been running some distance, their cheeks red with exertion.

"What is it?"

"We saw…"

"There were…"

"Lots o' them…"

"A whole group…"

Quin held up his hand. "Take a deep breath and start again, at the beginning. One at a time please!" He inclined his head toward Benjamin, who noisily sucked in air through his teeth before rattling off a string of words.

"We saw a whole lot o' men up by the tenants' cottages, sir, together like, in a big group, lookin' very fierce and up to no good."

Quin frowned. "A group of men you say?"

Benjamin nodded vigorously while Conor scrunched up his nose in thought.

"What is it Conor?" Quin asked.

"There may have been a woman or two," the boy said but was immediately rebuked by his friend.

"It was only men!" Benjamin insisted, shaking his head vigorously. "Vicious-lookin' men!"

"But Ben, don't ye recall that some o' them was wearin' skirts?"

"Hm, ye may be right."

"And I think one o' them was maybe holdin' a babe."

"No! Never! It was a fierce group o' men…maybe with one or two women."

"But…"

Quin lifted both hands this time to quell the argument. "What were they doing?"

Benjamin opened his mouth to respond but snapped it shut as a contemplative expression came over his face. The boys looked at each other for a moment before turning back to Quin.

"Nothin'," Benjamin said, sounding very disappointed.

"Nothing?"

"Well, they was walkin'…"

"I see," Quin said. "So you saw a group of people walking by the tenants' land?"

Benjamin huffed in irritation. "But sir, they were dirty and…scruffy and and…"

Quin lifted one brow as he assessed the boys standing in front of his desk. A streak of mud was smeared across Benjamin's cheek, and both sets of clothing sported assorted bits of filth. Becoming aware of Quin's scrutiny, Benjamin's cheeks blazed a red almost as bright as his hair. He started rubbing a hand over the stained cuff of his shirt, while Conor took one look at his dirt-encrusted fingers before hiding them behind his back.

Quin pressed his lips together to stop himself from laughing. "We'll go investigate, shall we?"

AS FAR AS dirty and scruffy was concerned, Benjamin's description had been accurate.

"Please, sir, we have nowhere else t' go." Tear tracks snaked down the grubby cheeks of the woman looking up at Quin with pleading eyes. Her hand held tightly to a scrawny girl at her side while clutching a small bundle to her chest—likely all they possessed in the world.

"They threw us out," a stooped old man kept muttering to himself in Gaelic. "They just threw us out." He shook his head slowly from side to side, his eyes unfocused as he relived the horrors he'd endured.

"Can ye help them, sir?"

Quin turned toward Mr Casey, one of his tenants who'd materialised beside him. The man looked at Quin anxiously before darting a glance to a few others who were observing them from a short distance away. Seeing the intensity in their eyes Quin understood why Benjamin and Conor had jumped to the conclusion that the men were up to no good. There was a seething anger lurking beneath the surface that Quin hoped wouldn't break loose.

"Do you know them?" Quin asked, looking back at Casey.

"Aye. It's a third cousin on me mother's side and his kin—or what's left o' them."

Quin compressed his lips as he looked at the twenty or so people assembled before him. Benjamin and Conor had been right in saying the group consisted mostly of men. The fact that there were so few women and children or elderly among them could mean only one thing.

"I'd heard many were taken by illness," Casey said, confirming Quin's suspicions. "And now this..."

"Where did they come from?"

"Near Baile an Scotaigh in Monaghan. Ah...ye'll know it as Scotstown."

Quin nodded, although he couldn't remember if he'd ever heard of Scotstown before. He had heard, though, that the neighbouring County Monaghan had been more severely affected by the ravages of the famine than County Tyrone—which nevertheless paled in comparison to the devastation wreaked in some other Irish counties, especially those in the southwest.

"It must have taken them some time to get here."

Casey shrugged. "One day, maybe two...under the circumstances." His eyes flitted to a small group huddled on the ground, most of whom were little more than skin and bones.

Only desperation would have made these people walk for miles to an unknown destination, Quin thought—and with no guarantee of what they'd find when they got there.

"They must've thought...I mean, with what I'd told 'em they would've hoped..." Casey drifted off, throwing Quin a sideways glance.

Quin could feel the tension coming off the other man and reached out a hand to squeeze his shoulder. "We'll find a place for them, Mr Casey. They won't be turned away."

"TWENTY-THREE MORE MOUTHS to feed."

Quin looked at the food on the plate in front of him, suddenly losing his appetite. It was a simple meal of meat and bread but one that thousands across Ireland would give anything for.

"We'll manage," Alannah said, reaching out to squeeze his hand while Evie babbled happily to herself in her chair.

Quin gave her a weak and fleeting smile. "At least they'll have a roof over their heads...even if it is just that of a mud hut."

"Mr Casey did offer to put up some of them in his own home and you suggested the empty overseer's cottage. It was their own choice to move into the abandoned huts closer to the other tenants. Besides, that's probably what they were living in before."

"I suppose you're right." Quin knew many such dwellings were scattered across the Irish countryside, the gloomy, one-roomed structures housing countless peasants and their beasts.

"Luckily they were still usable after all this time."

Quin nodded absently. While they'd torn down some of the mud huts the tenants had lived in before Quin's arrival at Glaslearg a few years earlier, others had been left standing, even after the new stone cottages had been built.

He sighed, rubbing a hand over his face.

"What is it?" Alannah asked in concern.

"These men and women we've taken in...they're broken. They've lost loved ones, many of them. They've been evicted from their homes...and they've lost their faith in humanity. There is a bone-deep sense of injustice simmering beneath the surface. One has to wonder where all of this is going to end."

"They're grateful you've given them a second chance."

"Perhaps."

While a number of the newcomers had expressed their gratitude, he couldn't shake the feeling that he was deeply resented by some, the looks on a few of the men's faces speaking volumes.

He couldn't blame them, he supposed. Across Ireland, thousands of peasants were being thrown off their land because they could no longer pay their rent. The fact that many landowners themselves were on the brink of ruin from the lack of income was no comfort to the evicted. Especially so, as even those tenants who could scrape together what they owed might find themselves being shown the door.

In some cases the evicted were lucky enough to be given a few coins for their peaceful surrender or be allowed to take away their thatch, while many more were left with nothing. Oftentimes, neighbours were ruthlessly punished for harbouring the evicted, meaning that those without a home to return to found themselves having to construct temporary shelters using whatever material they could salvage. Without even the debris from their tumbled cabins to do that, the less fortunate resorted to digging holes in the ground and covering them with turf or sticks, leaving many to die in these ghastly hovels by the roadside.

Such misery was difficult to imagine and horrified many on both sides of the Irish sea. It was hardly surprising that the agitation of the poor soared along with the number of evictions, especially so as the British government refused to intervene, allowing the ruthless—and often illegal—clearances and destruction of houses to continue across Ireland, despite protests even among their own ranks.

In the face of the ongoing hostility from those in power, some Irishmen had started whispering of revolution, calling on country folk to rise up against British tyranny, emboldened by recent events in France.

"They'll come around," Alannah said, breaking into Quin's thoughts. "Even your existing tenants didn't like you very much when you first arrived here. And that's certainly changed."

Quin gave her a half-hearted smile. "You're right. Perhaps I'm feeling overly gloomy." While the situation across Ireland remained dire, at least conditions on his own estate weren't nearly so bleak.

Alannah grasped his hand once more. "We're living in gloomy times."

"That certainly is true." He ran a thumb over Alannah's knuckles, holding her eyes. Finally, he took a deep breath and turned back to his plate. "Let's not allow this food go to waste," he said, picking up his fork at last. "Lord knows that's one thing nobody in Ireland can afford."

# 26.

WITH A FRESH coat of whitewash on the walls, Glaslearg's old mud huts were made as habitable as they were ever likely to get, and the estate's newest residents soon settled into their new homes. Tending fields and beasts was likely much the same anywhere in Ireland, Quin supposed. With none of their own yet to care for, the newcomers assisted the old tenants where they could while they tried to get on with their lives.

The cluster of huts they'd moved into was at the edge of the estate, close to the Murphys' stone cottage and not far from the Caseys. Quin visited the newcomers periodically as they went about their business. They seemed to be faring reasonably well, all things considered, although Quin couldn't fail to see the wary glances thrown his way occasionally when they thought he wasn't looking.

When he came to the huts that evening, about a week after their arrival, some of the men were huddled close together outside, so engrossed in conversation they barely noticed his approach. Only when he called out in greeting did a few heads rise in acknowledgement. Quin saw a flash of irritation cross one of the faces, while another was strongly tinged with dislike. One or two of the men barely looked at him, studying their scuffed shoes instead. As Quin got closer a woman appeared in the doorway behind the men. When she saw him, her eyes went wide, and she quickly ducked back inside.

Quin tried his best to ignore the lack of enthusiasm for his appearance but found it even more difficult when he noticed Mr Murphy among the group of men, his features marred with undisguised hatred. Quin held the man's eyes and lifted his chin, until Murphy finally looked away, his cheeks flushed.

Clenching his jaws briefly in annoyance Quin ignored Murphy and addressed the others. But while he was telling the men of the portion of oats he'd set aside for their use, he found himself getting more and more irritated. If ever there'd been a time when Murphy had thought of Quin with respect, that had long since vanished. What he might now be telling Casey's kin about their new landlord, Quin could only guess, but he knew it would be none too favourable.

Not much to be done about it, though, he thought—except to continue as before, hoping the newcomers would judge him for himself.

"I shall ask Mr Connell to assist you in repairing the roofs," he said to them now, having noticed how patchy the thatch was looking in places. If they insisted on living in mud huts, they should at least be kept dry! "And if you come down to the granary tomorrow, I'll have the oats ready for you to transport."

Some of the men nodded, looking moderately pleased, while a few others continued to avoid meeting his eyes.

Murphy's scowl hadn't altered one bit.

Trying to dismiss their middling reactions from his mind Quin turned away. There was enough to keep him busy on the estate. His popularity with his tenants was the least of his concerns.

# 27.

WITH OUR NEW tenants reasonably well settled, the busy spring season soon turned into summer. Although Quin remained a little wary of our new residents his apprehensions slowly lessened, and I was happy to see him smiling at me on a beautiful sunny afternoon.

"Would you like to go for a walk?" he asked as he came through the drawing room door, lifting his chin in Eveline's direction.

Seven months old, she was rapidly mastering the art of crawling and was wreaking havoc everywhere she went. At this moment she was heading toward a potted plant that stood in the corner of the room, a determined expression on her small face.

"No, Evie!" I said sternly, setting aside the newspaper I'd been trying unsuccessfully to read all day.

She paused with her hand lifted toward the rim of the large pot. Her eyes swivelled from me to the plant and back again before she pulled herself up by the rim and started reaching for the pot's enticing contents.

"Evie!" I rushed to her side and quickly scooped her up before she could scatter soil all over the floor, making her squawk in protest.

Hearing a chuckle behind me I turned to Quin. "A walk is an excellent idea," I said, thinking it would do all of us good to get out of the house. After several days of near-constant rainfall the clear weather was a welcome respite.

I quickly told Geraldine and Mary we were going out and fetched bonnets for Evie and me. Once outside I blinked in the bright sunshine, unused to it as I was after the recent gloom. Evie wriggled on my hip and I adjusted her weight. She huffed in annoyance at being restrained, her small face contorted into a grimace.

"Ready?" Quin asked, placing a hand on my arm.

"Yes," I said, leaning back to dislodge small fingers from my hair. As I straightened up Evie slapped my cheek with one pudgy hand, making me laugh.

Quin looked at us in amusement as we set off, walking leisurely across the courtyard.

A screech up ahead made all of us turn toward the stable, where Emmett came pelting out the door, being chased closely by Benjamin. Bits of hay were clinging to the boys' clothing and hair, scattering here and there as they raced around the outbuildings grinning from ear to ear. Clearly, they too were taking advantage of the sunny weather, interrupting their duties with a little outdoor activity.

Noticing us watching them Emmett came to a sudden stop, Benjamin almost crashing into him. Looking a little sheepish they both hunched their shoulders when John appeared at the stable door and gruffly called them back to work. Dragging their heels the boys obeyed, throwing us guilty glances. Seeing Quin and me smiling at them, though, they grinned once more before going back inside, while John doffed his hat and followed his charges.

Looking after the three of them as they disappeared into the stable I found myself thinking about how little I had ridden in recent months. I had previously enjoyed taking my mare, Milly, out almost every day but hadn't had much opportunity to do so since Evie's birth. But with her a little older now and Geraldine, Mary and even Mrs O'Sullivan more than happy to watch her for a time, perhaps I could get back into the habit. I would be glad to have a little more time to myself and was sure Milly would appreciate the change in scenery as much as I, having endured most of her exercise at the end of a lead rope since midway through my pregnancy.

Determined to make it so I followed Quin along the path that led to the stream.

When we crossed the wooden bridge Evie squirmed in my arms, leaning toward the water as it bubbled past. Quin took her from me, and we walked a little further until we got to a flat bank, where he placed her gently down onto the grass. Evie held stock-still for a moment before slowly rocking back and forth on her hands and knees while kneading her fingers into the strange green ribbons beneath her palms. She lifted one arm high to propel herself forward, only to stop once more, distracted by the novel sensation of trying to crawl on grass.

Quin's eyes crinkled into triangles that made my heart leap with joy. I took his hand, and we followed Evie's slow progress along the bank.

After a minute or two Quin cocked his head in my direction. "Do you think Evie will have a brother or a sister one day?"

"I don't know." Not too long ago it had seemed impossible for us to have even one child. I hadn't thought too much about having any more. "Although the midwife didn't seem to think there was anything standing in the way of more pregnancies."

"Would you want to have a house full of children?"

"I don't know about a house full but one or two more might be nice."

"I never had any siblings growing up. I always wondered what it would be like."

"It's wonderful," I said with a small sigh, thinking of Kieran. "You always have somebody to play with, somebody who will stand by you.—At least until you both want to play with the same toy and try to tear each other's hair out," I added wryly, remembering a few scuffles my brother and I had gotten into when we were children.

Quin laughed and pulled me close to his side.

"It would be nice for Evie to have a brother," I said softly, imagining a small boy with Quin's green eyes and a dimple when he smiled.

Quin kissed the top of my head before letting go of me when Evie's speed increased as she neared the edge of the stream. He quickly snatched her up before she could crawl into the water, making her squawk and strain against his grasp. Holding her with one arm Quin carefully squatted down by a flat spot and suspended her over the water. She slapped her hand onto the surface, making a splash. Delighted, she did it again, faster and faster until droplets were flying everywhere.

I laughed as she squealed in delight while her smock and Quin's trousers became soaked. He looked back at me and grinned.

"She certainly is enjoying herself," I said, delighted myself at the spectacle.

"And so am I." Quin's eyes softened, even as more water sloshed onto his clothing and his feet squelched on the wet bank.

"Rupert will be thrilled at the state of your shoes," I said, tilting my chin toward the mud-encrusted specimens.

Quin lifted a dismissive shoulder. "I am no longer a London gentleman so he shouldn't complain."

"Do you miss it?"

"What? London?"

I nodded.

"Occasionally," he admitted, but chuckled when Evie spluttered as a big splash of water landed on her face. "It hasn't exactly been all smooth sailing here." His face clouded briefly before he continued, "And there certainly are conveniences to be had in London but…to live simply like this with you and Eveline…what more could a man want?"

I held his eyes for a moment. "Dry trousers, for one thing," I said wryly.

He laughed. "There is that."

With the two of them dripping by now Quin got up, to Evie's dismay. He walked a short distance from the stream, where he laid her down and removed his jacket. Before she could crawl back to the water, he wrapped her up in the jacket and tucked her into the crook of his arm.

She blinked at him, looking rather surprised at this turn of events, but soon settled against his shoulder and stuck her thumb into her mouth. Her eyelids drooped as we started walking back to the house.

"It looks like she's ready for her afternoon nap," Quin said.

I smiled at the sight of the two of them. "A nap will do her good."

As we crossed back over the wooden bridge a cool breeze came up, making me glad I'd thought to bring my shawl.

"Are you cold?" I asked, glancing sideways at Quin.

Although it was a pleasant day for early summer, the water of the stream was anything but warm.

He gave me a quizzical look before shaking his head, dislodging a few tendrils of wet hair that had been plastered to his forehead. "Why would I be cold?"

"Because you're drenched in cold water?" I suggested, amused.

"I'm hardly drenched." He dismissed his noticeably wet clothing with a wave of his hand. "Although I can't say the same for Evie." A tender expression bloomed on his face as he looked down at his daughter, whose eyes were mere slits by now. "Besides, most days I find it unbearably hot set up in full rig. It's a great relief to be walking about in my shirtsleeves!"

"Well, that's one more benefit to living in the countryside," I said. "Nobody will think less of you for going about your day half dressed!"

ONCE THEY WERE back at the house Alannah changed Eveline out of her wet clothes and put her down for a nap. Having dried off himself Quin settled in the study for a few hours' work, feeling quite content.

Despite the challenges of living in Ireland during these difficult times he wanted for nothing and had a wife and daughter he adored. He'd thoroughly enjoyed himself that afternoon and was determined to repeat the experience as soon as possible. With many others not nearly so fortunate he knew to treasure the times he could spend with his family.

When he went into the dining room a little later, Alannah and Eveline were already there.

"With all the excitement of the afternoon Evie woke up half starved," Alannah said, laying aside the newspaper she's been perusing, "so we decided on an early supper." She waved her hand at the food on the table.

Quin sat down while Eveline crammed a piece of bread into her mouth, making him smile.

"Have you already eaten?" he asked, eyeing Alannah's plate.

"Yes, I'm sorry." She nodded apologetically but he was unconcerned.

Helping himself to a slice of beef he found he had quite an appetite himself and quickly settled down to his meal. As Eveline babbled happily to herself in her highchair she started smacking her hands onto the tabletop. When she squealed in delight Quin chuckled, meeting Alannah's eyes. They shared an amused look before he turned his attention back to his supper and Alannah picked up her newspaper once more.

Mrs O'Sullivan brought him some wine and he ate peacefully for several minutes. He was just reaching for his second helping when Alannah made a strangled sound.

He looked up, startled, glancing at Eveline, who was happily playing with a spoon. Alannah, though, wore an expression of such despair that his heart squeezed tight at the sight.

"What is it?" he asked, reaching a hand toward her.

She shook her head wordlessly and pushed the newspaper across the table, her fingers trembling. Getting up, she took Evie out of her chair and crushed the small body to her chest, eliciting a surprised squawk. Quin stared at the sight for a moment before looking down at the page in front of him. It didn't take him long to find what had upset Alannah—a few unassuming printed words that summarised an unimaginable horror.

An inquest was being held into the death of a five-year-old boy who'd been found with his family in such ghastly circumstances that it had caused widespread outrage.

Quin's throat felt tight as he continued reading:

*On entering the cabin, a sight calculated to horrify the most callous heart presented itself. One child was lying on its back, opposite a few lighted sods of turf, being deprived of the use of both his feet and hands by mortification of the extremities. On a straw bed in a corner lay two others, who from an utter prostration of all physical ability, resulting (as in the case of the other boy) from a want of food, never left that miserable pallet for the last six weeks, save when taken out by their mother to crawl about for food!! Two others, not so deeply afflicted, but yet presenting an extremely emaciated appearance, stood on the floor, well nigh completely naked; and to complete the melancholy picture, the mother had lost the use of the right arm and was paralysed on the right side from the same cause also!! The body of the dead child was stretched on a table in the midst of the floor.*

According to the article, the mother and her children had been entered onto the relief roll but had nevertheless received no relief, despite the fact that they'd subsisted on nothing but a pitiful quantity of turnips for the six weeks prior to their discovery. At least three of the other children were expected to soon join their brother in death, and Quin found it doubtful a better end awaited the remaining members of that doomed family.

He sighed deeply, closing his eyes, the joy he'd experienced only a few minutes earlier suddenly feeling like a distant memory.

How many more such stories would they come across before this nightmare would come to an end? How many more lives would be lost in the face of cruel, unwavering laws that denied desperately needed relief to so many? And how many more of those deemed destitute or infirm enough to merit relief would not receive it in time?

Quin ran a hand over his face, the unimaginable suffering that surrounded him daily oppressing him anew, like so many times before.

Looking across at his own family, he had to swallow heavily. Alannah's face was buried in Eveline's dark hair as she held on tightly to the sturdy little back. Quin walked around the table, his legs feeling like lead, heavy with hopelessness. He wrapped his arms around his wife and child, wishing he could draw them into himself to keep them safe.

The three of them stood locked together for a moment until Evie started fussing, irritated at being squashed between her parents. When Alannah lifted her head, her jaws were clamped tight, her eyes shiny with tears.

Quin tightened his arms once more, even as Evie continued to squirm.

At last, he could let them go.

He ran a hand across Alannah's cheek, wiping away the fallen tears, and placed a kiss onto the soft crown of his daughter's head. "Time to take care of the living."

# 28.

AS DREADFUL AS it was learning of others' suffering, they had no choice but to continue with their own lives, doing the best they could, reminding themselves over and over again that they couldn't help everyone.

The people of Glaslearg fared well enough. Hoping it would stay that way Quin had set aside a section of land for the new tenants and was having lease agreements written up. While many of them seemed grateful there were others who could barely conceal their ongoing distrust of their new English landlord. And while Quin did his best to shake it off, Robert Murphy continued to be a thorn in his side. Although the man barely spoke to him, Murphy couldn't hide his intense dislike of Quin and, in the same way, Quin couldn't contain his growing irritation every time they crossed paths. He vacillated constantly between ignoring Murphy's existence and wanting to throw him bodily off his land, his promise to Alannah be damned.

In the end, though, he did neither. He could hardly avoid the man entirely and nor could he leave the rest of the Murphys out to starve—besides, other than being a wholly unlikeable character Mr Murphy hadn't actually done anything worthy of being evicted since the altercation after the Bealtaine festival.

Contemplating having to deal with Murphy when he collected the tenants' rent in two weeks' time Quin shoved aside the bedcovers and rubbed a hand vigorously over his face. With the precarious situation the tenants had found themselves in since the first failed potato harvest, rent collection could turn into a delicate negotiation, with Quin having to carefully toe the line between collecting what was due and making sure the payment didn't leave the tenants with nothing—being, of course, one of the few landlords who entertained such thoughts at all.

Quin shook his head to clear it before sliding to the edge of the bed.

Alannah's side was empty, and he got up to go in search of her. He found her in the nursery with Eveline, who was sitting on a rug playing with wooden blocks. When she saw him, she gave him a gummy smile, showing off two small white teeth in her bottom jaw. She reached her arms toward him, and he swung her up into the air, making her giggle.

He did it a few more times before putting her back down on the rug. Walking up to Alannah in the nursing chair, he placed a kiss on the top of her head. "I didn't hear you get up."

"That's hardly surprising, you sleep like the dead. Nothing short of cannon fire is likely to wake you up."

Quin chuckled at Alannah's observation, although it was probably true. As a former soldier he'd learnt how to get efficient shuteye when he could. Instantly alert when faced with any threat to his person or those around him, he could just as easily sleep through any number of minor disturbances.

Such as the crying of his own daughter, he thought with a touch of chagrin.

He must have looked sheepish for Alannah laughed. "Come," she said as she got up, "let's go down to breakfast."

Dressed and seated at the dining table a short time later they chatted of this and that as they enjoyed their morning meal.

While Quin was buttering his second slice of toast Denis, the elderly butler, tottered in with a small tray bearing several letters, which he presented to Quin.

"Thank you, Denis."

Quin placed the letters next to his plate, intending to read them later in the study. Seeing one from his father on top of the pile, though, he took the butter knife, wiped it carefully on a napkin and used it to slit open the envelope.

Alannah quirked one brow but didn't say anything as she passed Evie a small piece of toast. Quin unfolded the baron's missive and started reading, his eyes widening as he did so.

Alannah leaned forward in her chair. "What is it?"

"My father," Quin started slowly, shaking his head, "is coming to Ireland."

"Your father...is coming to *Ireland*?"

"Apparently." Quin handed Alannah the baron's letter, feeling as stunned as Alannah looked.

"But why?" she asked, scanning the page.

"He doesn't say." Suddenly, Quin chuckled, making Alannah give him a quizzical look. "The fact that neither of us thinks my father could simply want to visit us is quite amusing."

"You're right. But it's hardly surprising based on his previous letters."

Quin nodded as he recalled the numerous times his father had urged them to come to England amid the crisis surrounding them, frequently resorting to varying degrees of ridicule when they'd refused.

"I am looking forward to seeing him, though," Alannah said.

"Me too. Quite to my own surprise." Quin grinned, making Alannah laugh.

But while it was true that Quin was looking forward to seeing his father he did wonder what it would be like to have the baron living under his roof for an extended period of time. The two of them hadn't always gotten along, the baron having disagreed with numerous choices Quin had made, not least of all Quin's decision to resign his commission with the British Army. And while it was also true that he'd repeatedly urged Quin and Alannah to come to London since the start of the famine, the baron had never been particularly enamoured by Ireland in the first place. In fact, the acquisition of Glaslearg by his father years earlier had been a monetary incentive rather than one based on any love for the Irish people or the Irish countryside—which was why he'd been less than thrilled when his only son had decided to take an Irish wife and settle down in Ireland on the land that had come to him upon his marriage.

In short, there were several contentious subjects between father and son that might make for an interesting visit.

A huff from across the table made him look at Alannah, who was staring down at the baron's letter.

"I see Trevelyan's been knighted," she said, unable to hide the derision in her voice.

"Oh?"

Quin took back the sheet of paper and scanned the bottom of the page, having read no further than the announcement of the baron's intended visit in mid-June. There, penned in his father's neat hand was a brief postscript notation that the head of London's treasury had recently been awarded that highest honour of being dubbed *Sir* Charles Edward Trevelyan, apparently as a just reward for his achievements in dealing with the Irish famine.

"I rather doubt the Irish people he supposedly assisted would agree that his efforts were valiant." Alannah shook her head in annoyance.

"No, I suppose not."

Insensitive and uncompromising, the man's *laissez-faire* approach to the Irish crisis could hardly be deemed laudable, in Quin's opinion. In fact, Trevelyan's insistence that the Irish populace become self-sufficient instead of relying on charity clearly showed the depth of his ignorance about Irish affairs.

"My father told me he once overheard the former Irish chief secretary say that Trevelyan knows as much about Ireland as his baby, if he has one." Quin gave a brief snort at this apt description of the man's infantile knowledge of the land he presumed to reign over.

"Well, he's certainly proven as much.—And the fact that he was knighted for his so-called heroics surely demonstrates the ignorance of the Queen herself." Alannah threw Quin a sideways glance.

He shrugged. "I suppose. Although she's contributed relief funds herself, inspiring others to do the same, Queen Victoria and her cabinet likely hold any number of the same prejudiced beliefs of so many others."

"Hmph."

Still visibly irritated Alannah stabbed the butter knife into the dish before vigorously scraping a blob of butter over her toast, scattering crumbs onto the tabletop. She took a bite and sighed, laying the toast aside and wiping her hands.

When her eyes fell onto the remaining letters she pulled the small tray toward her.

"Oh, here's a letter from Mr Dunne."

Visibly brightening she set the remaining two or three letters aside and handed Quin an envelope. Lifting her chin toward the much-used butter knife she wiped it clean and gave it to Quin. He made quick work of their former overseer's missive, pulling out a neatly folded piece of paper and beginning to read.

*Boston, Mass., April 10th, 1848.*

Mr Quinton Williams,
The estate of Glaslearg,
County Tyrone, Ulster P.

*Sir,—I have found her! I can scarcely believe I am writing these words but I have found Miss Thompson, living right here in Boston. With what little money she had available she had no choice but to stay near the port where she landed and make the best of her circumstances. Having concluded as much when I located her name on the ship's register I had steeled myself to knock on every door in the city in search of her whereabouts. Alas, my efforts were to be delayed by an ague that struck me down shortly after my own arrival, seeing me confined to my inn room for a week. For several days I fevered in my bed, afraid I would soon expire like so many of my fellow travellers. When at last the fever had broken I was too weak to do anything but sip broth and gather my strength until I was finally well enough to embark upon my quest. I began asking about Miss Thompson at every inn and boarding house in Boston, until it became apparent my funds would not last forever and that I would soon require alternative means of supporting myself. Fortunately, I was able to secure a position as a clerk at the port to earn a little coin for food and board. And so my days were spent recording cargo and passenger lists while my nights were spent traipsing through the city in search of a woman I had once known and loved.*

*When my efforts had yielded no results after several months I began to fear I had been wrong in my assumption that Miss Thompson was still in Boston. But just when I was about to despair I found her at last! I had already begun to broaden my search and finally located her in a house of ill repute. I imagine you will be as surprised to read of this as I was at experiencing it first-hand, but Miss Thompson assured me she was employed at the house as a maid. Although I dare to say I would have been pleased to find her under any circumstances I have to admit I was relieved to hear she had not debased herself to survive. I was further relieved at her joy at seeing me and her assurance that her feelings for me had not changed. Such was our mutual joy that I soon whisked her away and made her my wife!! My elation at these circumstances can scarcely be described. And yet, we are now faced with the difficulty of having to decide on our future. While there are opportunities to be had in Boston, neither of us feels the land to be our home and we miss the familiar comforts of Ireland. But do we want to risk crossing the Atlantic to return to Ireland amidst the ongoing suffering, and bring any children we may have into it? These are questions we ask ourselves daily, making the best of what we have and continuing with our lives here while waiting for answers.*

*One answer I have finally been granted is to the question of who inflicted the multiple bruises on Mr Thompson after my encounter with him when he told me he was sending his daughter away. In fact, it was Miss Thompson herself who caused her father's injuries, as she lashed out at him and struggled bodily when he informed her of his plans, finally having to be dragged away from him by a servant who had heard his cries. While the thought pleased me to no end, my wife was distraught at hearing that I had been punished for her actions. I assured her I would do it again in a heartbeat, just as I would repeat the perilous journey to find her. My only regret is having to leave your employ, sir, when you had made me feel like family in the two years I spent at Glaslearg. But perhaps I shall return one day and we shall reminisce about old times.*

*I do hope all at the estate are well and that you are weathering the ongoing storm. The news that reaches us from across the ocean makes me despair at the fate of my countrymen, and yet I am comforted knowing that those on your land are being given at least a fighting chance.*

*Please send my warmest regards to all at the estate, most especially your wife. I trust she is well and I look forward to hearing news of the safe delivery of your child.*

*As ever, your most obedient servant,*
   *Lachlan Dunne.*

Quin finished the letter and passed it across to Alannah, who read it quickly. When she put it down she looked up at Quin with an amused expression on her face.

"So Miss Thompson was the one who inflicted all those bruises on her father. Mr Dunne did insist all along that he'd hit Mr Thompson only the once."

She laughed at the thought, making Quin grin as he recalled how he'd tried to assure her that using one's fists was, in fact, a perfectly gentlemanly form of communication under certain circumstances, including—most naturally—the circumstance of Mr Dunne applying his fist to his former employer after being faced with the knowledge that his beloved Miss Thompson was being sent away.

"She must have been in quite a fury to manage it!" Quin said with some admiration, wondering if he'd ever get the chance to meet the woman himself. "And it's no wonder Mr Thompson didn't bring forward any other charges. He would never have wanted to admit he'd been assaulted by a woman, much less his own daughter!"

"Because he would then also have to admit he was sending her to America against her wishes.—Although I don't suppose the courts would care overly much about that."

"I don't suppose they would." A young woman's father could do with her just about whatever he wanted to, without so much as asking for her opinion.

Alannah clamped her lips together for a moment before shaking off her irritation. "Do you think she really was employed only as a maid at a house of ill repute?"

"I suppose it's possible. Presumably brothels do actually employ maids…" In fact, Quin knew they did, having seen at least two of them during his visit to the Dublin brothel with Archie. He wasn't about to remind his wife of that night, though. Besides, who knew what services a maid in a brothel was expected to provide.

"Hm." Alannah didn't look convinced. "Would she have admitted to Mr Dunne if she had been employed as something else?"

"I don't know. Having never met Miss Thompson I can't account for her character, much less say whether she would admit to the man she loved—whom she hadn't seen in several years and who crossed a perilous ocean to find her—that she was, in fact, prostituting herself to survive." He glanced briefly at Evie, but she was babbling happily to herself in her chair, oblivious to the adults' conversation.

"When you put it like that it does seem rather unlikely she'd tell him the truth if so."

"And perhaps he'd prefer it that way."

"Perhaps." Alannah paused before turning her blue eyes on him. "Would you want to know?"

"Me?" Quite unintentionally Quin's hands clenched into fists. "You mean, if you had..." He clamped his mouth shut and frowned, unable to finish the sentence. The thought of Alannah with a different man each night made a sudden rage bloom in his chest. "I would hope you would never stoop that low!"

"Stoop that low?" Alannah gave him a disbelieving look. "Do you really think women would choose such a profession if they had any other choice?"

"There is always a choice!"

"Is there?" She leaned across the table and narrowed her eyes at him. "When women barely have any rights as it is and there are hardly any options for those who have nothing? Sometimes doing what you must is the only choice!"

They were both quiet for a moment.

"I wouldn't want to know," Quin finally grumbled, making Alannah's lips twitch.

She reached a hand across the table and clasped his fingers. "Then perhaps it's better if Mr Dunne never asks Miss Thompson for the truth."

"Hmph."

"Do you think they will return to Ireland?"

"I can't say. It's as Mr Dunne said, Ireland is their home. But would they have a better life if they stayed in Boston? Nobody can know for sure."

"And would we have a better life if we moved to England as your father suggests? Would Evie?"

Quin held Alannah's eyes before looking at his daughter. "There are days I am convinced of it. And then there are days when I know we are doing the right thing by staying here." Despite having made the choice to stay in Ireland long ago he was sometimes plagued with doubt, especially now that a child was involved. But he waved a hand toward the window. "We have everything we need here. Evie is taken care of, she wants for nothing, just like she would in London.—And there are people here who need us." His mouth quirked into a smile. "Sometimes doing what you must is the only choice."

Alannah's eyes softened and she took his hand once more. "And we are doing what we must."

"I *WOULD* WANT to know."

"I beg your pardon?" I turned toward Quin, who was lying on his back on our bed, looking up at the ceiling, his outline dim in the darkness.

"You asked me earlier if I'd want to know if you'd been forced to work in a brothel to survive." He rolled onto his side to face me and sought my hand beneath the covers. "I said I didn't want to know…but I would."

I was quiet for a moment. "Why?"

He pulled me closer. "So I could share your burden. And so there'd be no lies between us."

"Even if it meant hurting you with the truth?"

"The truth can be dealt with. Lies will only lead to more lies."

I nodded, thinking suddenly of Kieran and the many lies he'd told himself to continue treating me like dirt. It was only when he realised the truth that he'd been set free of his hatred.

Quin ran a hand along my back. "And I would hope you'd know you could trust me with the truth."

"I've trusted you from the start," I said, placing my mouth against his.

His lips lingered on mine, softly at first, until he deepened the kiss and pressed himself against me. "And I trust you, with all of myself. Until the day I die."

# 29.

WITH THE BARON'S visit imminent a frenzy of activity descended upon Glaslearg. It was only a few weeks until his expected arrival in mid-June and the servants spent their days scrubbing and polishing every surface of the house and tidying the outbuildings until our surroundings gleamed. Even the normally stoic Mrs O'Sullivan was visibly flustered at the thought of welcoming a peer of the realm into her domain, fussing about the proposed menus and the preparation of the guestrooms.

"He's only a man, Mrs O'Sullivan," I said to the cook one afternoon, trying to soothe her concerns as she faced the difficult task of deciding which bedding was suitable for such an important personage.

She gave me an affronted look. "He's a *baron*," she insisted, clearly horrified at my audacity to compare the two. "He'll be expecting the best."

"He'll be expecting to spend time with his son and his family."

"Hmph."

With a brief shake of the head Mrs O'Sullivan left the study and returned to her work.

I smiled after her, although I couldn't help feeling a little apprehensive myself. While the baron and I had parted on good terms when Quin and I had left London there was no question that he wasn't the easiest man to please—as I had noticed quite clearly upon our very first meeting, when he'd barely acknowledged my existence. I had no idea what he might be expecting from this visit. We had every intention of making him feel at home, of course, but we were simply not in a position to provide him with some of the fineries he was no doubt accustomed to in London. Most of our supplies came from the estate, with the rest obtained at the local market. Fanciful imports to impress distinguished guests were out of the question.

"Perhaps we should have a dinner party," I said to myself, thinking we could invite some of the surrounding landowners to provide the baron with a little entertainment during his visit.

"Perhaps we should."

I turned toward Quin, who had poked his head through the study door.

I nodded slowly as he came into the room. "I suspect, though, that Mrs O'Sullivan would be appalled at having to arrange a dinner party with only our meagre supplies to hand." By meagre I meant limited in variety, but to our cook it would probably be much the same as having limited quantities of food which to prepare.

"Or perhaps she'll enjoy the challenge of providing a marvellous feast even so. I have no doubt she could."

"I have no doubt you're right.—I'll discuss it with her later." I glanced at the small clock on the desk and started getting up. "Evie should be waking from her nap soon." Coming around the desk I lifted onto my toes and placed a kiss on Quin's cheek. "I wonder what she'll think of her grandfather. And what he will think of her."

"I suspect she'll have him wrapped around her little finger in no time." His eyes softened and he returned the kiss. "Just like her father."

I WAS STILL thinking about the likely relationship between the Baron Williams of Wadlow and his granddaughter as I walked toward the drawing room with Evie on my hip that evening. Supper would soon be ready and I thought I'd let her play for a few minutes until then. Crossing the threshold I spotted Emmett standing by the window. I could see him only in profile but the sullen expression on his face was evident, even so.

"I don't trust 'em," he grumbled as I got closer.

Suddenly noticing that he had an audience he gave a start.

"Who don't you trust, Emmett?" I asked as I put Evie down on the rug.

"Oh...nobody." He waved a hand, which caught Evie's attention. She gave him a toothy smile and he flopped onto the rug in front of her, making faces until she laughed.

He looked up at me and grinned, which made me laugh too. I hadn't forgotten his mutterings, though. "Who don't you trust?" I asked once more while I fetched Evie's wooden blocks.

"Some of 'em new folks."

"New folks? You mean the new tenants?" Mr Casey's kin had been with us for a few months by now but I supposed they might still be considered new.

Emmett gave a curt nod.

"Why don't you trust some of the new tenants?" I placed the wooden blocks in front of Evie who immediately started banging two of them together.

This seemed to amuse Emmett and he took a moment to respond to my question. When he noticed me watching him patiently he sat up a little straighter. "They're always lurkin' about, huddlin' close together." He huffed, as if such behaviour were intolerable.

"Do you not think they may simply be turning to each other in support during this trying time?"

"Oh no, that's not it.—At least not all o' the time," he added, conceding the possibility there might be something to my suggestion. "And when that Murphy's about there's trouble afoot."

"Mr Murphy is…lurking about with some of the new tenants?"

"Oh, aye." The grimace on Emmett's face made it clear he hadn't forgotten the scolding he and his friends had received from Mr Murphy at the Bealtaine festival the previous year. "And they're always lookin' grim, wi' faces like sour apples."

"I can't disagree with you there," I said in some amusement. It certainly was an apt description of Robert Murphy's general demeanour. Still, Glaslearg's newest residents hadn't had much to smile about in recent times. With all they'd been through it was only natural they might turn to their new neighbour to air some of their grievances, no doubt finding in Mr Murphy a most willing ear.

"Just this afternoon Ben and me saw a few o' them by a field on the way t' Conor's house. They scowled at us as we passed. And we didn't even do nothin'!" Emmett looked outraged at such rudeness, as if he were the soul of courtesy himself. "They was up t' somethin', I'm sure."

I thought it just as likely that Mr Murphy had simply been telling the new tenants unfavourable stories about the three friends—all of which would probably be true—but decided not to say anything.

"Mayhap I'll tell Mr Williams," Emmett said, jumping up suddenly, a determined look in his eye. "He'll know what t' do about 'em."

I looked after him as he sped out the door, doubting he would find a willing accomplice in Quin. While I was of course aware of Quin's intense dislike of Robert Murphy—and, indeed, shared it—I was also aware he wouldn't interfere with the tenants as long as the agreement of tenancy was upheld. Any personal grievances they may have, were irrelevant. And he could hardly stop them from complaining among themselves—even if it was about him.

With a small sigh I sat down next to Evie who was now trying to cram the wooden blocks into her mouth.

"Are you hungry?" I asked, running a hand over her head. She bobbed up and down as if in agreement, making me laugh. "Come along, then. We'll see if we can find you something to eat.—And we'd best make sure to work on your table manners. You'll want to be on your best behaviour when your grandfather arrives."

# 30.

"WILFRED."

Alannah smiled at Quin's father as he climbed out of the carriage that had pulled up at Glaslearg's courtyard moments earlier under a grey sky.

"Alannah." The baron looked only mildly startled when Alannah embraced him, quickly returning the gesture with a smile of his own. "And Quinton."

Quin came to stand in front of his father and extended his hand. The baron shook it firmly before pulling Quin closer and thumping him heartily on the back, looking undeniably pleased at seeing him. The greeting was so in contrast to the sort of distant welcome Quin had come to expect since his adolescence that he felt himself flush with pleasure.

"It's good to see you, father," he said with feeling, grateful to see how their relationship had changed for the better since Quin and Alannah's visit to London.

"It's good to see you both. But where are you hiding my granddaughter?" The baron looked around the courtyard expectantly as a few raindrops started to fall.

"I'm afraid she's having her afternoon nap," Alannah said. "But she'll be up soon, I'm sure.—Perhaps you'd like to settle in in the meantime?"

The baron nodded and followed Quin into the house while his footman started unloading his luggage with Finnian's assistance, the two of them rushing to get the job done in the rain that was now falling steadily from the sky.

Having heard the commotion of the baron's arrival the other servants were waiting in the entrance hall, and much bowing and curtsying ensued at welcoming such a distinguished guest at the estate.

Spotting Emmett among the group the baron turned toward him. "I'd heard you'd come to Ireland, young man. You're not going to confuse me with the Queen again, are you?"

Emmett's face went bright red at the question and Quin suppressed a chuckle. When he'd met the baron in London Emmett had been so flustered that he'd called him "your majesty", having no idea how a baron should be addressed.

"No, sir," he squeaked now, shaking his head and looking down.

When the baron laughed Emmett's eyes went wide and he glanced uncertainly at Quin. Seeing his employer's amused expression the boy visibly relaxed, his lips quirking up ever so slightly.

"If you'll follow me, sir, I'll show you to your rooms."

Denis bowed to the baron and upon his acquiescence led him up the stairs, the valet's slow movements and proud bearing making for a stately procession that may well have been worthy of royalty.

While his father settled in Quin spoke to Mrs O'Sullivan about the footman and valet being accommodated in the staff quarters in the attic. The cook had, of course, already seen to everything, including the evening meal, having been prepared for the baron's arrival for several days now.

Quin smiled to himself as he left the kitchen, thinking the woman could probably deal with anything. Why none of them referred to Mrs O'Sullivan as the housekeeper, he had no idea, the woman still being lauded only as their cook. His smile grew wider when he came into the entrance hall and saw Alannah at the bottom of the staircase with Eveline on her hip. Seeing him Evie gave a toothy grin and reached for him.

Quin scooped her up and she wrapped her arms around his neck, her thick hair tickling his ear. He nuzzled her cheek and she giggled, the sound lightening his heart.

"And who is this delightful creature?"

Quin turned toward the baron, who was coming down the stairs, wearing an enchanted expression on his face.

"Father, I'd like you to meet your granddaughter, Eveline."

The baron came to stand in front of them and reached out a hand but stopped before touching Evie, who had pulled closer to Quin and was eying the newcomer sceptically. Her small black brows drew together and she popped her thumb into her mouth, making the baron laugh.

"You're right to be suspicious of strangers, Eveline," he said approvingly. "It never hurts to be cautious.—But I do hope I'll meet with your approval during my stay here and that we might become friends."

Quin met Alannah's eyes over Evie's head. Her lips quirked in amusement at this formal speech but she came forward and indicated the drawing room with one hand. "Why don't we make ourselves comfortable? I'm sure Evie will warm up to you shortly."

Quin sat down with Evie on his lap, her eyes following his father as he settled into one of the wingchairs.

"The place looks much improved to when I purchased it," the baron said, looking around in appreciation.

"I dare say you're right." In fact, Glaslearg's manor was hardly recognisable from the neglected and starkly empty house Quin had first moved into. "I'll show you the grounds tomorrow. Then you'll really be astounded." He grinned, recalling the wildly unkempt fields that had yielded hardly any produce and the overgrown lawn at the back of the house.

"I hope you had a good journey from London, Wilfred."

The baron turned toward Alannah and nodded. "As good as can be expected."

While the adults made casual conversation Evie started wriggling on Quin's lap, wanting to get down. He placed her on the rug and went to fetch some of her wooden blocks from the chest against the wall. She started babbling happily to herself as she alternately tried stacking one block on top of another and placing it into her mouth.

"That reminds me, I brought Eveline a gift," the baron said and excused himself before leaving the room.

When he returned a few minutes later he crouched in front of his granddaughter and held out his hand. Quin could see he was holding a beautifully carved miniature rocking horse painted in bright colours. Evie reached out a pudgy hand, her earlier apprehension forgotten. The baron placed the wooden horse onto the rug and set it rocking, making her coo in delight. His face softened and he sat down on his haunches in front of her, showing her how to do it again.

The two of them were quickly absorbed in their game. Watching them Quin's heart filled with joy. Never would he have expected to see such a scene. While his father had spent time with him while he was growing up it was usually in pursuit of some useful task, such as learning to ride a horse or use a sword, never in something so frivolous as playing with wooden toys.

"No, no." The baron shook his head and gently pulled the horse away from Evie's mouth. "You'll ruin the paintwork."

She looked at him with big eyes for a moment and placed her thumb into her mouth instead.

"That's better."

Quin chuckled and his father smiled and ran a hand over Evie's head.

"I think we'll get along just fine."

And, in fact, they did. By the time they got up to go to the dining room Eveline was happy in her grandfather's arms. He carried her proudly and settled her in her chair before taking his own seat. They passed a pleasant dinner talking about the estate and reminiscing about Quin and Alannah's visit to London.

"Of course, your attempted murder was quite a superfluous item on the itinerary," the baron said at one point, frowning in remembrance.

Quin grimaced and rubbed a hand over the site of the bullet wound on the right side of his chest. But although he would have preferred never having been shot by Herbert Andrews' agent he had to admit it was that very act that had precipitated the improved relations between father and son. Facing the prospect of Quin's death the two men had been honest with each other for the first time in years, which had finally allowed them to move past some of their differences.

"That's true," Alannah said, her jaws tight as she threw Quin a quick glance. "But at least it led to Herbert Andrews' arrest."

The baron nodded.

"I had meant to thank you again," she said, leaning forward, "for seeing Talamh na Niall returned to me after Andrews' death. I can't tell you how much it means to me."

To Quin's amusement his father's cheeks flushed.

"It was the least I could do." The baron cleared his throat. "But you evidently haven't lost your penchant for adventure, Quinton," he said, neatly changing the topic and turning back toward his son, "even now that you're a father.—How do you and your friends manage to get mixed up with murder and mayhem at every turn?" He shook his head in disapproval. "And death by crossbow? It sounds like a tale from the middle ages."

"It does indeed," Quin agreed and launched into a recounting of how he, Archie, Ham and Ollie had apprehended Mr Cartwright's murderous cousin on the dark streets of Dublin some months before.

Although Quin had written to his father with a brief summary of events the baron wanted to hear all the details, asking numerous questions and shaking his head at regular intervals.

"George Cartwright was hanged a few weeks later," Quin concluded solemnly after several minutes, making the table go silent at this reminder that two lives had been lost.

At last Alannah rose from her chair. "I need to take Eveline up to bed," she said, looking at her daughter, who was rubbing her eyes with her fists.

The two of them left and Quin and his father returned to the drawing room. Quin made for the whiskey decanter and poured two ample portions. The baron sighed in contentment and they started sipping in quiet companionship.

"Now tell me honestly, Quinton," his father said suddenly, "what is the state of affairs in Ireland?" He placed his glass on a small table and looked intently at Quin.

Quin paused before answering. The baron had evidently been waiting to be alone with his son to have this conversation. "The situation is still dire."

"Whereas England has convinced herself the land is on the cusp of greatness, requiring only a little local industry to tap into its multitudinous resources now that the famine is over."

Quin narrowed his eyes despite the note of cynicism marring his father's voice. "And is that what *you* believe?"

"Hardly." The baron waved a hand. "I've had your personal correspondence telling me otherwise, for one thing." He paused before continuing, "For another, I've had the misfortune of recently having to travel halfway across the island.—And I had my eyes open the entire time."

Quin gave a snort. "Plenty of others have had their eyes open these past three years and have seen not a thing."

"I don't doubt that. And I doubt any description you might have sent could have quite prepared me for the wretchedness I encountered on my way to the estate." The baron shook his head. "The dozens of beggars on the roadsides and flocking to the houses of the gentry looking emaciated? What a ghastly sight!"

Quin compressed his lips, thinking of the desperate people who'd shown up at their own estate over the last few months, and the group of beggars they'd encountered at Cornac House. "Perhaps if we sent the members of parliament to the Irish countryside the English would stop ignoring the state of the land or blaming it on the Irish themselves."

"Perhaps," the baron echoed, not bothering to hide his scepticism. "But even if they stopped blaming the poor for their own misery, the British government and much of the populace is of the opinion that the landowners ought to be the ones providing employment and relief outside of the workhouses, believing, of course, that the historic neglect of their estates by Irish landlords is responsible for the widespread devastation caused by the famine in the first place.—Not to mention their resentment of the landlords for the vast influx of Ireland's evicted tenants onto English shores, whose dreadful state means thousands more are crowding into *our* workhouses and hospitals and being provided for under *our* poor laws."

The expression on the baron's face made Quin wonder whether his father held some of these opinions himself.

"*Irish property must support Irish poverty*," the older man continued. "It's a much-favoured maxim of politicians and civil servants in England these days."

"Yes, it's also a very convenient method for the government to take no responsibility at all," Quin said drily, "even if Irish landlords aren't entirely without blame." For it was true that many Irish estates had been poorly managed in the past, contributing to the wretched state of the vast majority of Irish peasants even before the start of the famine. "And the quarter-acre clause has become the perfect excuse for landowners to clear their estates." Although greatly desired by the British, the act that required local Irish communities to alleviate local destitution had been bitterly contested by the landowners who would be left footing the bill. To get the act passed, the government had made numerous concessions, including allowing landowners to deny relief to tenants who rented more than a quarter acre of land—which many took as liberty to evict those who rented less, whom they would otherwise have to support.

"I'm sure there are many landlords who needed no such excuse," the baron said, "being more than happy to evict those smallholders for whom they would otherwise have to pay poor rates from their own dwindling coffers. Besides, I've heard the opinion expressed that Ireland's vast population needs to be thinned to allow agricultural development to take place—with the remaining population all under the appropriate social control, of course."

"Of course, yes, quite ignoring the fact that those *surplus individuals* are in fact living and breathing people."

The baron shrugged. "Putting that aside, one can't deny that the land is, in fact, grossly overpopulated, which no doubt contributed to this entire mess." Quin opened his mouth to respond to this statement but before he could say anything his father went on, "Perhaps emigration is the humane solution, after all, as it at least provides the hope of a better future."

"Certainly, particularly when many never reach their destination in the first place and when those who do, end up arriving in a strange and unknown land with nothing but the clothes on their backs. That is indeed an excellent solution to the problem…for the British!"

"There's no need for that tone, Quinton."

"Oh, I do apologise. I hadn't realised that callous disregard for human life was an acceptable trait."

The baron pursed his lips as he breathed in heavily through his nose. "I believe many Irish people are themselves making the choice to cross the Atlantic."

"It's not much of a choice if they've been evicted from their homes."

"And yet they do still *choose* to get on the ship."

"As opposed to staying here to starve?"

The baron shook his head and sighed. "This is a nonsensical argument. We each will do as we must. Some will live and some will die.—It is as it has always been."

"And what would you do? Would you get on a ship? Giving up any hope of ever seeing your home again, knowing full well that you might die on the voyage, and with no assurance that your life will be any better once you reach your destination?"

His father was quiet for a moment. "I don't know," he said finally, his voice soft. "And I thank the Lord that I don't need to make that choice."

He held Quin's eyes briefly before looking away. As silence settled around them Quin glanced outside the window. A light rain was falling in the darkness, making the drawing room feel like an inviting cocoon.

With the comforts of home all around him Quin asked himself the same question: what would he do? If nothing remained here for them, would he take Alannah and Eveline and get on a ship headed to an unknown land and an uncertain future?

The thought alone made his heart speed up and he swallowed heavily, feeling like the baron had—glad that he didn't need to make that choice.

"Why do you insist on staying here?"

His father's voice pulled Quin out of his reverie.

"This is my home," he said simply, feeling the truth of the statement keenly.

The baron gave him an annoyed look. "*England* is your home."

"Not anymore."

"You are an *Englishman*, Quinton," his father said intently. "You were born and raised in England, you have English forefathers, you served in her majesty's army.—*England* is your home," he insisted, giving Quin a penetrating glare.

"Not anymore," Quin repeated, shaking his head.

"Hmph." The muscles in the baron's cheeks bunched in evident displeasure at his son's views.

The sight made Quin's nostrils flare in irritation. Even after all these years, his father still didn't understand.

"Ireland is my home now," he said, a little more forcefully. "My wife has lived here all her life, my daughter was born in this very house, and we have made a life for ourselves here.—Should I simply turn a blind eye to the suffering around us? Should I act like so many of my countrymen, men who own land in Ireland they've never set foot upon and who leave their Irish agents to the dirty business of evicting their tenants in difficult times?" Quin shook his head. "I can't believe you would expect me to be so cold, father."

The baron's features darkened as he threw Quin another angry look. "You would have the resources to help them from afar."

Quin gave a dismissive snort, but his father suddenly sat forward in his chair.

"I worry about you, Quinton, about all of you."

The words were spoken softly as the baron held Quin's eyes. Seeing the depth of feeling in his father's gaze Quin's earlier irritation disappeared. He laid a hand on the baron's arm, startled to realise suddenly that his father was no longer a young man. Veins showed on the backs of his hands and a few knuckles were thickened with age.

"I know you do," Quin said, his throat feeling tight. "And I'm grateful for your concern. But this is our home…and we care about the people who live here. We cannot abandon them."

"Hmph."

The baron looked away and Quin suppressed a sigh, wishing his father would understand.

"It's late," he said. "Why don't we retire? You've had a long journey."

The baron nodded and got up. Standing in front of Quin he clasped his shoulder, gripping it firmly for a moment before turning away without another word.

# 31.

"YOU'VE DONE WELL, Quinton."

Quin looked sideways at his father as they sat on their horses on a rise overlooking the farmland the following day. He nodded in silent acknowledgement of the rare compliment before clearing his throat.

"We repaired the walls the first year and cleared much of the land," he said, waving a hand toward the neatly demarcated fields. "There wasn't much growing here when I arrived.—At least not much in the way of crops, Mr Brennan having been entirely preoccupied with his own interests."

"Hmph." The baron huffed at mention of Glaslearg's former overseer, who'd let the estate slide to the brink of ruin. "Should you not appoint another, more competent steward to run the estate for you?" he asked after a moment.

"Alannah and I have managed well enough since Mr Dunne's departure and enjoy being involved ourselves.—Besides, there's not much money to spare to hire anyone else."

"Hmph."

When his father said no more Quin turned Gambit toward the path that led through the fields, the baron following behind him. With each lost in their own thoughts they ambled slowly over the rolling farmland. In the distance, thin tendrils of smoke rose into the sky from the tenants' cottages.

"We plant the fields in rotation to preserve the soil," Quin said a short while later, breaking the silence, "leaving them fallow at intervals. We get a good yield of wheat and oats, and a bit of barley too."

The baron nodded as he looked over the golden stalks swaying in the breeze.

"Before the famine much of our produce was exported to England but now a good portion goes to our tenants. We sell most of what's left on the local market where it's desperately needed, although it isn't always of help even so, with the poor having no coin to spare to buy it."

"And you'll be running at a loss, no doubt." The baron scowled in disapproval once more. Likely he would have handled thing differently.

Quin took a deep breath, trying not to get irritated. "We get by."

They rode in silence for several minutes more. When they reached a patch of land that was overrun with scraggly growth the baron stopped and looked curiously across at Quin.

"These fields were set aside for conacre—small parcels of farmland rented seasonally to labourers to grow potatoes to feed their families," Quin explained. "The system has largely collapsed, the labourers dispersed to the towns or ports to await passage aboard ship, and many of them dead. Those who are left want to be paid in coin for their work, not arable land that may yield nothing, especially not when they're forced to pay the exorbitantly high rent before they've even planted their seeds, with no guarantee of a healthy harvest—and a high likelihood of its failure."

The baron slowly shook his head. "It seems impossible that the failure of a single crop could have such far-reaching consequences. *Why don't they simply eat something else?* I've heard many an Englishman ask."

"Because they have nothing else. And no money to buy it, either."

Quin looked across the land that had once fed dozens of people, feeling—as always—the oppression of Ireland's fate. Dark clouds were amassing over a distant hill, reflecting the darkening of his mood.

Perhaps they should be heading back to the house, he thought.

"I should like to see these stone cottages you've told me so much about." His father's voice cut into his gloomy thoughts. "I can't quite picture my son building walls and putting up roofs"—the baron's lips quirked briefly at the corners—"much less imagine the hovels your tenants lived in before."

Quin gave his father a surprised look. "I'd have thought you would have seen the mud huts when you visited Glaslearg before purchasing it."

The baron lifted one shoulder dismissively. "I visited the manor house and surveyed the land from a distance. I never meant to settle in Ireland and so it was a question of numbers, income and expenditures, that would assure I made a good investment. I was told how many tenants lived on the estate and how much rent they paid, and left it at that."

"I see." Quin clenched his jaws to prevent himself from accusing his father of not caring about the people who lived on his estate. From the start the baron had seen the value of his tenants from a pecuniary perspective, insisting the large number of tenants assured him of a steady income, regardless of their living conditions. But having never seen those conditions for himself he could easily plead ignorance of their horrid circumstances.

"The cottages are just over the next rise," Quin muttered, waving a hand toward the plumes of smoke. "And several mud huts are still standing, awaiting your inspection."

With a huff of annoyance he set off toward the tenants' land at the edge of the estate—at a convenient distance from the manor house to allow lofty landowners to ignore their existence if they so chose.

Several of the men were working their potato fields and Quin greeted them as he and his father rode past. They exchanged a few words here and there, the tenants looking at the baron with wide eyes before getting back to work.

They stopped at an abandoned mud hut, and the baron got off his horse to get a closer look. He walked around the outside of the small structure before peeking inside.

"Rather dismal, isn't it?" He scuffed one shoe along the earthen floor at the threshold and ran a hand over the crumbling wall. "And you say your new arrivals have chosen to live in these?"

Quin shrugged. "It's all they've ever known. And I suppose some of them are grateful to be made to feel at home even in these ghastly constructions."

"Some of them?" The baron gave Quin a quizzical look at his word choice.

"A few others are…less than thrilled at their circumstances."

"I suppose they would be."

"True. But I get the feeling some of them are harbouring a great deal of resentment against me in particular."

"Misdirected anger at their former landlord, perhaps?" The baron glanced at the nearby cluster of stone cottages and their occupants.

"Perhaps."

Quin frowned but looked up suddenly when a drop of water landed on his nose. The sky was dark and brooding and the gentle breeze had picked up pace, lashing the potato vines back and forth. A few more plump raindrops fell around them, stippling the packed earth in front of the hut. He looked toward the horses, which were standing close together with their heads down, but realised quickly it would do no good to leap upon their sturdy backs. They were caught amid the oncoming storm and had no hope of returning to the manor house unscathed.

"Mr Williams."

Quin squinted in the direction of the voice and made out a figure in one of the stone doorways. He recognised Grandfather O'Reilly, who was beckoning him with one gnarled hand while a few others made for the entrance.

"Come, father." With one last look at the hobbled horses Quin led the baron to the O'Reilly's cottage. "Thank you, Mr O'Reilly," he said, carefully wiping his feet on a thick mat before stepping inside.

The old man nodded and pointed toward a table and chairs that stood in the centre of the main room. Quin ran a hand across his damp face and went to stand in front of the fire before sitting down. Although it wasn't exactly cold, he was glad of the fire's warmth and relieved not to be getting soaked outside. The rain was coming down in earnest now, thrumming on the thatch roof and lashing against the windows, making even the most hardened Irishman seek shelter.

Grandfather O'Reilly closed the door behind the last straggler, dimming the noise of the downpour.

Quin smiled at Mr and Mrs O'Reilly and their adolescent son, Thomas, who looked a little startled at having his landlord show up in his family's house—and even more so at having a baron standing a few steps in front of him. The boy self-consciously patted his wet hair and swallowed heavily, before executing an awkward bow, while his parents fussed around their guests.

"Please, don't trouble yourselves," Quin insisted in response to an offer of a hot cup of broth.

But Mrs O'Reilly shook her head. "No trouble, no trouble." Vigorously bobbing her head she led Quin and his father to the table before turning her attention to a large cauldron, which she hung over the hearth.

Quin looked around the inside of the cottage with interest. He'd helped several of his tenants with the building, hauling rocks, assembling door and window frames, and laying thatch. It gave him a feeling of contentment seeing the finished house from the inside, and the home he'd enabled the people on his land to create. Although it was rather dark outside with the storm, the windows let in natural light, and the stone walls and foundation made for a solid construction that radiated warmth.

"Sir."

He looked up at Thomas, who'd come to stand in front of him with a steaming cup in hand.

"Thank you, Thomas."

The boy's cheeks bloomed at the use of his given name. Having served his guests and family he took his own cup and sat at the table, fidgeting self-consciously. An awkward silence descended as they all sipped their broth.

"Delicious," Quin said after a few minutes, placing his empty cup on the table.

Mrs O'Reilly beamed and gestured to the cauldron, offering more, but he declined.

"Do you think the storm will last long?" his father asked.

He'd been talking to nobody in particular but all the O'Reillys sat up a little straighter, looking rather terrified at the thought of making conversation with a baron.

Quin suppressed a grin. "I don't think so. Ireland's weather tends to change from one minute to the next. I'm sure the storm will blow over shortly."

"Unless the Sidhe are involved," Thomas said earnestly.

"Oh?" The baron cocked his head toward the youth, making the latter's face go bright red at the scrutiny.

He rallied bravely, though, swallowing heavily before going on. "Yes, sir. The Sidhe often cause mischief and can even cause great storms t' swell in the sky."

"And the...Shee"—the baron glanced at Quin as he stumbled over the strange word—"are...supernatural creatures?"

Thomas nodded vigorously. "Oh, yes, sir. They have great power...t' do harm or good, as they choose."

"I see. And you say they can affect the weather?"

"Aye, sir. Even not so long ago the Sidhe caused a great storm, like nobody in Ireland had ever seen before."

Quin's lips quirked as he watched Thomas. Clearly, the young man had inherited his grandfather's way with words—a natural storyteller, Grandfather O'Reilly often held the people of Glaslearg captive with tales of Ireland's folklore and the secrets of its past, delivered in his native Gaelic, which Alannah was usually kind enough to translate for Quin. No translation was necessary in this case, though—and a good thing, too, since Quin's understanding of the Irish language remained limited at best. But like so many other younger folks, Thomas was almost entirely fluent in English. Realising it was the language of the future many of Ireland's people were making the effort to learn.

"It was on a January night not so long ago," Thomas began his tale. The baron leaned forward intently, while the O'Reillys exchanged an amused look. In the corner of the room Grandfather O'Reilly swayed gently on a wooden rocking chair with his eyes closed. "It had snowed earlier that day but in the afternoon, a strange stillness came over the land. The clouds seemed frozen in the sky and there was no wind, makin' some feel a sense o' forebodin' for what was t' come." Thomas paused, looking around at his audience. "As the evenin' came on it started t' rain and the wind that was absent before picked up. It quickly turned int' a howlin' gale so ye couldn't hear the man standin' right next t' ye. In no time at all it thundered over the land, tearin' roofs off houses and topplin' chimneys or causin' fires t' break out in the thatch. The great wind pulled trees out o' the ground and scattered livestock while the waves from the sea grew many times higher than a man, crashin' t' the land t' destroy anythin' in their path and smashin' boats upon the rocks. Sand and salt were carried far inland and for days after fish were found miles away from the sea."

Thomas was silent for a moment, his head bowed. The others sat quietly, the sombre tone of the tale spreading through the cabin like the harsh wind of that dark winter night.

"There was no comfort for those who'd lost everythin', maybe even their lives," Thomas continued softly. "It's said the destruction was caused by the Sidhe. It's said they left Ireland in great numbers that night, perhaps driven out o' their home by their English enemies"—he glanced briefly at Quin and his father before going on—"and carried away on their magical whirlwinds, the *sidhe chora*, which caused the *Óiche na Gaoithe Móire*, the night o' the big wind."

The hair on Quin's arms stood up and he could almost believe fairies must have been to blame for the supernatural destruction Thomas had described. A gruff sound in the corner made him look toward Grandfather O'Reilly. His eyes were open, staring into the distance as he muttered something to himself in Gaelic.

"Grandfather says it was the leavin' o' the Sidhe that night that's t' blame for all that's befallen Ireland since then. Famine, sickness, death. There are too many o' them gone, the land we once knew is no more."

A sense of doom settled on Quin at the old man's words. He breathed in deeply and looked across at his father. The baron was sitting quite still with an unreadable expression on his face. His eyes met Quin's and held them for a long time. Finally, his brow twitched, making Quin look toward one of the windows. Outside, a few white clouds were visible, floating in a blue sky.

The storm had passed.

With the spell broken Mrs O'Reilly got up and started clearing away the cups and the rest of the broth. In quiet unison Quin and his father rose from their chairs and thanked Mr O'Reilly for his hospitality before bidding them all farewell.

Outside, a pale rainbow spread across the sky while drops of water glistened in streaks of sunlight, the only signs of the recent storm. The horses' coats were wet but they seemed comfortable enough, nickering softly at the men's approach.

Quin stroked Gambit's neck. "You'll get a good rubbing down back at the stable," he promised and swung onto the horse's back.

They rode quietly for a few minutes through the softly dripping crops, the horses' hooves squelching on the muddy path. They'd just passed the last of the tenant's fields when Quin spotted a group of men coming toward them on foot. Recognising Mr Murphy leading a few of Glaslearg's newcomers he groaned, his nostrils flaring in instant irritation. His father gave him a strange look but didn't say anything.

"Mr Murphy." Quin nodded toward the man when they came alongside.

"Mr Williams." Murphy's lips twitched as he regarded Quin atop his perch.

Quin straightened to his full height and looked down his nose, holding the man's eyes for a moment before greeting his companions, whose own salutations weren't markedly friendlier.

"The Baron Williams of Wadlow, my father," Quin said, extending a hand.

He noticed that the men's clothes were wet. Clearly they'd been caught in the storm. Caught doing what, he wondered? His distrust was getting the better of him, especially since Emmett's insistence that some of Glaslearg's tenants were up to no good. No doubt they'd simply been working the estate's fields, Quin told himself, returning his attention to the grim-looking group. As he'd tried to explain to Emmett, he couldn't have anyone arrested for being bad-tempered or ill-mannered—much as he might like to do so at times.

"Gentlemen." The baron bowed his head toward the men, receiving a smattering of acknowledgment in return.

"We wish you a good day." With another curt nod Quin flicked the reins and started back along the path, his father following behind him.

"At a guess I'd say those were the men you feel bear you some resentment."

"Whatever gave you that idea?" Quin gave a snort before leading Gambit toward the river. Taking the more scenic route back to the house might improve his mood.

"What are you going to do about them?"

Quin breathed out heavily at the baron's question. "I could throw them off my land, of course, but what will become of them then? Murphy has a family that depends on him and the others..." He shook his head.

"Have already lost their homes once?"

"And far more than that." Quin sighed and rubbed a hand over his face. "I've warned Murphy I'll evict him if he puts another foot wrong. As for the others...I can only hope they'll come around. Just like the other tenants did when I first arrived."

"Hmph." His father didn't seem entirely convinced of the merits of Quin's approach but didn't question him further.

They'd reached the waterway by now. The sun had come out in full, making the stream sparkle as it bubbled past. On the banks birds were flitting to and fro, eager to return to their business after the storm.

"I will admit that it's beautiful here," the baron said, looking around appreciatively.

"It is."

Silence descended as they continued along the path, Quin settling comfortably into Gambit's gently rolling gait, his irritation steadily subsiding. He inhaled deeply, enjoying the fresh scent of the rain-damp earth and starting to feel quite content once more.

How peculiar it was, Man's changeable mood.

Caught up in Thomas' supernatural tale of destruction Quin had felt the hopelessness that so often accosted him when faced with the fate of the many people around him. And yet now, only a short while later and despite the unwelcome appearance of Mr Murphy and an uncertain future, he was at peace and happy with his lot in life.

But perhaps it was his ability to see the beauty in everyday things that allowed him to feel such joy even during times of hardship. It was a skill he'd had to hone over the years, one that didn't come naturally to many, he knew.

He glanced at his father, wondering what he'd been like as a younger man. Hard to please and quick to anger, he'd not been easy to live with while Quin was growing up.

"Did you always know you wanted to join the army?"

The baron looked across at Quin, a contemplative expression on his face. "I suppose so." He pursed his lips in thought before continuing, "It was something of a family tradition, after all, your great grandfather having earned the baronial title on the battlefield. I don't think I felt I had much choice about it. It was expected of me"—he held Quin's eyes briefly—"although I dare say my father and grandfather made it all sound terribly exciting."

Quin gave a short laugh. "It sounds as though you were talking about me."

The baron's mouth quirked into a brief smile. "The excitement wore off, though, didn't it?"

Quin's eyes flashed to his father's, sure he'd detected a note of bitterness in his tone, the baron's disappointment in his son's decision to resign his commission being no secret. The older man's face was expressionless, though, and so Quin didn't say anything.

"Do the Irish really believe in all that nonsense about the supernatural?" the baron asked, neatly changing the topic.

Quin nodded slowly. "Many of them do, yes." Having lived in Ireland for several years now he had to admit he felt a little annoyed at his father's obvious disdain for local beliefs. "Any number of small tasks are performed every day with the sole aim of keeping the fairies happy.—But of course you should never call them that for fear of incurring their wrath." He looked around a little guiltily at having broken that very rule. "And there are plenty of folks who firmly believe that misfortune arises from not showing the Sidhe their due respect."

"I see." Although the baron's expression remained largely impassive he couldn't quite hide the scepticism in his voice.

"It isn't really any different from people believing in the wrath of God for punishment of their sins, is it?"

"I suppose not. Although I'd like to see you convince the archbishop that God Almighty and Irish fairies are much the same."

Quin grinned. "I think I'll leave that task to someone else." A thought suddenly occurred to him. "Let me show you something."

They had reached the wooden bridge that led to the path past the outbuildings and back to the house but instead of crossing over the river Quin followed it further upstream. With a curious tilt of the head his father followed.

"There's a hill fort on the estate," Quin said. "The Irish believe they're the underground dwelling places of the Sidhe."

The baron made a noncommittal noise at the back of his throat.

"There it is." Quin pointed a little ahead, where a distinctly rounded, elevated patch of grass was discernible between the surrounding stalks of wheat. Getting closer, a ring of bushes became visible at its base.

The baron rode slowly around the perimeter, perusing the green mound. "It is peculiar, I'll give you that."

"It certainly is. The Irish believe that disturbing the forts will anger the Sidhe, resulting in a host of terrible consequences for those foolish enough to do so."

"And an unsuspecting traveller such as myself?"

"I doubt you'd be let off easily on account of your ignorance." Although he didn't believe in fairies any more than his father did Quin found he had no desire to step foot on that hill even so.

"Hmph."

The baron got off his horse and walked up to the circle of bushes. He crouched down, running a hand along the soil. "There are some stones here."

Quin dismounted and stooped down next to him. "I see." Looking carefully he spotted several irregularly shaped stones scattered between the bushes. "I've never been this close to it before. The people on the estate tend to give it a wide berth."

"A peculiar place, indeed." The baron stood up and rubbed dirt off his hands. "Although I don't know about the fairies."

They returned to the horses and rode back toward the bridge, discussing the possible origins of fairy mounds as the sun started setting behind them.

"Just refrain from telling the locals that you don't believe in the hill folk," Quin advised his father as they rode up to the stables a short while later.

John and Bryan emerged from the building at the sound of the horses' hoofbeats, murmuring a brief greeting before carefully looking down.

"Because I'm so very popular with them now?"

Quin suppressed a laugh at the low-voiced comment. "Just give it a little time."

# 32.

OVER THE NEXT few days they settled into something of a routine. To Quin's surprise his father often accompanied him on his rounds across the estate, showing a greater amount of interest in Glaslearg's workings than Quin would have thought. Even the wet weather didn't put him off, the baron simply donning his hat when he stepped outside, ignoring the rainfall that frequently accompanied them.

Quin liked to flatter himself into thinking the baron wanted to spend time with him and that he was proud of everything his son had achieved over the past few years. But then, his father's old self would reappear and Quin would reassess that assumption as the older man questioned his choices—vociferously and unapologetically so. Fortunately, Quin usually managed to bite his tongue at some of the baron's cutting remarks, knowing the older man was unlikely to change.

All in all they got on well enough and Quin was glad of his father's visit.

Eveline, too, was clearly enjoying the baron's company. Having overcome her initial shyness of her grandfather she now couldn't get enough of him. The two of them were often found together, playing on the floor or enjoying a rare sunny afternoon on the porch.

After she went to bed in the evenings, the adults would retire to the drawing room, where they'd spend a few hours in pleasant conversation or playing a round of cards.

That evening Quin was the last one to arrive, having seen to some correspondence in the study after supper. Coming through the drawing room door he smiled at Alannah and the baron, who were deep in conversation, but he suddenly stopped short.

"You were *where*?" He looked at his father, sure he must have misunderstood what he'd said.

"At a mummy unwrapping party," the baron enunciated patiently.

"A mummy…"

"I've heard of those," Alannah said, making Quin gape at her instead.

"You mean…those actually exist?"

"Oh yes," Alannah said as Quin finally dropped onto the seat he'd been hovering over. "My tutor, Mr Henderson, told me all about them. The mummy is slowly unwrapped before an audience, revealing myriad treasures buried within the bindings, not to mention the mummy itself.—But you were there, Wilfred, tell us about it!" She looked eagerly at the older man, who turned toward Quin.

"Such parties were very popular in the 30s, Quinton, with large assemblies gathering to witness the mummy's unwrapping. But I suppose you wouldn't have paid much attention to such things then."

Quin nodded absently, thinking back to his youth, which was filled with dreams of military glory rather than the Egyptomania that had taken root in Europe since Napoleon's invasion of Egypt. While the idea of mummified bodies and long-lost treasure was certainly appealing to an adolescent boy, Quin hadn't been nearly as obsessed with the topic as some and had always assumed much of what he'd heard must be exaggerated.

"I'd never had the opportunity to attend such an event before," the baron went on, "and not much interest either, I must admit. The practice did become a little more subdued over the years but when I received a personal invite to Lord Featherston's private parlour to witness what he called…the unrolling of a mummy from Thebes at half-past two…well, my curiosity was piqued after all."

"And?" Alannah leaned forward in her seat.

"Hm. It's certainly something I'll never forget. Featherston had Thomas Pettigrew himself perform the unwrapping.—He's the surgeon and antiquarian who introduced such parties to the world," the baron explained, evidently for Quin's benefit. "The man quite lived up to his moniker, Mummy Pettigrew, and I dare say he took great pleasure in ruthlessly tearing off each layer of encrusted bandages to reveal the shrunken body beneath. Poor Mr Ackland was quite overcome by what he deemed the undignified treatment of human remains and stormed off, looking rather green." He shrugged. "I'm not sure what else he would have expected at the unwrapping of a mummy but either way, his departure didn't distract Pettigrew in the least."

"What did the mummy look like?" Quin asked, not sure if he should be fascinated or horrified.

"Quite unlike any body I'd ever seen. Desiccated and gaunt…but clearly human, nonetheless. It did give me a strange feeling to gaze upon a face that hadn't seen the light of day in thousands of years." The baron was quiet for a moment before continuing. "Pettigrew was thrilled at the mummy's *excellent condition*, as he called it, having informed us beforehand that such a thing could never be guaranteed."

"And were there any hidden treasures?" Alannah asked.

"Several amulets—meant to protect the deceased and ensure their safe passage to the afterlife, or so Pettigrew told us. But some of the linens the mummy was wrapped in were adorned with a great number of mysterious symbols that had the man quite beside himself with excitement."

"Hieroglyphs?" Quin found he was rather engrossed in the topic himself by now.

His father nodded. "He said they were spells from the Book of the Dead, which were supposed to aid the deceased on their journey."

"He was able to decipher the symbols?"

"Oh yes, Pettigrew quite prided himself on his abilities."

"Did he tell you how the symbols were decoded in the first place?" Alannah asked, eyes bright with excitement.

"He did but I shall leave it to you to enlighten the ignorant among us." The baron's lips twitched into an amused smile as he glanced briefly at Quin, while Alannah's cheeks turned pink.

"A stone was discovered several years ago," she said to Quin, "inscribed with what turned out to be the same text in hieroglyphs, Greek and a third language, which was used to interpret the meaning of the Egyptian symbols—or at least a number of them."

"Precisely," the baron said. "Pettigrew told us the pharaohs who were descended from the Greek-speaking conquerors of Egypt still used the Greek language at the time, while hieroglyphs had become reserved for priests and temples by then. That turned out to be rather a stroke of luck as it meant the decree issued by the pharaoh was inscribed in both hieroglyphs and Greek, allowing for the hieroglyph's translation."

"What about the third language?" Quin asked, intrigued.

"Pettigrew said there was some speculation that the third language may be the written form of the time's common tongue."

"How fascinating."

"It certainly was an enlightening afternoon," the baron agreed.

"Fascinating and enlightening no doubt," Alannah said, "but I'm not sure I'd want to be unwrapped in front of an audience if I were the mummy in question."

Quin grinned. "No, I suppose not."

"Neither would I," the baron said. "Then again, being unwrapped in front of an audience is a far better fate than some other mummies have had to endure. Just think, being ground up into questionable medicine or ending up on an artist's palette as a pigment of mummy brown. So much for resting in peace!"

"And so much for the mummy's curse," Quin said, getting up and heading to the whiskey decanter, pouring them each a glass. "If there were such a thing none of these mummies would have been taken out of Egypt in the first place."

"Those stories are probably the result of the tomb robbers' guilty consciences," Alannah said.

The baron slowly moved his head from side to side. "Perhaps. Pettigrew did inform us, though, that what amounts to curses have been discovered carved into some tomb walls. Potential desecrators of the grave are warned they'll face a painful earthly death or the wrath of the gods if they persist."

"Well, that doesn't seem to have scared off Mr Pettigrew," Quin said drily as he sat back down.

The baron huffed a laugh. "Not at all.—Although I don't believe he's actually raided any tombs himself. Quite convenient, isn't it, letting someone else deal with the curse before stepping in to claim the glory."

"Hm." Alannah nodded absently, taking a sip of her whiskey before turning to Quin. "I've just thought of Mrs Lewes' story at the house party. You recall, about her husband finding a body in a bog?—Hearing about the mummy makes me think the body in the bog must have looked quite similar."

"So...the body was mummified in the bog?" Quin asked.

"I suppose so. Or at least, preserved somehow in a similar way."

Seeing his father looking curiously between the two of them Quin quickly told him about the fascinating—and morbid—conversation they'd had at Cornac House.

"Well," the baron said when he was done, "I dare say there is entertainment to be had in Ireland after all. If you're entertained by ancient, dead bodies, that is.—But tell me more about this house party where such topics were discussed."

Quin and Alannah obliged, regaling the baron with a recounting of some of the events at the Cartwright's country home.

"That's where we first met George Cartwright," Quin said a few minutes later, frowning into his half-empty glass.

Alannah's expression matched his own. "I never would have taken him for a murderer."

The man hadn't struck Quin as violent, either, but who knew what people might resort to when they were desperate. "I think most of us are capable of murder under the right circumstances."

"The right circumstances?" Alannah repeated in some surprise.

"Or the wrong ones, perhaps." Quin sighed. "Filled with fury and desperation George snapped. He's not the first man ever to have done so."

A sudden vision of his hands wrapped around Martin Doyle's throat flashed vividly across Quin's mind, the sensation of squeezing the life out of the man prickling at his fingertips.

"That was entirely different."

Alannah's soft voice made him look up. Her eyes held his for a moment, open and trusting, before dropping down to his hands. With some surprise Quin noticed their clawed appearance, as if they were enveloping Doyle's scrawny neck at that very moment.

He gave a curt nod and uncurled his fingers. Although he'd never regretted the action that had resulted in Doyle's death he did regret the need for it.

"I dare say he won't be the last one either," his father said, throwing Quin and Alannah a curious glance. "I can only hope to remain in full control of my own senses under any and all circumstances.—To avoid becoming one of those who lose themselves in a murderous rage."

His lips twitched into a smile, although a haunted look flashed briefly across his face. The baron had fought with the British Army and had no doubt killed men during his service. Ending someone's life never left a man unscathed, even when acting upon a commander's orders to obliterate the enemy or when ridding the world of a vile creature such as Martin Doyle.

"But right now I believe I shall retire." The baron suppressed a yawn as he set aside his empty whiskey glass. "I hope to be safe from such testing circumstances in my bed," he said, winking at Alannah as he got to his feet.

"Good night, Wilfred," she called after him as he left the room.

"Good night, father."

Quin stretched out his arms, thinking he would retire soon too.

"Do you think your father would be a different man today if he hadn't served in the army?"

Quin looked at Alannah, not surprised her thoughts had followed his own. "I suspect so. One can hardly come through the horrors of war and remain unchanged."

Alannah held his eyes for a moment. "And you? How did it change you?"

"I..." Quin paused as he gathered his thoughts. "I became...more cynical, having seen what violence men are capable of, what violence I'm capable of myself. And less carefree, I suppose."

"It's what happens to most of us in the end, isn't it? Losing the carefreeness of youth." Alannah sighed, a distant look on her face. "Even my own father, who never served in the army and who'd always been an optimist, often despaired in the last few years of his life.—At the state of Ireland and what was happening to its people, the lack of compassion shown by so many and the desperate need of so many more, even then."

Quin sat forward in his chair and reached for Alannah's hands. "Each tragedy lived or heard of leaves a mark on the soul. A lifetime spent accumulating such scars means there's little room for joy in the end."

"But there has to be."

Quin ran a thumb across the smooth, patterned surface of Alannah's wedding band, remembering the joy he'd felt when he'd placed the ring onto her finger a few years earlier, his hopes for the future symbolised as much by the act as by the design of the Claddagh ring itself—two hands joined in friendship, clasping a heart in love; a loyal crown to guide them and an endless knot to bind them.

"There is," he said, squeezing her fingers, a reminder of the hardships they'd already endured—and overcome. "Because we choose it. We choose it every day and hope to God it helps us remember how fortunate we are."

# 33.

"IT'S AN ODD mixture of guests," Quin said the following morning as he perused the list of names I'd written down.

"It's *our* dinner party," I said a little defensively, "we can invite whomever we want."

Quin chuckled. "Of course we can."

Having decided to hold a dinner party while the baron was visiting I'd been faced with sending out the invitations, only to realise our pool of acquaintances had shrunk in recent years. Several landowners in our vicinity had relocated to their town mansions or escaped Ireland altogether with the advent of the famine, leaving the running of their estates to their agents. With fewer people of so-called importance to invite I had decided to simply invite our friends instead.

"Did you really want to spend the evening with Sir Spencer?" I scowled at the thought of the pompous man who owned a sizeable plot of land nearby. Although he'd previously rented out a large portion of his estate to tenant farmers, he'd evicted every last one of them and turned the land to pasture—without batting an eye.

"I can't say I would," Quin said, shaking his head. "Although I'm sure he'd be delighted at the opportunity to boast how his fortune is growing."

I gave an unladylike snort. "I'm sure he would. He did tell me livestock farming was the business to be in. And I suppose he's right, if his own wealth is any indication.—I've heard his Dublin townhouse is the size of a small palace."

"Still, it might have been entertaining to see his reaction to sharing a meal with tenant farmers such as the Lynches."

"Not as entertaining for them, I'm sure."

Since Joan's visit to the manor house following Evie's birth we'd met with Niall's tenants several times more, and Joan and I had become fast friends. This would have meant nothing to Sir Spencer, though, who believed himself to be vastly superior to anyone who didn't own any land, even those tenant farmers who rented large acreages and were wealthy in their own right.

"You realise the Lynches might find the experience uncomfortable even so?" Quin said softly.

"I do," I admitted, having had this discussion with Joan herself. "But they've agreed to come and I'll do my best to make it a pleasant evening for all of our guests."

Quin smiled and squeezed my hand. "I'm sure you will."

BY THE TIME the day of the dinner party arrived I was having doubts.

Joan had been on the verge of cancelling on me the afternoon before, pointing out that she and her husband had never interacted with lofty personages such as barons before and had no idea how to behave. Looking rather terrified she'd told me they'd both come from families of smallholders and that it had taken a considerable amount of grit and good fortune for the two of them to be able to rent a farm as sizeable as Niall. I'd assured her my own family had hardly been anything akin to royalty even though we'd owned the land we lived on, all the while thinking Herbert Andrews' scheming undertakings had in some ways been a stroke of luck for the Lynches, who would otherwise never have ended up being our neighbours.

I'd said no such thing, of course, only promising once more that everything would be alright and that nobody would stand on ceremony.

But what if I was wrong? What if the baron himself acted deplorably toward some of our guests? Although I'd never seen him be cruel toward a servant he did tend to rule them with an iron fist, barely acknowledging them for the most part as they went about their business. What if he acted the same way toward other people he considered beneath his station?

Was this evening going to be a disaster?

I muttered to myself as I prepared to get dressed, wondering if I'd made a mistake and contemplating whether there would ever come a time when people would be judged on their character rather than their standing in society.

I highly doubted it, human nature being what it was.

I did my best to brush aside the thought, and with Mary's assistance was soon wrapped in blue silk—the finest I owned—with my hair piled stylishly on top of my head.

I smiled at the maid as she pinned the last strand of my dark locks into place. Her eyes barely met mine in the mirror, though, before she looked away and started tidying the dressing table.

"Are you alright, Mary?" I asked, standing up.

She nodded but still avoided looking at me, her hands flying across the dresser.

"If there's something bothering you, you can talk to me. You know that don't you?"

Mary paused for a moment as if contemplating what I'd said. While I was sure she knew I meant it she was confiding in me less and less of late. Although she was careful never to criticise Mr Murphy in front of me it was obvious that the strained relationship between her husband and Quin weighed heavily on her, and that she didn't want to do or say anything to make it worse.

"Thank you, Mrs Williams." She seemed about to say something else but instead compressed her lips into a tight line. She darted me a quick glance, the brief glimpse of her eyes revealing the turmoil within her—a turmoil she clearly didn't want to bother me with.

"It will be alright," I said for lack of anything better to say. What else *could* I say? She couldn't change the man she'd married, nor could she undo his behaviour of the last several months or the damage he was doing to his family and others around him even now. I ran my eyes over her unobtrusively to assure myself of her physical wellbeing—no visible bruising, at least.

I clasped her hand and patted her fingers in what I hoped was a gesture of comfort. I would make an effort to speak to her in the next few days, I decided. If nothing else, having someone to talk to might ease her burden.

A soft sigh escaped her lips as her fingers tightened briefly on mine and she gave herself a visible shake. Soon, she started scrutinising me from head to toe, tucking in a stray curl here and adjusting an unruly hem there, until she was finally satisfied with my appearance.

"You are ready to receive your guests," she declared at last.

"Thank you, Mary."

The corners of her mouth lifted in what I thought was a genuine smile as she curtsied and left the room.

I looked after her for a moment before turning back to the dressing table and inspecting myself in the mirror. I had to admit the overall effect was flattering, especially in contrast to the plain clothes I tended to wear on an everyday basis. Quin seemed to feel the same, if the look on his face as he came through the door a minute later was any indication.

His eyes travelled slowly over me before meeting mine with an undisguised look of longing in their depths.

I lifted one brow. "Would you prefer to spend the evening up here?" Finding him just as appealing in his fine dinner jacket, I almost wished we could do just that.

"The idea has considerable merit," he said, coming closer and placing his hands on my waist. He pulled me against his chest and kissed me thoroughly, leaving me a little breathless. "Alas"—his face drooped—"I suspect our peculiar assortment of dinner guests would be at something of a loss without your guidance."

I laughed. "I'll be there in a minute."

While Quin made his way downstairs I headed to the nursery to check on Eveline. I could hear her giggling from the hallway. Geraldine was a wonderful caretaker and Evie adored her. Seeing me, though, she squealed in delight and crawled toward me at speed. I picked her up and settled her carefully against my hip, leaning back a little to avoid her grabbing handfuls of my carefully arranged hair.

"You look beautiful, Mrs Williams," Geraldine said, her eyes shining.

"Thank you, Geraldine." I placed a kiss on top of Evie's head. "Will you bring her down a little later?" Evie would make a brief appearance at the dinner party before Geraldine put her to bed, something I usually enjoyed doing myself.

"I will. I hope you have a lovely evening."

I thanked her and opened the door to the hallway, where Rupert was just passing by. Looking a little startled at my sudden appearance he glanced into the nursery and at Geraldine, who was standing next to me. His cheeks blazed as he bobbed his head, while Geraldine observed him under lowered lashes. Neither acknowledged the other further, though, and Rupert quickly dashed away.

Shaking my head in amusement I followed Rupert downstairs, where I found the valet standing next to Benjamin in the entrance hall. The latter was wearing something resembling a footman's livery that was clearly one or two sizes too big.

"Where's Finnian?" I addressed the two of them.

The young man was supposed to have helped Rupert with the serving, Benjamin and Emmett having been given strict instructions by Mrs O'Sullivan to stay out of the way. Already daunted by the prospect of arranging a dinner party using nothing but peasants' fare, as she called it, the cook had wanted to take no chances of anything spoiling the evening—least of all the presence of two often mischievous young boys.

"Abed with a headache," Benjamin said. "I'm t' assist this evenin' instead." He puffed out his chest and lifted his chin.

"Mrs O'Sullivan sent Finnian to get ready after he'd been helping around the house all day," Rupert said, "but he never came back downstairs. When I went to check on him I found him in his bed with the shutters closed and a damp towel over his face."

"Oh dear." I looked toward the attic, where Finnian had his room. "I hope he'll be alright."

"Oh, he'll be fine, Mrs Williams," Rupert assured me, sounding rather dismissive of Finnian's troubles.

Seeing the expression on my face the valet cleared his throat as his cheeks turned pink.

"He'll be fine," he repeated, this time a little more heartfelt. "I'll look in on him when I have a chance."

"Thank you, Rupert."

"The guests will arrive any minute." Quin's voice came from the drawing room door. He smiled at me before turning toward Benjamin. "I hear you've been called into service to replace Finnian."

Quin gave the boy a rather dubious look. While Benjamin was eager to please, his excitement at even the most mundane of tasks could quickly turn him into something of a hazard. I could only guess what the unparalleled privilege of acting as a footman at a dinner party would do to his constitution. I glanced down briefly at my gown, wondering whether I should cover myself with sack cloth, the spilling of food onto my person being a distinct possibility.

"Yes, sir." Benjamin beamed up at his master. "I won't disappoint you, sir."

Quin's mouth twitched with amusement. "Of course not."

Benjamin executed a brief bow before rushing off in the direction of the kitchen.

"Don't run, Benjamin," Quin called after him, making the boy come up short before taking deliberately slow steps that made him look like a young stork walking across a swamp.

I met Quin's eyes and we both laughed, just as there was a knock on the door.

Denis strode forward with dignity on his aged legs to admit our first visitors and soon the entrance hall was filled with the soft chatter of our guests. Several—like the Dochertys, Mr O'Malley and Mr Byrne—were already acquainted and quickly started exchanging pleasantries, while others—like the Lynches—stayed in the background, looking a little wary of the rest of the party. When the baron descended the staircase rather regally a few minutes later I held my breath. There was a brief lull in conversation while introductions were made, the Lynches in particular looking flustered at making his acquaintance. The baron greeted everyone cordially, though, and I felt hopeful that Quin's father would be able to behave himself for the duration of the evening.

The thought made me smile as I linked my arm with Joan's and led her toward the dining room. "You'll be sitting next to me," I said, showing her to her chair.

She gave me a grateful look as we all settled into our seats and Quin thanked everyone for coming.

When Rupert and Benjamin started serving the soup a moment later I watched them closely, expecting the latter to slop a portion onto somebody's lap. Benjamin held his nerve, though, only spilling a few drops onto the tabletop, which nevertheless made him look immediately at Quin, face aghast. Quin waved away his concern and Benjamin quickly retreated, throwing a nervous glance at the baron, who didn't look terribly impressed, truth be told.

I lowered my face to hide my amused expression while pretending to peruse my bowl. Looking back up a moment later I realised that it had become rather quiet around the table as we started in on the first course, with only the clinking of spoons against crockery to be heard. I experienced a moment of panic, convinced that nobody would speak another word the entire evening. What if they'd already said all there was to say to each other in the entrance hall? I was frantically thinking of a topic of conversation I might introduce when the elderly Mr Docherty beat me to it.

"Have ye been long in Ireland, Baron Wadlow?" he asked his table companion between spoonfuls.

"About a week, Mr Docherty," the baron said, laying aside his napkin as a few more conversations sprung up among our guests.

Perhaps the dinner party wouldn't be a disaster after all, I thought with some relief.

Mr Docherty nodded. "And how are ye finding our fine land?"

"It certainly is beautiful," the baron started slowly, "but...not without its difficulties."

"Aye, aye. That's true enough." The older man's face drooped.

"And have you lived here long yourself, Mr Docherty?"

"Och aye. I was born here."

"You were?" The baron couldn't hide his surprise.

Mr Docherty chuckled. "Ye wouldna think so hearing me talk but I was born and raised in Ireland, and me parents besides. But bein' o' Scots descent they learnt t' talk like a Scot and as for me...well I suppose it feels like home t' do the same." A nostalgic expression appeared on the old man's face as the soup plates were cleared away and the talk turned to other topics.

I glanced at Joan next to me, glad to see her engaged in conversation with Mr and Mrs O'Malley. The older O'Malley brother had married a few years earlier and had recently taken over the family estate not far from Glaslearg, while his younger brother had moved to County Cork with his new bride.

I had only met Mrs O'Malley once before. Fairly young, she looked younger still with the freckles that covered her cheeks and stubby nose. She'd been reserved and had hardly spoken to me then, but seemed a lot more relaxed tonight.

"My husband's family likes to claim kinship with Grace O'Malley," she was saying to Joan, leaning conspiratorially toward her.

"Grace O'Malley? The Pirate Queen?" Joan's eyes widened in amazement.

"One and the same," Mrs O'Malley said, undeniably pleased. "His family did move to Ulster from County Mayo many years before so perhaps it's true— even if it is likely to be a distant connection." She gave her husband an indulgent look. A rather stoic sort he didn't respond, only flashing her what may have been meant as a smile.

"Grace O'Malley...did she not sail to London to petition Queen Elizabeth?"

I turned toward the baron, who was looking expectantly between Mrs O'Malley and Joan, the latter's eyes widening at being so addressed.

To my surprise it was Joan herself who responded. "She did. She led her clan from aboard ship for decades, defending their territory against other clans and English invaders"—she glanced at the baron and then at Quin, her cheeks going pink—"but she lost everything when an English general destroyed her fleet, plundered her land, killed one of her sons and kidnapped another. She requested an audience with the Queen to demand back her prisoners and her lands, and her right to sail the seas." Suddenly realising that everyone else at the table had gone quiet and was hanging on her every word Joan blushed furiously. "Um...most of her requests were granted," she concluded hurriedly, blinking down at her plate before throwing a quick glance at her husband, whose lips twitched briefly up at the corners.

"You seem to know a lot about this remarkable woman," Quin observed.

Joan nodded, squaring her shoulders and lifting her head as her courage returned. "As it happens I do. Even from a young age Grace O'Malley loved the sea, cutting off her long hair so her chieftain father would allow her to set sail with him." She sighed and looked into the distance before once again focusing on the here and now. "I grew up on the shores of a small town in Londonderry. I used to dream of following in *Granuaile's* footsteps."

Quin gave me a curious look.

"*Granuaile* means Bald Grace," I said, "a moniker bestowed on her for shaving her head to be allowed aboard ship as a girl."

"It is said she sailed even while heavy with child and that she rallied her men to defend her ship shortly after giving birth on board."

There was a gleam in Joan's eyes as she spoke, which was mirrored to a lesser extent by Mrs O'Malley, who laid a hand unobtrusively over her abdomen.

Perhaps the O'Malleys would soon be welcoming their first child, I thought. Would they call her Grace, I wondered, if it was a daughter?

"Pirate Queen," Mr Byrne muttered suddenly to himself, shaking his head and pulling me from my thoughts.

I had noticed before that the wealthy tenant farmer was not particularly fond of women stepping out of line, as it were, but realised looking around the table that he was not the only guest who seemed a little startled at the recent conversation. The Dochertys sat rigidly on their chairs, their mouths looking rather pinched. Rebellious female pirates, pregnancy, delivery aboard ship? Such were not topics to be discussed at a dinner party amongst polite company.

Fortunately, the next course arrived to distract those who were disgruntled, Benjamin doing his best to lighten the mood by tripping over his own feet and toppling forward with the gravy boat held out in front of him, eyes wide at the impending disaster. Faster than I would have thought him capable of moving Mr Docherty leapt from his seat and snatched the gravy boat out of Benjamin's hands, placing it on the table with a flourish. A smattering of applause ensued and he gave a small bow, a twinkle in his aged eyes, his good humour restored.

I was glad to see our guests were taking the incident with a dash of humour—or at least, most of them seemed to be doing so. The baron frowned as he observed Benjamin's flustered reaction, perhaps thinking he'd never encounter such ineptitude in his own home. Not able to do anything about it, though, I dismissed the thought from my mind, although I did hope Benjamin would be put in charge of less hazardous edibles—such as the breadbasket, perhaps—upon his next venture into the dining room. Quin was clearly thinking the same thing as he watched Benjamin make a quick retreat, shaking his head with the long-suffering air of a man despairing at the competence of his staff, although his lips were turned up at the corners even so. I gave him an amused look and he grinned, lifting one shoulder in resignation.

"Ah, there's my granddaughter."

I turned toward the baron, who'd gotten up and was taking Evie from Geraldine's arms.

"Ready for bed, are you, sweetheart?"

Evie laid her head against the baron's shoulder and stuck her thumb into her mouth, looking around the dining room with big eyes, not sure what to make of the company.

"What a beautiful child," Mrs Docherty said, looking fondly at Evie. A nostalgic expression flashed across her face as she turned toward her husband. "Our own youngest granddaughter had just such wispy black hair at that age, did she not?—And now she'll be eighteen next spring."

Mr Docherty patted his wife's hand. "It seems like only yesterday she was such a wee girl herself."

"Good night, darling," I said, taking Evie from the baron and kissing the top of her head. Quin came to stand next to me and Evie reached her arms toward him.

"Thank you for bringing her down," I said to Geraldine as Quin handed Evie back to her a few minutes later.

Geraldine bobbed a quick curtsy and headed toward the stairs. I looked after them for a moment, thinking I ought to follow them, wanting to put my daughter to bed myself as I usually did. I managed to stay seated, though, deciding I would leave Geraldine to it. She would call me if Eveline made a fuss.

Turning back to my guests I met the expectant gaze of Mrs Docherty, who was clearly waiting for me to respond to something she'd said. Apologising, I asked her to repeat herself, making her give me an indulgent look that warmed my heart.

Despite being distracted by thoughts of my daughter I found I was quite enjoying the company, my previous concerns about the dinner party proving unfounded. Our guests were talking animatedly among themselves, the food was simple yet delicious and everyone seemed content. Having a good portion of my focus permanently on my offspring even so was simply an unavoidable consequence of motherhood, I supposed. But Evie was tucked safely into her bed upstairs and dinner parties didn't come around every day—especially not in the times we lived in.

I returned the older woman's smile, determined to make the most of the rest of the evening.

THEY HAD REACHED the dessert course without any major disasters and Quin found he was quite enjoying himself. Although Mr Byrne tended to be a little too sure of his own importance the rest of their small assembly were pleasant enough folks. Without Sir Spencer's pomposity dampening the mood, the dinner party had proceeded smoothly, with conversation flowing freely among all concerned, whether landowner, tenant farmer or English baron.

The baron himself had been on his best behaviour, for which Quin was most grateful. Benjamin, too, had acquitted himself well of his new duties, bar a few near calamities that had provided everyone with a good laugh.

All in all, Quin was content. Popping a bite of sweet pudding into his mouth he savoured the delicious morsel, looking toward the window where the last slivers of sunlight held back the darkness on this long summer's day.

He turned back to his plate only to suddenly swivel toward the window once more, his brain registering belatedly what he'd seen.

His heart gave a lurch at the sight of the pale face looking in on them, barely visible in the rapidly growing gloom.

As calmly as he could Quin got up. "Please excuse me for a moment."

Without waiting for a response or acknowledging the curious looks aimed in his direction he hurried toward the drawing room. Pulling open one of the large double doors he rushed onto the portico and toward the corner of the house. He stopped when he heard a rustling sound.

"Who's there?"

Getting no reply he took another step forward. He peered around the side of the house where the dining room window was situated but couldn't make out anything in the growing gloom.

"What's the matter, Quinton?"

Quin whirled around, to see his father striding toward him, a look of concern on his face.

"I thought I saw someone at the window," Quin explained without preliminaries, making the baron's eyes widen.

He came to stand next to Quin, looking back and forth.

"There!" the baron hissed, pointing at one of the shrubs that grew along the side of the terrace, which appeared to be moving as someone—or something—tried to hide behind it.

Quin nodded and lifted his chin in one direction, while indicating the other with his hand. In silent understanding father and son approached their prey from either side. Almost instantly there came the sounds of a scuffle from his father's side and within moments the baron emerged, holding the perpetrator by the scruff of the neck—and the scruff of the neck it literally was, there being no collar or any other stitch of clothing to take hold of.

"Finnian?" Quin gaped at their captive, who was squirming in the baron's grasp. "What in God's name are you doing?"

The baron let go of Finnian's scrawny neck and the young man hunched over, his hands clasped protectively in front of him. "Um...sir..." He looked down his skinny chest, clearly wishing himself to be anywhere else.

"Explain yourself, Finnian," Quin demanded. "Last I heard you were tucked up in your bed with a headache."

"Ah…um…and so I was, sir, but well…"

"Yes?" The baron added his stern voice to Quin's, making Finnian swallow heavily.

"I got hungry, sir."

"So hungry you forgot to get dressed?"

"Um…no…"

Finnian was visibly shaking at the baron's scrutiny, making Quin hopeful he'd soon spit out the truth. "What happened, Finnian?" Quin asked, taking a step closer and staring down his nose at the footman.

"Well, sir, ye see…Mr Docherty's coachman and me…well, we had a bit of a misunderstandin', we did."

"And so he took your clothes and locked you out of the house?"

"More o' less."

"And what was this misunderstanding about?"

"Ah, well, ye see, his sister and me, we…um…" Finnian cleared his throat, looking down as his cheeks started to blaze.

"I seem to recall having a similar conversation with you once before," Quin said. That time the object of Finnian's affections had found her way into Rupert's arms as well, causing the two young men to lay into each other with their fists amid the outbuildings one fine afternoon. "And I assume, as then, that the girl in question was receptive to your advances?"

"Oh, yes, sir, very very much so." Finnian paused, a dreamy look appearing on his face before his eyes widened suddenly. "Ah…I mean…yes, she was, sir."

"I see. But her brother took exception to your actions?"

"He did, sir."

Quin nodded slowly to himself. "You never had a headache, did you?"

Finnian threw him a guilty look. "Um…well…no, sir. But when I realised he'd likely be here tonight, well…I thought I'd better make meself scarce."

"A wise choice," the baron said drily. "And yet, your resolve seems to have failed you."

"I got hungry, sir, as I said. Only, Mrs O'Sullivan made a fuss o' me, thinkin' I was ill, and when I tried t' sneak past the back room by the kitchen where the servants was all waitin' they saw me. I ran off straightaway but...well..." Finnian's eyes dropped down to his bare toes.

"You're lucky you got away without being beaten black and blue," Quin said, wondering whether the girl's brother would demand that the two of them marry.

"Oh, no, sir." Finnian vigorously shook his head. "He'd never do that. We're friends, we are."

"If you say so."

"Oh, aye, sir. They was only tryin' t' rile me, hopin' I'd have t' steal past the drawin' room with me bare backside showin' while all o' you fine folks were inside. Um...beggin' yer pardon, sir." Finnian bowed awkwardly to the baron, whose stony expression remained unchanged.

"Right," Quin said, trying to keep a straight face. "So you were looking into the dining room window to assure yourself we were still seated at the table so that you could make your escape around the side of the house—the way through the kitchen being barred by your...friends, of course?"

"That's the way of it, sir."

Quin looked at his father, whose lips twitched in the slightest hint of amusement. "A spot of humiliation as a form of revenge? Why not?"

"Why not, indeed?" Quin agreed.

Watching Finnian's gangly limbs twitch as he tried to hide his bare nether regions made him think Mr Docherty's coachman had achieved the desired effect. Although he'd managed to avoid the scrutiny of the entire dinner party Quin suspected it would take Finnian some time until he could once more meet his employer's eye.

"Well, Finnian, I'd advise you as I did the last time, that you take a little more care with your actions, else you may find yourself in a worse situation than prancing around the estate in the nude. Now"—Quin waved an arm at the drawing room—"I'll fetch you something to cover yourself so you can get back to your room."

Finnian sagged in relief as Quin darted inside and collected a throw from the backrest of one of the armchairs.

"Here." He tossed the fabric to the footman, who snatched it up and quickly wrapped it around his middle. "You're lucky it isn't raining." It had been a rare sunny day in what was turning into yet another wet summer.

Finnian gave a brief nod, although he didn't look convinced that a drizzle would have made his situation any worse. With one last awkward look at Quin and his father he started dashing across the portico, only to come up short when Quin called after him.

"Do you have a key to the servants' door?"

Finnian's face took on a look of horror as he shook his head. "No, sir," he squeaked, his eyes going ever wider as he no doubt realised his attempted escape would have been thwarted at the last hurdle. While the servants' door was usually left open during the day it was always locked at sunset.

"There's only one thing to do," Quin said cheerfully. He tilted his head in the other direction, back toward the kitchen and the waiting audience.

Finnian gave him a pleading look.

"I'm sorry, Finnian, but I'm afraid you'll have to face your enemies once more.—Pardon me, your friends."

Resigned to his fate the young man walked back the way he'd come, dragging his dusty feet across the terrace and around the side of the house. Once he'd rounded the corner Quin looked at his father and grinned.

The baron gave a brief snort as they started heading back inside. "Wherever did you find him?"

"He was something of an inheritance," Quin admitted, "from Alannah's household before we were married."

"I see." The baron shook his head. "He's a character, that's for sure."

"He is that. In fact, we seem to have a number of those at the estate.—But I suppose life would be boring otherwise."

"I suppose so."

The baron shrugged dismissively, making Quin wonder whether he'd ever had to deal with such antics from his own staff. Quin couldn't remember hearing anything of the sort and assumed his father had his employees under tight control.

"Are you going to punish him?"

Quin's eyes widened in surprise at the question.

"For pretending to be ill to get out of his duties?" the baron specified brusquely, as if it should have been obvious what he meant.

"Oh." Quin had almost forgotten that Finnian had lied about having a headache. "I doubt it." Remembering the sight of the young man as he dashed away with a blanket wrapped around his loins, Quin chuckled. "I think he's been punished enough."

"Hmph." The baron didn't seem convinced of the merits of his son's approach.

"Things are different here," Quin said. "With all that's happened over the last few years, our staff aren't only staff to us.—They're people we care about, friends even."

"That may be so, Quinton, but they *are* your employees and should behave as such. You shouldn't let them forget that."

With a sniff the baron entered the dining room, Quin following close behind. Their appearance was greeted by curious glances.

"Is everything alright?" Alannah asked, searching Quin's face.

He smiled at her and nodded around the table. "Everything is fine, just a small matter with one of our staff members to resolve.—Now, shall we ring for the brandy, gentlemen? And sherry for the ladies?"

ALANNAH LAUGHED, THE sound reverberating through Quin's chest. They'd retired for the night after their guests had gone home, but weren't yet ready for sleep.

"I wish I'd seen it!"

Quin had told Alannah about Finnian's adventures, to no small amount of amusement on her part.

"And lay eyes upon an unclothed man who isn't your husband?" he scoffed, feigning shock. "I think not!" He grinned at her and she slapped him lightly on the arm.

"I wish I'd seen the expression on his face."

"It was amusing, I can assure you of that."

"I'm only surprised Emmett didn't cause any further mayhem himself."

"I suspect Mrs O'Sullivan threatened him with death and dismemberment if he so much as showed his face around the house this evening." Quin's smile faded as he remembered what his father had said earlier. "Do you think I'm too lenient?"

Alannah lifted her head a little to look at him. "Too lenient?"

"With our staff. My father thinks Finnian ought to be punished for lying to me about being ill."

"By the sounds of it he was punished enough."

Quin chuckled. "That's precisely what I said." He tightened his arm around her and she ran a hand over his chest.

"The people who work for us don't do so only out of duty. They know they are treated fairly here, meaning they are also loyal. You can't achieve that by forgetting they are human and make mistakes just like we do."

Quin kissed Alannah's forehead before breaking into a smile once more. "Although not all mistakes are equal. Only some end in one's backside being paraded about for all to see."

"Which may be considered a grave sin by some."

"No doubt. Nakedness is the height of indecency, of course, particularly to those who don't even see their own spouse in the nude, undressing only in the safety of the dark."

"How unfortunate for them." Alannah gave him a suggestive look and shoved back the blanket. Still holding his eyes, she undid the drawstring at the top of her night dress and slowly pushed it down past her hips. The candle flickered, making Alannah's skin glow with a golden light.

"I have no objections to nudity myself," Quin said, quickly removing his own nightshirt to prove it. He lowered his mouth to her neck and ran a hand across one breast. "In fact, I much prefer it when in bed with my wife."

Alannah laughed softly and pulled him to her so his naked body covered hers. "Fortunately, so do I."

# 34.

THE FOLLOWING MORNING I woke up to a steady drizzle falling outside the window. The bed next to me was empty and I lay still for a few minutes, enjoying the sound of the rain. I found the wet weather quite pleasant while ensconced cosily indoors as I was now, but I did hope it would clear later in the day so I could take Eveline outside.

Thinking of Evie I got up and went to the nursery. She was lying awake in her cot, babbling happily to herself. Seeing me as I came closer she pulled herself up by the railing and started bouncing her knees up and down in excitement. I scooped her up, making her giggle.

Once she'd had her fill of milk I got us both dressed before going downstairs. In the entrance hall we passed Finnian as he came out of the dining room where breakfast had already been set up—if the smell of fresh toast and bacon was anything to go by.

"Good morning, Finnian."

"Good morning, Mrs Williams."

Finnian barely met my eyes before quickly looking away, a soft blush creeping up his neck. Seeing movement behind him in the doorway to the dining room I spotted Benjamin. The boy had a grin on his face as he watched Finnian hurry away, making me wonder how much mockery the footman had already had to endure that morning. No doubt the whole household—and perhaps the entire neighbourhood—had heard of his unclad adventures the previous night.

Feeling a little sorry for Finnian I cleared my throat to get Benjamin's attention. The boy's eyes went wide and he gave me a quick bow before dashing away himself. I laughed and shook my head as I went into the dining room.

"Good morning," I said to Quin and his father, who were already present.

They both rose from their seats, greeting Evie and me as they did so. Quin took Eveline from me, kissed her cheek and deposited her in her highchair.

"I see Evie decided to sleep in this morning," Quin said, running a hand over his daughter's dark hair. "I hope you also enjoyed having a bit of a lie-in?" Quin cocked his head toward me in question as he sat back down.

"I did, and gladly so. Being awoken at the crack of dawn can be a little taxing, especially when the sun rises as early as it does during the summer."

"Does Eveline's nursemaid not care for her in the early hours?" the baron asked, a puzzled look on his face.

I shook my head. "Geraldine assists me mostly during the day, and less so now than after Evie was first born. I mostly take care of her myself."

The baron's brows rose on his forehead. Clearly, his own experience with childrearing was quite different to what I was describing. But with aristocratic views on the matter being what they were it was no surprise.

"I'm just glad she's sleeping through the night now. Waking up every few hours each night for several months is not conducive to a restful sleep!"

The baron's brows rose even higher at this statement. I suppressed a smile, wondering how he'd react if I told him I not only attended to Evie's needs myself during the night but also breastfed my own child.

No doubt such a thought had never crossed his mind.

Seeing his father's reaction Quin gave me an amused look. He offered me the dish of eggs and I helped myself to a small portion, finding I wasn't particularly hungry after the previous night's excesses. I handed Evie a piece of toast and we ate companionably for several minutes.

"I dare say it was an interesting evening yesterday," the baron said after he'd swallowed a mouthful of bacon.

There was a small crease between his eyes, making me throw a quick glance at Quin.

"Did you not enjoy yourself, father?" Quin cocked his head expectantly.

"Well, it was certainly entertaining, although...rather unorthodox."

I detected a hint of disapproval in his tone. "Were our friends not good company, then?" I asked, placing my fork on the plate, done eating. I wasn't sure what I would say if the baron's answer was no. Would I dare to defend myself on my choice of dinner guests or would it be better simply to apologise and move on?

The baron waved his hand, though. "They were pleasant enough. Some of them quite interesting, actually. I found it refreshing to discuss topics one doesn't encounter on a daily basis in London.—But the behaviour of some of your staff members on the other hand…" He shook his head while his mouth turned down at the corners. "I would have dismissed them long since."

"You're welcome to act thusly in your own home," Quin said cheerfully. "Here in the Irish countryside we choose to be a bit more…"

"Lax in your duties?" the baron suggested stiffly.

Quin sighed. "I was going to say easy-going but feel free to make of it what you will." Seeing me looking at him he rolled his eyes. "And while you're doing that please pass the strawberry preserve."

To his credit the baron managed this small task with only a minimal amount of grumbling and without making further disparaging comments. Quin spread the preserve on a piece of toast, being watched closely by Eveline. When she smacked her lips together Quin cut her a small square, which she crammed into her mouth, her fingers and lips coming away sticky. As I was cleaning her with a napkin Finnian entered the dining room carrying a fresh pot of tea, making a rather pinched look appear on the baron's face. The footman glanced at the older man out of the corner of his eye, his shoulders slumping when he saw the hostile expression.

The sight made Quin compress his lips. "Thank you, Finnian," he said, ignoring his father.

Finnian bobbed his head briefly and scuttled away, no doubt hoping the baron's visit would soon come to an end.

I smiled at the thought and Quin threw me a curious look.

"I had hoped to take Eveline outside today," I said, deciding there was no point in further addressing the issue. We were getting on well enough for the most part and Quin's father simply was who he was—intractable on some issues and impossible on others—and nothing was ever going to change that. I waved toward the window, where the rain was still falling steadily. "Unfortunately, it doesn't look like the weather is cooperating."

"It may brighten up this afternoon," Quin said, putting on a hopeful air. "Although it has been raining rather a lot of late"—he paused as he perused the blurry scenery outside—"even for a land as damp as Ireland."

"It has, hasn't it?" An uneasy feeling suddenly stirred in the pit of my stomach. "The last time the summer was so wet…" I stopped abruptly, swallowing heavily.

"Was in '45, when the potato harvest failed for the first time."

I held Quin's eyes for a moment before nodding slowly at his conclusion, my heart thumping dully in my chest as a prickling sensation crept over my skin. "The Irish people have barely begun to recover from two years of blight. It would be unthinkable if…"

Quin clenched his jaws. "It won't come to that," he said stubbornly. "Surely the harvest will not be ruined again, not after countless peasants across Ireland made such an enormous effort to increase the number of seed potatoes to be sown in the spring."

The baron gave Quin a quizzical look.

"With the blight having wiped out much of the harvest for two consecutive years, there were very few potatoes left to plant the following spring," Quin explained. "It meant that, even though last year's harvest was healthy, the overall yield was small—far too small to feed the thousands who are dependent on potatoes for their sustenance. To try and increase the yield of the upcoming harvest many of the poor saved every last potato possible from the little they had, even fasting for up to forty-eight hours at a time, or so I've been told."

I breathed in heavily, imagining the sacrifice thousands of people across Ireland had made in an attempt to claw themselves out of their desperate circumstances. Watching the raindrops continue to splatter against the windowpane I hoped to God it hadn't all been in vain.

"Did it work?" the baron asked, pulling my attention back to the dining room.

"By all reports, yes." Quin handed another piece of toast to Evie, who was fidgeting in her chair. She scowled and threw it onto the table, making Quin shake his head at her even as he visibly suppressed a smile. "I've heard it estimated that the acreage sown this spring was more than three times that sown the year before."

"So if the harvest is successful," the baron said, "the peasants may once again have enough to eat."

Quin gave a curt nod. "And if it isn't..."

He broke off and the room fell silent, none of us willing to put into words the devastation that would result from yet another failed harvest.

THE RAIN CONTINUED to come down after breakfast, restricting the household to indoor activities. By late morning it had lessened to a drizzle at last and I hoped Quin's prediction of a dry afternoon would come true. For the moment, though, I found I was quite enjoying the snug atmosphere created by the grey sky outside as I sat down in one of the wingchairs in Glaslearg's small library. With Eveline happy in her grandfather's company and Quin working in the study, I had decided to take a few moments for myself.

I reached for the book on the small table next to me and ran my fingers over the title page. Knowing my fondness for reading the baron had brought me a copy of *Wuthering Heights* from London. The novel had been published the year before and was widely described by critics as a *strange book*, although one that was purportedly also hard to put down and hard to forget.

Being only a few pages in I hadn't made up my own mind about Ellis Bell's work but found I was eager to return to the West Yorkshire moors. Throwing a shawl around my shoulders against the chill in the air, I settled into my seat.

By the time Heathcliff was vowing to take revenge on Hindley for all the cruelties bestowed upon him over the years, I understood what the critics had meant, finding myself both fascinated and appalled by the story in equal measure. The selfishness and utter savagery portrayed by some of the characters made me want to put the book aside immediately, while simultaneously preventing me from doing so as I yearned to reach its conclusion.

I pondered the mind that had created such a tale, wondering what the story said about its author. Were the characters a reflection of the writer? Were the hatred and violence described traits Bells possessed himself, or had perhaps been exposed to in his lifetime?

Lost in thought I was a little startled to hear someone giggling outside the library door, which I'd left ajar in case somebody needed me. Curious, I got up and looked into the entrance hall. I spotted Emmett and Benjamin standing close by with their heads together, talking in an excited whisper. A moment later Benjamin tiptoed to the dining room and peeked around the half-open door before dashing back to Emmett with a big grin on his face.

Wondering what they were up to I stepped out of the library and headed toward them. They were so distracted, though, that they didn't even hear me. Only when I cleared my throat when I was almost upon them did they both look up. Benjamin's eyes widened in surprise while Emmett threw a glance toward the dining room, his cheeks going pink.

I looked toward the dining room myself but when I took a step in that direction Emmett waved his hands as if he were trying to stop me from heading that way. Of course, this only made me even more curious and so I quickly covered the short distance to the door. I looked around the edge like Benjamin had done a few minutes before and found what I saw startling indeed.

The table was only half set in preparation for dinner, the napkins not yet placed next to the plates and the glasses waiting on the tray on which they must have been brought there. What was more surprising, though, was the sight of Rupert and Geraldine standing on the far side of the room, locked in a passionate embrace.

Emmett made a strangled sound as he came up next to me, his eyes flashing back and forth between his brother and me, clearly worried about my reaction to this unexpected spectacle.

I smiled briefly and he sagged in relief.

In truth, I was glad Rupert and Geraldine had finally acknowledged their feelings for each other instead of skulking around and ignoring each other as they had been doing these past months—although that didn't mean I wanted them getting better acquainted in the physical sense in the room where my food was about to be served.

For the second time in as many minutes I cleared my throat to get someone's attention.

The reaction was abrupt and immediate, the two young people springing apart as though they'd been run through with a hot poker. Rupert hunched his shoulders while Geraldine clasped her hands tightly in front of her, their bright red faces and wide eyes uniting them in their obvious mortification at being discovered in such a compromising position.

"Mrs Williams… I…um… We…that is… Ah…"

I raised my hand to put a stop to Rupert's blathering.

"Is everything alright?"

I turned at the sound of Quin's voice. He must have heard us from the study and come to investigate.

"Everything is fine," I assured him even as Rupert threw him a guilty look and Geraldine avoided his eye altogether.

Quin looked from one to the other and back again. His mouth soon quirked up as he realised what they must have been doing, the expression on both of their faces speaking volumes—not to mention Geraldine's slightly swollen lips.

"Is there something you would like to tell us, Rupert?" Quin cocked his head as he perused his valet, whose round cheeks reddened once more.

"Ah…yes…yes I would." Getting himself under control at last Rupert stood up a little straighter. "Miss O'Hagan and I…well…we are to be courting, sir." He peeked sideways at Geraldine at this audacious statement.

Unexpectedly, though, she shook her head. "No," she said, "we are not."

I exchanged a startled glance with Quin as Rupert's face drooped and he looked down at his shoes.

Geraldine stepped a little closer to the valet and entwined her fingers with his. "We are to be *married*, sir."

Rupert's head shot up and he gaped at Geraldine with his mouth hanging open. When she gave him a small smile a dreamy look appeared on his face. He stared at his future bride for a moment longer before turning to Quin and me, as if to assure himself that we, too, had heard her declaration.

I laughed, as much delighted as surprised by this rapid turn of events after the exceedingly slow start to their relationship. "How wonderful," I said, clapping my hands together like a young girl while Rupert continued to look stunned.

"Rupert? Where are ye, ye old scallywag? I asked ye t' do the one thing..." Mrs O'Sullivan's voice faded when she came into the dining room and saw all of us standing there. "Ah...pardon me." She dipped into a brief curtsy as she eyed Rupert suspiciously.

"What has he done, Mrs O'Sullivan?" Quin asked in some amusement, seeming to enjoy watching the young man squirm.

"He was supposed t' finish settin' the table and come right back t' take the first dishes across t' the dining room."

"Are those the usual duties a valet is expected to perform in this household?"

We all turned once more toward the doorway, where the baron had appeared, looking rather unimpressed at what he'd overheard. Eveline was balanced on his hip, clutching her small rocking horse.

"Ah, no, not usually, sir," Mrs O'Sullivan stammered, looking noticeably flustered under the baron's scrutiny. "Although it is rather a *small* household, sir, and...well, with Finnian bein'...well..."

She fluttered an accusing hand toward Emmett and Benjamin, making the boys squirm. I took this to mean the two of them had teased Finnian mercilessly about the previous evening. Since he was nowhere to be seen now I assumed Mrs O'Sullivan had taken pity on the footman and sent him to perform some solitary duties elsewhere.

Quin sighed. "The duties of our staff members are loosely defined, father, as you've surely noticed. We can hardly stand on ceremony when we have so few employees serving the entire estate."

"You hardly stand on ceremony where their behaviour is concerned, either," the baron said, his face marred with distaste.

He looked down his nose at Emmett and Benjamin before turning his menacing gaze upon Rupert and Geraldine, who were still standing close together with their hands linked. Geraldine released Rupert's fingers, although not without a flash of defiance in her eyes.

Quin took a deep breath, clearly trying to muster some patience as he pointedly turned away from his father. "Rupert, Geraldine, you have my heartiest congratulations. I wish you every happiness." He smiled at the pair, making them visibly relax. "If you would all excuse us for a few minutes, please."

The staff were more than happy to oblige, hastily darting past the baron on their way to freedom. As soon as they'd gone Quin rounded on his father.

"I realise things are done differently in London, father, but I'd appreciate it if you'd leave the running of *my* household to *me*."

"Quinton, such behaviour…"

"The private behaviour of my staff members is none of your concern," Quin interrupted ruthlessly. "You have been welcomed into our home and provided every comfort. What they do in their personal lives has nothing to do with *you*."

"Then they should make sure to keep their personal lives private instead of airing their dirty laundry for all to see."

The baron huffed but Quin laughed. "You consider the announcement of a betrothal to be the airing of dirty laundry?"

"I consider it an affront to polite society to have the affianced firkytoodling in the dining room—not to mention to have a footman stalking around the manor house in the nude!" The baron's voice had been rising throughout this recitation, being watched closely by the wide eyes of Eveline, who'd put her thumb into her mouth.

Father and son stared at each other for several minutes until at last, Quin's lips quirked. The baron's mouth twitched in response. Finally, he shook his head and gave a snort.

"I suppose such antics provide some distraction, at least." He looked toward the window. The sky was still grey and brooding, although the rain had finally stopped. "Lord knows Ireland would be a depressing place otherwise."

I inhaled sharply at this statement, making him glance in my direction. He didn't say anything else, though, only clamped his lips together for a moment—to prevent himself from offering further unflattering observations about my home, perhaps. I rather doubted he was about to apologise, in any case. I had come to realise the baron's opinions were rather intractable. And as much as he seemed to appreciate the vast improvements we'd made to the estate it was clear he didn't think much of Ireland as a whole, and never had.

Fortunately, Evie started squirming on his arm, offering a suitable distraction from the potentially explosive topic. The baron placed her on the floor, where she crawled rapidly toward one of the chairs, toy horse still in hand. She pulled herself to her feet and, with her free hand, grasped the edge of the tablecloth. Quin darted to her side and pried her fingers from the fabric before she could tug the crockery down onto her head. She squawked in protest and glowered at him, making her look remarkably like her grandfather had a few moments earlier.

The thought made me suppress a laugh. "I'll let Mrs O'Sullivan know we're ready to eat," I said, exchanging a glance with Quin. He had been observing his father with a grimace on his face but now shrugged, clearly resigned, as I was, to experiencing a few more such encounters during the remainder of the baron's visit.

# 35.

SEVERAL DAYS LATER I was playing with Evie in the nursery when Quin came through the door, dressed for riding.

I gave him a questioning look as he picked up his daughter and swung her up into the air.

"I'm off to Ballygawley," he said, smiling at Evie's giggles. "I'd ordered some new gloves at the manufactory, which should be ready for collection. And I thought I'd visit the market while I'm there to have a look at the horse tack on offer. We could well use some new bridles and reins."

I nodded. "I'd forgotten it was Friday." Ballygawley's weekly market was well supplied with all kinds of provisions and Quin was likely to find what he sought.

"Is there anything else we need?" He lowered Eveline back onto the floor and ran a hand over her head before looking at me, his eyes soft.

"I don't believe so.—Will your father be joining you?"

Quin shook his head. "He was content with our visit the week before so it will just be Gambit and I.—Unless the two of you want to join me?"

"I think not. It's almost time for Evie's afternoon nap." As if to prove the truthfulness of my statement Evie rubbed her eyes with her fists. "Besides, I thought I'd have a look at the estate's ledgers, which I haven't done in some time."

Quin grimaced. "There's not much improvement, truth be told."

"I know. Still, getting to grips with the numbers makes me feel like I'm doing something useful at least, even if the effort is largely futile."

Quin offered me his hand and pulled me up from the rug, where I'd been sitting with Evie—entirely unladylike behaviour but enjoyable, nonetheless.

"We're managing. That's more than many others can say."

"That's true." I took a deep breath and squeezed Quin's hand.

"I'll be back by late afternoon," he said, kissing me on the cheek before doffing his hat and heading out the door.

I played with Evie for a few more minutes but when she started yawning and fussing I put her to bed. She usually slept for about two hours in the afternoon, which gave me enough time to peruse the modest—but not yet dismal, I hoped—state of Glaslearg's financial affairs.

Leaving the nursery I sought out Geraldine, asking her to keep an ear out for Eveline in case I should not hear her awakening after her nap. Downstairs, I found the baron ensconced in the drawing room and we spent a bit of time in conversation before I headed to the study.

As I was crossing the entrance hall Mary emerged from the library. I greeted her pleasantly in Gaelic but she gave a start at the sound of my voice. When she recognised me her shoulders drooped, although the nervous expression remained on her face.

"Is everything alright?" I asked, coming to stand in front of her. With the baron's visit I hadn't yet had a chance to speak to her since the dinner party but thought I must do so without further delay, if her current state was anything to go by.

She was clutching a few cleaning rags to her chest but now lowered her hands, evidently trying to make an effort to appear at ease.

"Of course, Mrs Williams." She gave me a curt nod and made as if to turn back to her work.

"Mary," I said, giving her a penetrating look, "I know something is bothering you."

She started shaking her head but a telling flush was rising in her cheeks.

"Is it Mr Murphy?" I asked brusquely, deciding there was no point in delicacy. "Has he hurt you or the children?"

Her eyes widened and she gasped but shook her head once more.

"Tell me!" When Mary squirmed at my tone I softened my voice and placed a hand on her arm. "Please."

"He hasn't hurt me...or the children."

As much as I was relieved to hear that Robert Murphy hadn't caused his wife and children any physical harm Mary was still clearly troubled—which I was sure must be caused by the wretched man she called her husband. "What *has* he done?" I demanded.

She was quiet for a moment before giving a deep sigh. "It's only words," she said at last. "Words of anger, words of hatred."

I could guess who Murphy's anger and hatred were aimed at—those who ruled over the Irish poor and his own English landlord, the man harbouring not an ounce of affection for Quin even after everything he'd done for him. As if in confirmation Mary darted me a quick glance before looking back down at her shoes.

"It's only words," I echoed what she'd said herself. "He can't hurt anyone with only words."

"No, I suppose not. Although I wish he wouldn't…and that the children could…"

I patted her arm when she drifted off. While it was true that words alone wouldn't hurt them Murphy's anger and hatred were damaging his family, nonetheless. I wished there was something I could say or do to ease her burden but knew my hands were tied—Mary's fate was irrevocably linked to the miserable man she'd married.

We looked at each other for a long moment, both mired in helplessness, before Mary dipped her head and prepared to return to her duties.

"Why don't you go home, Mary?" I called after her, struck by sudden inspiration as she started up the stairs. "Take the rest of the afternoon off."

Whether spending time in the company of Mr Murphy would do anyone any good was questionable, though, and, indeed, Mary looked at me as if I'd made an absurd suggestion.

"Take the afternoon off, Mrs Williams?"

"Yes. There's nothing urgent to be done around the house, in any case. Go home and rest, and try to take care of yourself for a change."

"Oh, aye, I suppose…I suppose I could do that." She still looked dubious but seemed to be warming up to the idea. "Robert and the children will 'ave tended the field and the beasts, and Bridget will 'ave seen to supper. And Robert, well he might be leavin' soon, after all."

"Leaving?"

Mary threw me a guilty look. "Um, aye. Leavin' to meet with his…um…friends." Distaste flashed across her features, making me nod in understanding.

"To spew anger and hatred?" I guessed, knowing the answer before she confirmed it with a quick jerk of the head.

I felt my own anger rising briefly at the thought of Robert Murphy sharing his loathing of my husband and others with several likeminded individuals.

Still, there was nothing I could do about it and so I assured Mary once more that she was free to go and wished her a pleasant afternoon before making my way to the study at last.

Sitting at the desk with an open ledger I had to make a conscious effort to focus on the numbers in front of me instead of returning over and over again in my thoughts to the recent conversation. Finally, though, with the house quiet around me I found myself immersed in calculations like so many times before. As I started going through the estate's income and expenditures, trying to locate every last penny we could possibly save, I quickly lost track of time.

And so it was that I was surprised when Geraldine came to the door in what felt like a matter of minutes after I'd sat down. She was carrying Evie, whose cheek was creased from her pillow.

"Shall I be entertainin' her whilst ye finish yer work?" Geraldine asked, her eyes perusing the open ledgers on the desk with interest.

I glanced between the columns of numbers and my daughter, feeling torn. "If you wouldn't mind," I said finally, deciding to finish what I'd started.

"Not at all. She's the sweetest girl in all the world!"

The young woman's eyes crinkled in delight as she smiled at Evie, who returned the smile and started bouncing up and down on Geraldine's hip.

"Perhaps you'll soon have a child of your own," I said, making Geraldine blush.

Following the bold announcement of her betrothal to Rupert the two of them had been carefully tiptoeing around each other, their furtive, loving gazes interrupted by sudden bouts of shyness as they navigated their new circumstances. When exactly they planned to marry I had no idea, Rupert becoming entirely flustered whenever the topic came up. I supposed Geraldine would simply inform the valet, and the rest of us, when their nuptials would take place.

"I'll leave ye to it, Mrs Williams," she said now, bowing out of the room, Evie waving to me over her shoulder.

I looked after them for a moment before turning back to my numbers, thinking how much easier it would all be if only money would grow on trees.

QUIN PERUSED THE leather straps on display at the saddler's stall, contemplating what the new tack would cost. There wasn't much to be done about it, of course, some of the old bridles and reins being quite worn. Better spend a few coins on sturdy replacements than hearing an inopportune snap while out on a brisk ride.

He selected the items he needed and paid what he had to admit was a fair price before wandering over to the neighbouring stalls.

The market was busy as usual, although less so in recent times. Walking slowly up and down the rows of provisions Quin became aware of another difference to years gone by. The trade in livestock had diminished substantially. Whereas before the famine, a good number of pigs, sheep and cattle would have been on offer—at the monthly livestock fair as well as, to a lesser extent, the weekly market—only a handful of animals were now penned together at the edge of the square.

With the peasants barely able to feed themselves many'd had no choice but to sell their livestock, in part because they desperately needed the money and partly because they simply had no means of feeding their animals. Pigs, especially, had been reared on the potatoes that sustained the family, with the income acquired by the beasts' sale some months later used to pay the tenants' rent. But with thousands having sold their animals after the first failed harvest and with no means of purchasing new ones, Ireland's livestock trade had plummeted. So widespread was the effect that the number of pigs in Ireland had fallen by more than half, or so Quin had heard.

Gone were the days of the crowded and boisterous pig fairs that had once been part of Irish life.

Quin sighed, wondering if there would ever be a return to what might be considered a normal existence after these troubled times.

A movement at the corner of his eye caught his attention and he turned his head, squinting between the stalls. He noticed a man on the far side of the square, rushing back and forth, stopping briefly to address marketgoers before hurrying away.

The man seemed strangely familiar and when Quin took a closer look, he recognised Mr Casey, one of his tenants. While it wasn't entirely unexpected to see one of Glaslearg's residents at the local market, something about the man's demeanour gave Quin pause. Casey seemed agitated as he stopped in front of a stall and spoke to the seller, leaning toward the other man with a sense of urgency, his hands fidgeting in front of him. The seller hesitated, looking left and right, before quickly jerking an arm in the direction of one of the lanes leading away from the marketplace.

Casey gave a brief nod as the seller waved him away irritably, looking for more profitable business. Casey headed off, his hands now fisted by his sides, his whole body tensed.

Quin frowned, wondering what was bothering the man. It was already late afternoon by now and Quin should have been setting off for home but without giving it much thought he started to follow instead, making his slow way through the cramped space as Casey headed into the narrow street. When Quin finally reached the lane Casey was already some way ahead. Not wanting to shout and cause a scene Quin picked up the pace but was unable to reach Casey before he disappeared into a run-down cottage on the edge of town.

When he got closer Quin could hear raised voices coming from inside the delipidated building, making him hesitate. The door was ajar, though, and so he pushed it open, hoping Mr Casey hadn't gotten himself into any trouble. As he stepped over the threshold all conversation stopped abruptly and numerous faces turned toward him, looking none too pleased.

Quin froze, feeling suddenly as if he'd stumbled upon something he had no right to be a part of.

"Gentlemen," he said slowly, doffing his hat and doing his best to look agreeable as he peered around the room.

With a small shock he recognised some of Glaslearg's newest residents among the cottage's scruffy looking occupants. He inclined his head toward them in acknowledgement, but one of the men lifted his upper lip in what could only be described as a snarl and Quin was sure he heard the word *Sasanach* hissed in disgust somewhere to his right. Heart hammering in his chest, he ignored both, instead continuing to search the sullen faces for Mr Casey. He finally spotted him on the other side of the room, looking even more uneasy than before. He was gripping the arm of his adolescent son, who seemed to be vibrating with excitement about something. Seeing Quin the boy quickly looked away. Mr Casey held Quin's eyes and slowly shook his head, a frightened expression on his face.

A scuttling feeling crept down Quin's back, made all the more pronounced by the sight of Mr Murphy among the men, staring at him with undisguised hatred. Perhaps Quin should have taken Emmett's suspicions more seriously, after all, he thought. Although, what he might have done to prevent a gathering such as this—or the loathing in the men's eyes—he didn't know.

"I apologise for the intrusion," he said to nobody in particular. "I thought I saw a friend heading this way."

He glanced once more at Casey, whose eyes flitted toward the door at Quin's back, clearly hoping for his imminent departure. The rest of the assembly mustered Quin with varying expressions of distrust.

"There's no friend o' yers 'ere," growled a gnarly looking man at the front of the room as he took an aggressive step toward Quin.

Something squeezed in Quin's gut at the man's demeanour, but he stood his ground, refusing to be intimidated. "I can see I was mistaken," he said. "I'll be on my way then. It's time to be heading home." Quin aimed a pointed look at the men from Glaslearg.

Relief flashed across Casey's face, while one or two of the other men looked down at their feet. Quin stood up a little straighter and turned away, only to be met with Mr Murphy's scowl as he leaned against the wall next to the door. Thinking he would have to do something about the man at last, Quin was about to take a step when he was pulled back roughly by a hand on his shoulder.

With a grunt of surprise Quin spun around, getting into a defensive stance as he eyed the gnarly looking man in front of him. The man glared back, undaunted.

"Our homes were taken from us," he snarled in surprisingly good English, eliciting a smattering of grumbled agreement behind him.

Quin lowered his fists, spreading his hands at his sides. "It's happened to many," he said with a nod. "And I'm sorry for it."

"Ye're sorry? When has yer kind ever been sorry for anythin'?"

"My *kind*?" Quin braced himself as the man leaned into him. Around them, feet were shuffling back and forth, murmurs flittering through the air.

"Folk with land…and money…who think they can do what they want."

"I can assure you I am not…"

"Ye can assure me o' nothin'!" the man interrupted Quin brusquely, spittle flying.

A few of the other men had come a little closer—whether to prevent a fight or cheer on their fellow as he attempted to beat him to a pulp, Quin didn't know. He lifted his hands, palms out.

"I am truly sorry for what you've endured. I hope you and your family…"

"My family is *dead*." The man's jaws clamped onto the last word and his eyes lanced through Quin with a hatred so acute he felt it burning into his soul. "And after me wife and the little ones died, they threw me and me last boy out and burned our hut to the ground so we wouldn't come back."

Quin's heart gave a painful thump. Out of the corner of his eye he saw a boy of about fourteen come nearer, wearing the same expression as the man in front of him.

Quin turned his attention back to the father. "I have no intention of..."

The man growled deep in his throat, suddenly rushing forward and swinging a fist at Quin's head. Quin ducked out of the way, dropping the parcel containing his purchases. He took a quick step forward and jabbed the side of his hand viciously at the man's throat, making him collapse onto the floor, wheezing and clutching his neck.

The boy let out a blood-curdling scream and launched himself at Quin, who reacted instinctively and soon had one scrawny arm pinned behind the youngster's back. He held the screeching boy in front of him, while several other men flexed their fingers and started edging toward him.

"Enough!" Quin yelled. "I am not the enemy!"

He looked around for Mr Casey, heart pounding. While he could quite ably defend himself against one or two assailants, he was currently outnumbered about twelve to one. And at least ten of those twelve had no particular liking for an English landlord, whom they would see as the personification of the cause of all their suffering.

The men were closing in around him, resentment and hatred marring their rough features. Quin was moving back toward the door, still holding the boy in front of him, trying to look left and right, anticipating attack.

He spotted Mr Casey, who was trying to push his way to the front of the crowd, his eyes wide with fright. Casey pulled at a man's arm but was shaken off, his entreaties to stop this madness lost in the rising voices. Quin heard a slam behind him and swivelled his head in the direction of the noise, meeting Murphy's leering face as he planted his feet squarely in front of the closed door, blocking Quin's escape.

He quickly turned into the cottage once more to face the snarling horde, only for a fist to slam into his lower back. The boy gave a sudden jerk to free himself, tearing out of Quin's weakened grasp. The youngster stumbled into the men in front of him, catching them briefly off balance. Quin dropped into a defensive crouch, sucking air through his teeth as pain shot up his back. He turned this way and that, trying to manoeuvre himself to stand in front of the wall.

It was no good.

There were too many of them, urging each other on in their rage against their circumstances. Quin blocked a hefty blow from a man on his left, but another landed below his ribcage on his right, followed by a swift jab to the kidney that had his legs buckling. With a groan, he scrambled to deflect a meaty fist swung at his face, only for the back of his head to explode in pain as something hard made contact with his skull. His vision blurred and his ears rang, and he dropped to one knee, arms raised above his head as blows continued to rain down on him.

"Stop! Stop!" Casey's shrieked pleas filtered through the din but soon faded as Quin collapsed onto the floor.

QUIN CAME TO with a jerk that made him groan as pain shot through his head, causing his stomach to heave violently. He quickly closed his eyes again and breathed deeply until the nausea subsided and the pain was at least bearable. After a moment he became aware of the smell of damp earth creeping up his nose and cautiously cracked open one eye. It was dark but there was a dim light above him that he eventually made out to be a section of sky visible through a hole in the roof. Turning slowly, he could see he was lying on the packed earth floor of a dilapidated mud hut with crumbling walls. He seemed to be alone, although he could hear voices somewhere outside that made him suddenly recall the cottage in Ballygawley.

He cautiously flexed his arms, which he found to be unbound, his captors probably believing he would pose little threat after the beating they'd given him. Trying to push himself up onto his elbows, Quin thought they were likely right. His arms wobbled and his whole body felt like a mass of bruises. When he was finally sitting upright, he carefully ran his hands over his face. A split lip, a bulge on his forehead and another high on his left cheek, plus the sizeable lump on the back of his head and any number of scrapes and scratches, and he must look a right sight. No broken teeth at least, he thought, probing the inside of his mouth with his tongue.

Not that his appearance was his greatest worry under the circumstances in any case.

The voices he'd heard earlier were rising in volume and Quin strained to make sense of them. Only able to understand one word in ten, he finally realised the men were speaking in Gaelic, or at least mostly so. He shuffled further back to lean his shoulders against the wall and closed his eyes. His knowledge of the language was sketchy at best but with a little concentration it was no great difficulty to figure out the gist of the argument.

It didn't surprise Quin to hear that the men were unhappy with their circumstances, including their treatment by their previous landlords. It also didn't surprise him that some of them wanted to do something about it, urging the others to violence.

And now Quin was caught in the middle.

Swallowing heavily, he looked around the cabin once more. Nothing that could be used as a weapon presented itself. And even if it did, Quin was unlikely to be able to fight off all the men by himself—even were he not hampered by his injuries.

A few raindrops started falling through the open roof and Quin wondered where exactly he was. There were any number of uninhabited cottages scattered across the Irish countryside, especially so after the countless evictions in recent months. While many homes had been destroyed, others had simply been abandoned, left to crumble slowly to dust.

There was a sudden shout outside, startling Quin. A second angry exclamation was followed by a meaty thud and a piercing cry, which descended into a continuous low moan as the sound of the beating continued. When it finally died away Quin held his breath, expecting the door of the hut to be thrown open and the men's anger to be turned upon him once more. It remained quiet, though, the silence finally broken by words hissed low and ominously before descending into a grumbling noise that steadily moved further and further away.

Quin was not so naïve to think he was alone. The men wouldn't have taken him with them in the first place if they intended now to simply leave him behind. What they did mean to do with him, he tried not to contemplate. Clearly, their general opinion of him was not too favourable—although he did hope Mr Casey at least would put in a good word for him if it came to it. And surely someone at home would soon notice his absence. Quin didn't think the men could have travelled very far from town, so it was only a question of time until he was found.

*And how will anyone looking for you overcome the angry mob outside?*

Quin pushed away the thought. Unfortunately, it was immediately replaced by another. For even if Alannah and his father had the foresight to enlist the Constabulary Police Force for help, that could take several hours, or even days, to organise.

And by that time, it may well be too late.

Quin shifted uncomfortably, sucking in his breath as the bruising on his ribs made itself felt.

He wondered what the men would do. Reports of disturbances had become commonplace across Ireland, with tenants trying to defend themselves against the ruthless evictions, desperate to at least have a home when they already had little else. In some cases, landlords had been murdered, most notably Major Denis Mahon of Roscommon, who'd forcefully evicted over six-hundred families comprising more than three-thousand individuals before meeting his violent end. The event had sparked a heated controversy in both Ireland and England about clearances and the government's response—or lack thereof—while other Irish landowners had demanded greater protection from the British. Of course, a number of tenants had also lost their lives during such encounters and any additional oppression was unlikely to lessen the outrage of the Irish people, some of whom had resorted to raiding food convoys and farms to survive.

Were these displaced men likely to take their anger out on Quin?

The voices outside started up again and Quin strained to hear what was being said. If he knew what the men were planning, maybe he could make his escape. The noise was getting closer, and the door of the cabin suddenly flew open, making Quin's heart give a hefty thump. He squinted into the lantern light that appeared in the doorway, making out the silhouettes of several men who started shuffling into the hut. Behind them he could see a sliver of darkening sky, the early evening gloom looking strangely bright compared to the cabin's dim interior. He pushed himself painfully to his feet but was clearly at a disadvantage even so. He counted thirteen of them, including a few who looked barely into their adolescence. Despite their youth, two of them eyed Quin with undisguised hatred, while the third youngster studiously avoided his eye. Quin recognised Mr Casey's son, who'd seemed so eager for adventure earlier in the day.

One of the men pushed his way in front of Quin, blocking his view. It was the gnarly ringleader from that afternoon and by the snarl on his face, his mood hadn't improved one bit. Quin was immediately on guard, but nevertheless stumbled backward when the man gave him a rough shove, weakened as he was. He braced himself against the wall of the cabin, raising his chin toward his adversary.

The man mustered him from top to toe before giving a mocking laugh. "I told ye that ye didn't 'ave any friends 'ere."

Quin ignored the barb. "What do you want with me?"

The man's upper lip lifted as he stared at Quin, before breaking into a cruel smile that made Quin's blood run cold. "Take 'im," he said with a jerk of the head behind him.

Two men came forward and took Quin by the arms, dragging him across the floor. They passed Mr Murphy, who made no effort to hide his satisfied smirk. Quin held his eyes defiantly but all the while, his heart was hammering in his chest.

What were they going to do to him?

His mind flitted to Alannah and Eveline, and he berated himself for following Mr Casey. What had he been thinking? And why had he entered the cottage when he'd immediately known he shouldn't be there?

He pushed the thought aside, knowing it would do him no good wishing he could change the past. He needed to focus on the present—and on staying alive. The murderous glances thrown his way from the men surrounding him left him in no doubt about how most of them felt about him.

A shove in the back made him stumble, kept from falling only by the men on either side of him. When he righted his footing and looked back up, it was straight into the face of Mr Casey's son. The youngster's eyes were huge with fright, and he quickly dropped his gaze. Quin looked around for his father but couldn't spot the elder Casey anywhere.

Another shove sent Quin crashing through the cottage door. Released from his captors, he sprawled in the dirt, suppressing a moan as his bruised body hit the hard ground. There were a few more men gathered outside, all of whom eyed him with varying degrees of distrust. Quin slowly started sitting up, expecting at any moment to be kicked or beaten. He was ignored though—for the moment—as the men started discussing what to do.

He edged toward the wall of the cottage, looking around in the fading daylight.

He was sitting in front of one of several mud huts that were clustered together at the edge of a small copse and surrounded by long-abandoned fields. The huts themselves could scarcely be described as liveable, with the one at his back being the only one still halfway intact. Clearly, nobody had lived here for years.

Seeing a small wagon behind the group of men, Quin wondered if he'd been thrown into it in Ballygawley, vaguely recalling the feeling of being jostled back and forth. A movement to his right caught his attention and he squinted into the growing darkness, making out what looked like a large bundle lying a short distance away. The bundle moaned and Quin crawled toward it, cautiously reaching out a hand. He carefully turned the figure on its back and gasped when he recognised Mr Casey. The man's face was a mass of bruises and dark clotted blood. His laboured breathing intensified as he tried to edge away from Quin.

"Shhh," Quin whispered close to his ear, patting his arm carefully. "It's alright, Mr Casey."

"Mr Williams?" Casey's eyes flitted back and forth, mere slits in his swollen face.

Quin nodded before glancing toward the group of men. They seemed to be in the middle of a heated discussion and so he turned back to Casey, helping him to sit up and lean against the cottage wall. Spotting a water skin by the door Quin retrieved it, pleased to hear liquid sloshing inside. He passed it to Casey, who cautiously took a few sips. When he handed it back, he gave Quin a curious look, studying him intently as if he were contemplating what to say.

"What are ye doin' here?" he finally asked, sounding exhausted.

Quin narrowed his eyes. "I thought I was helping *you*." A look of surprise flashed across Casey's face, making Quin shrug irritably. "I saw you at the market…looking distressed. So I followed you."

"Oh." Casey's shoulders slumped and he gave a deep sigh.

"You were looking for your son, weren't you?"

Casey nodded, his eyes darting to the other men. Quin couldn't make out the youngster in the growing gloom but assumed he was among them.

"He was meant t' be helpin' me on the fields today but he never came. And when I got home, he was gone. I feared then…" He trailed off, compressing his lips. "The others, my kin…they'd been fillin' his head with ideas…" He looked at Quin briefly before lowering his eyes.

"Ideas of rebellion?" Quin suggested, remembering the numerous times he'd come across some of the men, huddled together and looking grim, deep in conversation.

Casey gave a brief jerk of the head. "I thought it was just talk, men complainin' among themselves. And I tried t' tell them ye were a fair landlord even in these troubled times but…they wouldn't listen. They kept sayin' how much better everythin' would be if Ireland could be free. And Joseph…he thought it would all be a grand adventure…"

Quin gave a humourless laugh. "I suspect he's found out by now it's anything but."

Remembering the boy's frightened expression when he'd last seen him, Quin's mind flashed briefly to his own first military campaign, when he'd been as naïve as young Joseph, his head filled with glory. He was soon to realise there was nothing glorious about warfare.

"What are they planning to do?" Quin asked, lifting his chin toward the group of men.

It had started to drizzle in earnest now and Quin huddled closer to the wall as a small shiver ran through him, as much from the cold as from his circumstances.

"I thought it was just talk," Casey repeated what he'd said earlier, looking dazed. "But now…" He fidgeted with his hands for a moment. "My kin…and these other men…they're talkin'…they're talkin' o' joinin' others…"

"Other rebels?" Casey nodded, throwing Quin a sideways glance that made him feel uneasy. "And?"

"Ah…well…"

Quin growled, narrowing his eyes.

"Some o' them said they wanted t'…" Casey swallowed visibly before pulling himself together. "They wanted t'…make an example o' you when they joined the others." The words were barely above a whisper, but Casey gave Quin a telling look as he said them.

Quin's heart thumped violently as the man's meaning became clear. "I see."

"I thought it was just talk," Casey said for the third time, anguish flitting across his features as he perhaps wished he'd talked to Quin earlier about what he'd heard. "I tried t' tell them not t' harm ye but…" He waved a hand in front of his bruised face before letting it drop heavily into his lap.

Looking at the drooping figure beside him, Quin suddenly became filled with rage, and he opened his mouth to snarl a response. Surely, receiving a beating was fair punishment for leading Quin to his death—a death Casey might have prevented if he'd had the nerve to come forward with what he knew.

Quin's anger must have shown on his face, for Casey shrunk against the mud hut's wall, fear and misery stamped on his battered features. Quin clamped his lips together, breathing out heavily to get himself under control. It was hardly Mr Casey's fault that Quin had followed him to the cottage in Ballygawley.

"When are they meeting the others?" he asked as calmly as he could.

Casey shot him a nervous glance. "I don't know but…I heard them say they weren't far away…" He trailed off, looking down at the ground.

"Hmph. And I suppose we are to travel at night." It wasn't a question, but Casey confirmed it with a brief nod, nonetheless. The cover of darkness would help conceal the group of men. Quin hoped it would conceal him, too, as he made his escape.

If he didn't run out of time.

THE CHIMING OF the longcase clock across the hall made me glance outside the study window. My eyes widened when I realised it was already evening. I'd completely lost track of time. I jumped up from my chair, just as there was a soft knock on the door.

"Come in," I called, walking around the desk.

Geraldine poked her head into the room, Eveline balanced on her hip.

"Shall I be puttin' Evie down for the night, Mrs Williams?"

Rather startled that I hadn't noticed it was Evie's bedtime I came to stand in front of the two of them. I stroked my daughter's curly head but stopped suddenly as it occurred to me with a small shock to wonder where her father was. Quin had assured me he'd be back from Ballygawley by late afternoon, but it didn't look as if he'd returned yet.

"Mrs Williams?"

Geraldine's anxious voice pulled my attention back to the girl, whose face was marred with doubt.

"I only thought…as she's already eaten and is quite tired. And with you bein' busy and all…"

"It's quite alright, Geraldine," I assured her, making an effort to sound cheerful. "I was only lost in thought."

She must have been worried I'd be upset by her suggestion, as I usually insisted on putting Eveline to bed myself, savouring the time we spent together at the end of each day. I glanced outside the window once more, thinking about Quin, before looking back at Evie, who was rubbing her eyes with pudgy fists. Clearly, she was more than ready to be tucked in for the night.

"If you wouldn't mind getting her ready," I said. "I'll come up to say goodnight in a moment. Thank you." I smiled at the girl, who bobbed a small curtsy before leaving the room.

I followed her out the door and went into the drawing room, where I found the baron seated in one of the armchairs in front of the fireplace with a book on his lap.

"Is Quin back?" I asked as soon as he lifted his head. Perhaps Quin hadn't wanted to disturb me in the study and was even now freshening up for supper in our room.

The baron's eyes narrowed, and he slowly shook his head. My heart gave a sudden lurch. I hadn't really thought Quin could have returned home without me knowing about it, but it was disconcerting to have it confirmed, even so.

The baron and I looked at each other for a moment in silence.

"He may have met an acquaintance," I said, trying to sound hopeful while a sense of unease crept up my spine.

"Hmph." The baron didn't seem convinced—which did nothing to calm my nerves.

I took a deep breath. "Or he may have stayed to conduct some business." What business that may have been, I had no idea. Ballygawley was a small town and we visited it mostly on market days. Quin himself had said he only needed a few items, which was why he'd ridden there alone, without a wagon to bring back bigger purchases.

The baron still didn't seem convinced.

"Gambit may have thrown a shoe."

My father-in-law seemed a little less sceptical of my latest suggestion but remained doubtful, nonetheless. He gave a brief shake of the head and got up.

"I shall ride there," he announced and started marching toward the door. "You will remain here," he added as he passed me, giving me a stern look before continuing into the entrance hall.

I nodded reluctantly. "At least take John with you," I called after him, getting a grunt of ascent in return.

As the baron's footsteps receded, I looked around the room, feeling momentarily at a loss. Remembering that Eveline was waiting for me upstairs, I quickly made my way to the nursery. Exhausted from a day's exploring the little girl was already fast asleep. I smiled at Geraldine as she bade me goodnight on her way out before placing a gentle kiss on Evie's soft head.

Leaving the nursery, I wondered what I should do now. It was getting late but I knew I would never be able to continue on to supper as if nothing was amiss, much less go to sleep before Quin was safely home. I finally decided to go back into the study, where I busied myself with tidying up the ledgers I'd been working on earlier and restoring a sense of order to the shelves.

But while this activity kept my hands occupied, my mind was free to wander. Soon, I had worked myself into a frenzy, thinking of all the horrors that may have befallen Quin. Breathing deeply for a few minutes I reminded myself that the best explanation was often the simplest one. No doubt Quin's horse really had thrown a shoe and he was even now making his way back to Glaslearg on foot while I was standing here worrying about nothing.

Feeling a little better, I returned to the drawing room, only to find that hardly any time had passed at all. In fact, supper was only now being laid out and hearing the clinking of dishes coming from next door, I realised I'd neglected to inform Mrs O'Sullivan that neither Quin nor his father was currently at home. I headed to the dining room, where I found Finnian setting out the cutlery in Mary's absence.

"Is Mr Williams still not back then?" he asked when he saw me at the door. Clearly, the servants were quite aware of what went on in the house, whether I told them anything or not.

I silently shook my head.

"He'll be home soon," Finnian assured me, his youthful face radiating confidence in his master's safe return. "And he'll be hungry."

"Yes. I'm sure you're right," I said, giving him an attempted smile.

After Finnian left, I sat down at the dining table, staring at the empty plates. Despite my best efforts, my sense of unease was growing by the minute. What had befallen Quin to prevent him from coming home? It just wasn't like him to stay out this late without telling me.

Mrs O'Sullivan bustled into the room, briefly distracting me from my thoughts. She insisted on serving me supper despite my protestations that I wasn't hungry. Thanking her as kindly as I could, I picked at the food on my plate but was unable to conjure up an appetite. I gave up after a few mouthfuls and soon found myself back in the drawing room, where my attention kept straying between the longcase clock in the corner and the door to the entrance hall where I kept hoping for Quin to come in.

The seconds ticked by as the household slowly wound down around me. The concerned faces of the servants appeared intermittently at the door, but still there was no sign of Quin.

It was close to midnight when the sound of the front door opening made me jerk upright in my chair, having nodded off. I scrambled to my feet and rushed out of the drawing room, only to have to come to an abrupt halt when I almost collided with the baron, on his way in.

"Where is he?" I demanded, craning my neck to see behind him.

The baron shook his head and my stomach dropped. I searched his face for answers. "What…?"

"We found his horse but…Quinton wasn't there."

"What do you mean he wasn't there? Where is he?—WHERE IS HE?"

I was finding it hard to breathe and staggered backward. Wilfred took me gently by the arm and led me to one of the chairs by the fireplace, where I slumped down, my hands shaking. Clasping them together firmly I looked up at my father-in-law. For the first time I noticed the lines of worry around his eyes and mouth, and the rain soaking through his clothes, making me feel ashamed of my outburst. I hadn't even greeted him when he'd walked through the door.

"Tell me," I said, trying to keep all sound of reproach from my voice.

The baron rubbed a hand over his face before turning bloodshot eyes on me. "Gambit was tied to the hitching post by the market square but there was no sign of Quinton. And the sellers had long since packed up and dispersed."

"What happened to him?" I whispered, dread rising in my chest.

"We knocked on doors, disturbing folks at their supper. The first few didn't take too kindly to being interrupted by an Englishman in their own homes, so John started doing the talking." The baron gave a brief snort, but I leaned forward impatiently.

"What did you find out?"

"He was seen leaving the market and heading up one of the smaller surrounding streets."

"Why?"

"Nobody could tell us, although those who noticed him said he appeared to be looking for something…or perhaps someone." He lifted his hand to forestall my next question. "We don't know who or what it might have been. But…" He paused, evidently trying to decide what to tell me.

The sight made my throat feel tight. "What is it?" I breathed, almost afraid to hear the answer.

"John enquired at the local tavern, buying a few drinks to loosen some tongues and…there was talk. Nothing said outright, of course, but he understood. It appears there are those living around the town who are determined to change their circumstances…violently if necessary." The baron gave me a pointed look.

"You mean…an uprising?" I swallowed heavily. "And you think Quin somehow got himself entangled in it?" The baron nodded and I felt the blood drain from my face.

"One of the drunkards told John there's a meeting house of sorts that the dissenters frequent. He didn't reveal the exact location, describing it only as a run-down cottage toward the outskirts of town but…"

"You found such a cottage on the street Quin was heading down when last seen," I guessed, my voice barely audible.

The baron's curt nod made a cold sweat break out on my skin as I pictured Quin caught in the middle of an angry horde of men, none of whom would have reason to feel kindly toward a local landlord, much less an Englishman.

Movement at the door momentarily distracted me from my thoughts. Emmett was leaning into the room, one hand clasped tightly onto the doorframe as he listened to the adults' conversation with big eyes. I was about to send him away when the baron spoke once more.

"We found this." He handed me a parcel he must have been holding the whole time.

Tearing it open I forgot all about Emmett as my heart lurched when I saw the items it contained—a new pair of expertly crafted riding gloves and several leather straps I recognised as horse tack—exactly what Quin had gone to Ballygawley to purchase.

Trembling as I clutched the evidence of Quin's presence in the cottage to my chest, I looked back at the baron. He glanced briefly in my direction before dropping his eyes.

"What are you not telling me?" I whispered, clenching my hands into fists.

He started shaking his head, but I was in no mood to be treated like a child. "Tell me!"

The baron sat on the edge of the seat across from me and leaned forward to clasp one of my hands. The unexpected gesture made me want to recoil in denial of whatever he was about to tell me.

"There was blood," he said slowly, and my heart lurched. "And signs of a struggle..."

"It may not be his," I objected automatically. "And if he were..." I cut off, unable to say the word. "They wouldn't have taken him if he was gravely injured," I insisted, glaring at the baron before jumping up from my chair, making him follow suit.

"That may be the case..." he began but I rounded on him, suddenly filled with rage.

"Why are you not out looking for him? You're wasting precious time!"

"Alannah..."

"Quin needs you! Why did you come back here without him?"

"It was the last thing I wanted to do!" The baron's voice shook with emotion, and I dropped my eyes, suddenly feeling remorse. Quin was his son, after all.

"I am going to find him." The words were clipped, a statement of fact.

"But then why...?"

"John and I could hardly face a mob on our own."

"Where *is* John?" It occurred to me belatedly that I hadn't seen the groom return.

"He's gathering the men. I expect he'll return shortly."

I gave the baron a confused look.

"We spoke to an officer of the Constabulary Police Force after we'd gathered what information we could. Despite the hour he was not unsympathetic to our concerns, and I dare say the man was eager to appease a peer of the realm"—he gave me a meaningful look indicating he'd done all he could to bring Quin home—"but unfortunately, with all the unrest in Ireland, the Constabulary is rather short-handed at present."

"So they won't go looking for him?" My heart sank, making me feel helpless.

The baron shook his head. "They will. But they don't have many officers to spare. And with the number of men likely to have participated in the meeting Quinton seems to have interrupted, one or two officers simply won't be enough."

"I see. And so John…"

"…is gathering the men of Glaslearg to help bring him home."

I felt a small lightening of my spirits at his words but couldn't keep a little scepticism at bay. "Do you really think that will work?" While I hoped most of the men felt sufficient loyalty toward Quin to go looking for him, they were farmers, with no experience in facing down a rebellious horde.

A look of annoyance flashed across the baron's face. "My dear, I have led troops of the British Army through war." He squared his shoulders and lifted his chin, radiating confidence, making me feel instantly better. Suddenly, he gave me a brief grin, which made him look remarkably like Quin. "A few rabblerousers are hardly going to cause me trouble."

I smiled weakly and he patted my arm. "I must go," he said, turning away. When he reached the door, he looked back at me. "I promise you Alannah, I shall bring him home."

QUIN SHUFFLED ALONG behind his captors, assessing his surroundings as he went, trying to ignore the persistent pain in his head and side.

It was a dark night, with only a sliver of moon appearing intermittently between the clouds. Had the men planned their movements, knowing the darkness would hide them, or was their timing fortuitous?

The man in front of Quin cursed as he stumbled on an unseen rock, yanking on the rope that bound Quin's wrists.

Just fortuitous, Quin surmised as he lost his own balance.

The men didn't seem to have much of a plan, and he found it doubtful they were even aware of something as trivial as the lunar cycle. They'd argued until well past sunset before finally setting out, unsure which route to take to prevent detection and where exactly the other rebels were hiding. The latter had bolstered Quin's spirits, thinking it would win him some time.

But then the discussion had turned to him.

While there were indeed those who wanted to take him along, others preferred to leave him behind—conveniently silenced. With murderous glances aimed his way, accompanied by the flashing of knives and the shaking of clubs, Quin had been sure he was about to meet his maker. The argument had become quite heated but, in the end, the very man who'd gotten Quin into this predicament was the one who'd assured him of a stay of execution. The gnarly individual who'd thrown the first punch in Ballygawley had insisted they keep Quin for further entertainment when there were more of them to enjoy it and eventually, the rest of them had agreed.

And so, Quin had found himself trudging along the dark Irish countryside in the rain, thankful none of the men seemed to have guns, otherwise he'd probably long since have been shot. Not that this lack by any means assured his safety. And the men certainly didn't trust him to meekly do what he was told—which was why his hands had been tied in front of him and he was being led by a grimy individual of the persuasion that it would be better to be rid of him sooner rather than later.

"Watch it!" the man snarled, pulling on the rope as Quin struggled to stay upright, feeling dizzy.

Quin tightened his jaws, forcing himself to keep quiet while he regained his footing. It would do his circumstances no good to antagonise the man by pointing out he was the one who'd tripped first—and his chances of escaping were small enough as it was. Breathing out heavily, he continued along the small dirt track without saying a word as the drizzle finally subsided.

The sound of the other men's movements was all around him, but their hushed voiced faded as they made their way through the night. Not using torches meant progress was slow, with the rising sickle of moon the only indication of the passage of time—which seemed to stretch on and on in their cocoon of darkness. They passed a few burned-out huts and abandoned fields, making Quin feel like the rest of civilisation was a world away and that he'd been doomed to walk this dark and dreary landscape forevermore. He started swaying with exhaustion, his head throbbing with each step as his body reminded him of the beating he'd received not long before.

Not paying attention, Quin didn't notice when the man ahead of him came to a stop. Quin crashed into his back, earning himself a rough shove that sent him sprawling into the dirt, landing awkwardly on his bound wrists. He lay there with his eyes closed, not caring if they beat him again as long as he didn't have to take another step. No fists or boots accosted his person, though, and so he slowly opened his eyes and painfully pushed himself upright. He could make out a small group of men conferring to one side, talking in gruff voices. They seemed to be agitated, their dark shapes gesticulating animatedly against the inky sky.

Quin wondered what had caused them to halt their progress. It didn't look like they'd reached their rendezvous. He squinted into the darkness, noticing a tumbledown cottage a short distance away. As two of the men disappeared around the side of the building Quin thought he saw a light flashing nearby. He trained his eyes on the crumbling walls, hoping against hope that someone was about to come to his aid.

A loud shout suddenly rent the night air, making Quin's heart leap into his throat.

The men who'd inspected the cottage emerged in a scramble, along with two others. Even in the dark Quin recognised the uniforms of the Irish

Constabulary with their pointed hats. He experienced a surge of relief, sure the police had been sent to rescue him. One of the men brandished a sword and the other a gun, and Quin was grateful for once that the government felt Ireland's policing required something akin to military force, as it meant the men from the constabulary were heavily armed.

Quin's captors were quick to respond to the officers' appearance with raised fists and clubs. Perhaps they'd realised earlier they were being followed, Quin thought. He tried to shuffle out of the way, but it rapidly became evident that there wasn't likely to be much of a fight. His heart sank as he watched the rebels circle around his would-be rescuers, who received no backup from the dilapidated cottage.

The two constables had come alone.

The other men were cautious of the officers' weapons, but soon started taunting them when they realised they far outnumbered their foe. The constable with the sword lashed out at one of the youngsters, who'd dashed forward to attempt a strike. "Give yourselves up!" the man demanded, sword raised high.

The command was met with a few sneers but no attempt to follow it. Instead, the rebels got braver in their attacks, hounding the constables in twos and threes. One of the men fell back with a screech as the point of a sword hit home, causing the others to surge forward.

Quin tried to scramble to his feet, thinking he may at least be able to make his escape during the scuffle. He soon found himself back in the dirt, though, as a well-placed boot from one of the onlookers tripped him up. Suppressing a groan of pain and frustration, he started pulling viciously on the rope binding his hands while his chance of rescue vanished before his eyes.

The officers were quickly overrun. With blows raining down on them, they disappeared under the angry horde. Suddenly, the gun went off with a loud bang, followed by a piercing scream that caused the hair on the back of Quin's neck to stand on end.

It didn't take long after that.

The constables' muffled cries soon faded, along with Quin's hope, even as he finally managed to free one of his hands. He turned away from the sight of the two men being kicked and beaten long past the point of resistance, a terrible sense of guilt creeping over him.

The officers were likely dead—because of him.

A low moan and a rattling breath close by pulled him out of his thoughts. He shuffled over to the crumpled figure on the ground surrounded by two or three others, who were kneeling next to the fallen man, looking helpless. Quin placed a hand on the man's shoulder, realising with a small shock that he was only a boy, one of the youngsters he'd seen earlier. His heart sank when he saw the large, dark patch of wetness spreading across his shirt. He carefully ran his hand over the boy's narrow chest, pausing when he encountered the bullet wound in its centre. The ribcage under Quin's hand rose for another laboured breath while more blood seeped through his fingers.

Swallowing heavily Quin leaned over the boy. "What's your name?" he asked softly, grasping one of his hands.

The boy struggled to speak, dark-tinged spittle spotting his chin. "Dan...iel," he finally whispered. His eyes rolled back and forth in fear and Quin gripped his hand more firmly.

"It's going to be alright, Daniel." The lie tasted like acid on Quin's tongue, but he kept his voice steady.

Daniel's eyes locked with Quin's, pleading even as their light faded and his body stilled.

Quin clenched his jaws hard, causing pain to radiate down his neck. He looked up, meeting the shocked face of Mr Casey's son. A continuous tremor was running through the youngster, and his cheeks were wet with tears. Quin gave Joseph's arm a gentle squeeze but was suddenly flung backward.

"Get away from him!" an angry voice snarled above him.

The newcomer knelt next to the dead boy, gripping him by the shoulders. "Daniel! Daniel!" He started shaking him, willing him to respond until finally, with a heart-wrenching sob, he pulled the still body into his arms.

Quin turned his head, leaving the man to his grief.

A short distance away a few more figures lay on the ground, motionless. Whether they were dead or merely injured, he couldn't tell. The rest of the men were huddled together in small groups, presumably deciding what to do next.

Quin looked back to the crumbled cottage, wishing he could have made a run for it.

A noise behind him had him turn his head, just in time to duck out of the way of an angry fist aimed at his temple.

"This is your fault!" The man who'd wept over the dead boy launched himself at Quin, cursing and screaming.

Quin lifted his arms over his head and tried to roll out of the way, but the man came after him, berserk with anger and despair. Weakened as he was already there was nothing Quin could do but try to fend off the worst of the blows. He groaned as a kick landed on his midriff, followed by a jab to the side of the head that had his ears ringing. He felt himself slipping into unconsciousness but suddenly the beating stopped.

He lay still, struggling against the heaviness that threatened to pull him under. He heard a noise through the buzzing in his ears and braced himself for further violence. When he felt a gentle touch on his arm instead, he opened his eyes, finding himself looking into the frightened face of Mr Casey. The man's lips were moving but Quin couldn't make out the words.

He slowly shook his head and slumped back onto the ground, trying not to think, just to breathe.

He opened his eyes again some time later when Casey held a water skin to his lips, in a reversal of their roles earlier. Quin took a few cautious sips, wincing at the stinging of his split lip.

Gradually, his head started to clear, and he began to make out the murmured voices of the other men. A suppressed whimpering filled with despair tugged at his heart, but he held his breath as a low moan reached his ears. He'd encountered his share of dying men on the battlefield and he knew the sound of someone who'd been mortally wounded.

Very carefully, he pushed himself off the ground, fighting against nausea and vertigo until he was finally seated upright. He turned toward the deathly sound, making out a dark shape that was writhing slowly in the dirt, hands scrabbling in helpless agony. Quin swallowed heavily but couldn't look away.

"It's Mr Murphy."

Quin startled at the sound of Casey's voice. With a violent thump of his heart, he registered what the man had said.

"Mr Murphy?" He looked back at the pitiful form, conflicting emotions flittering through his mind.

Casey gave a curt nod. "He took a sword to the gut."

They were both silent for a moment, lost in their own thoughts. With no doctor at hand Murphy's chances were slim to none. Even with the best medical care such abdominal wounds were usually fatal, festering and oozing until the recipient died an agonising death.

The best Murphy could hope for would be to bleed out before then.

Quin's thoughts flitted to Murphy's wife and children. The man hadn't been the best husband or father but how would his family survive without him?

Another moan escaped Murphy's lips and a feeling of dread scuttled down Quin's back as the sound seemed to go on and on, echoing through the night. He suddenly wanted nothing more than to end the man's suffering that very instant—with his bare hands, if necessary—if only the ghastly keening would stop.

The same sense of unease seemed to be rippling through the other men, their jerky movements and tense postures betraying their edginess even in the dark. Quin kept his head down, not wanting to catch anyone's attention. One man had already beaten him after their run-in with the constables and he was sure the others would do the same if given half a chance.

Raised voices to his right made him hunch his shoulders but he was ignored—for now.

He tried to follow what the men were saying but struggled through the thick sludge that seemed to fill his brain, the few English words flittering away on the wind amidst the rapid onslaught of Gaelic.

"They're arguin' about what t' do wi' the bodies."

Quin startled at the soft voice in his ear, having forgotten Mr Casey was there. He made an interrogatory sound at the back of his throat, waiting for his heart to slow.

"The boy's father wants t' bury him. He says there's a small burial plot on the hill from the family what use t' live here." Casey swallowed heavily before continuing in a voice that shook with emotion. "It'd be consecrated ground at least." He paused once more, taking a deep breath. "Some o' the others don't want t' take the time. They just want t' leave him.—And him," Casey added, waving a hand toward Mr Murphy.

Quin glanced at the writhing body on the ground as a scuffle broke out among the arguing men. Somebody threw a punch, but the fight was over quickly after that. It soon became clear they'd be staying where they were a little longer, as Daniel's father located a spade and got to work.

The sound of the sharp edge hitting the earth reverberated through Quin's skull, mingling with Murphy's agonised cries. His head started spinning and he lay back down with a dull thump, the noises of the other men retreating mercifully to the distance.

He must have lost consciousness for he woke up with a jerk as he was pulled roughly to his feet. Pain lanced through his head and his stomach heaved. Bile spewed out of his mouth, earning him a shove that had him staggering. He tried to lift his arms, but they felt like lead, and he could do little more than wave his hands feebly as he was propelled forward.

The small wagon appeared suddenly in front of him and when he made sense of the rest of the scene his heart gave a violent thump. He started struggling in earnest, his body relying on its last reserves in its fight for survival. His captors tried to shove him onto the wagon bed, but he stemmed himself against it with his hands and feet, jabbing his elbows left and right as he shouted for help from the top of his voice.

Surely, somebody somewhere would hear him and come to his aid.

A final vicious push sent him crashing onto the wood, landing heavily on his side, facing the single accursed tree far and wide. A sudden blast of wind rattled the branches above him, making the rope that dangled there sway ominously in a mocking foretelling of his imminent demise.

Hands reached for him and pulled him upright even as he fought against them with every ounce of strength he had left, the wagon shuddering beneath him with his efforts. His arms were soon tied behind him, though, and his head yanked back painfully by his hair. The leering face of the rebels' leader loomed in front of him, an unmistakable sense of satisfaction marking his features as he took hold of the noose. Clearly, he'd changed his mind about keeping Quin as a captive for later use.

The rope descended upon Quin's head—so slowly that surely, he must be able to stop it—and he felt a tide of despair and regret wash over him.

"Forgive me, Alannah," he whispered, the last of his hope vanishing as the rough fibres settled against his neck.

He closed his eyes, picturing his wife and child as he waited for the noose to be pulled tight.

He hoped his end would be quick.

There was a sudden loud crack, and something wet splattered across his cheeks, making him jerk. The rope still lay loosely around his collarbone, and he opened his eyes. The man who'd been standing next to him was crumpled in the wagon bed, the dim moonlight doing little to hide the grim mess that was all that was left of his face.

Quin stared at the gruesome sight, his mind a complete blank.

A hand on his arm made him lurch in the opposite direction, his heart pounding furiously. He blinked when he recognised the youngster standing next to him as the son of one of his tenants, while slowly becoming aware of a great deal of noise surrounding him. The boy's lips twitched into an attempted smile while his eyes kept straying to the body at his feet, before finally turning his attention to Quin and removing the rope around his neck. While young Thomas O'Reilly worked on freeing his hands, Quin looked at the heaving mass of men that had materialised around him. He could make out a few of his tenants as they grappled with his captors, who seemed to be outnumbered—or at least

Quin hoped so. In the thick of it was his father, back ramrod straight as he wielded a pair of pistols to good effect while barking orders.

The sight made Quin's knees buckle with relief. Feeling himself about to fall he realised it wasn't just his own constitution that was causing him to be unsteady on his feet, but rather the efforts of the mule hitched to the wagon he was still standing on. Patient though the poor animal may usually be, it had clearly had enough of the mayhem surrounding it and was desperately trying to escape.

Quin quickly started scrambling off the wagon bed, pushing Thomas ahead of him to do the same.

They landed in the dirt while the mule bucked and strained, finally succeeding in dragging the wagon across the stones that had been keeping the wheels in place until it rocked into motion. Sensing freedom the panicked animal picked up speed, leaving trampled bodies and fleeing men in its wake as it disappeared into the distance.

Quin had no time to admire the mule's prowess, having to jump to his feet when a group of grappling men stumbled upon him. He recognised one of his captors and didn't hesitate to smash his fist into the man's face. Taken unawares the man crumpled to the ground but was soon replaced by another. Fuelled by his growing rage Quin promptly dispatched the second man and then a third, until—to his immense frustration—there was no further foe forthcoming. He looked around wildly, his blood roaring in his ears. The fighting was winding down around him, though, and the last of his abductors was soon subdued.

A smattering of cheers from his tenants confirmed their victory and Quin quite suddenly found himself exhausted, his legs giving way beneath him. He slumped to the ground, breathing heavily, dark spots appearing before his eyes.

"Here, son."

The potent smell of fine whiskey scorched Quin's nose as a flask was pressed to his mouth, a strong hand holding him steady. He gratefully took a few restorative sips.

"You came for me," Quin murmured, trying to focus on his father's face, which was looking rather blurry.

"Of course, I did." The baron's voice was gruff but his hand on Quin's arm tightened almost painfully. "I promised your wife I'd bring you home."

Quin placed his own hand over his father's and gave a gentle squeeze. "Thank you."

"Hmph." The baron shrugged dismissively, not one for sentimentality.

Quin lifted his chin in the direction of the other men, his head feeling terribly heavy. "How many injured?"

"Not many. Some scrapes and bruises, but we took them unawares."

"I noticed," Quin said drily, running a hand over his blood-encrusted face. "You might have shot *me*, you know."

His father gave a brief snort. "It was either that or see you dangling from the end of a rope. I took my chances.—Besides, I knew I wouldn't miss."

Grateful his father's aim had, in fact, been true Quin looked around him once more. He was startled to see Emmett, who was prancing back and forth next to a pair of captives looking very pleased with himself.

"I told the boy to stay behind." The baron's voice was tinged with irritation. "By the time I realised he'd followed us it was too late to send him back. I suppose his loyalty towards his master might be commended.—Although his listening skills leave something to be desired!"

Quin started to chuckle but was cut short by an agonised screech that silenced everyone else around him.

"That must be Mr Murphy," he said quietly as subdued murmurs broke out among the men.

The baron gave him a quizzical look.

"He was with the rebels. He was run through by one of the men from the constabulary who tried to come to my aid.—I don't think they survived the scuffle, and nor will he."

The baron wrinkled his brow as another long wail rent the night air. He started moving toward the sound.

"I'll come with you," Quin called after him, getting laboriously to his feet, swaying with dizziness. His father grasped him firmly by the arm. He gave Quin a stern look but didn't say anything.

Murphy was lying a short distance away, thrashing his limbs weakly, his head lolling from side to side. The sharp tang of blood coated the back of Quin's throat, underlaid by a hint of putrefaction that made him want to gag. He was glad the cover of night hid the man's gruesome injury. Or at least, it mostly did so, Quin amended as he quickly tore his eyes away from Murphy's gaping abdomen.

A few of the tenants were standing around awkwardly, unsure what to do.

Quin knelt down next to Murphy and the baron did the same on the man's other side. A sheen of sweat covered Murphy's forehead, while his eyes rolled back and forth beneath closed lids.

"Mr Murphy," Quin said softly, placing a hand on the man's shoulder, which shuddered continuously under his touch.

Murphy opened his eyes. When he recognised Quin, undisguised hatred flashed across his features. His lips started moving and Quin cautiously leaned toward him, although he wasn't sure he wanted to hear what the man was trying to say. It wasn't words that came out of his mouth, though, but spit.

Quin reared back as a thick globule landed on his face.

Murphy snarled in satisfaction but stopped suddenly. A long groan escaped his lips and his heels started digging into the ground as his body arched upward. When he slumped back down again, he lay still, and Quin held his breath.

The man wasn't dead though—not yet.

His glazed eyes locked onto Quin's, filled with loathing. "Get...away...from me."

Quin hesitated, feeling torn, unwilling to leave a dying man alone but knowing his presence would bring the opposite of comfort.

"Get away...from me." Despite his mortal wounds Murphy's voice was rising, until he was shrieking at Quin while lashing out at him with his hands. "Get away!"

Quin scrambled backward and glanced at his father, who lifted one shoulder before getting up and walking away. Swallowing heavily Quin followed. Murphy continued to screech behind him until his cries were drowned out by another deathly moan.

"We'll put him on the wagon. Take him home." The baron's voice cut in on Quin's thoughts.

He nodded slowly. "If he lives that long."

"I suspect his hatred alone will sustain him for a while longer."

Quin frowned but couldn't fault his father's observation. Even in death, Murphy's loathing of him ran bone deep.

"It's not your fault, son." The baron patted Quin's back. "The other men know what you've done for them and their families. They were glad to be able to come to *your* aid for a change."

Quin was surprised to detect a hint of admiration in his father's voice. It seemed the baron may have realised the men would never have gone with him to rescue their employer and landlord if Quin had dealt differently with his staff and tenants—even though his father hadn't necessary approved of some of his actions before. Quin's lips twitched briefly at the thought as he looked around the clearing, where his tenants were now standing in small groups, watching over their captives. Quin saw that someone had retrieved the panicked mule and tethered it a short distance away. The wagon was standing a little further back, looking like it had survived its boisterous ride.

As Quin's eyes travelled over his surroundings, some of the men grinned at him, while others lifted their chins in acknowledgment. Quin nodded back gratefully, trying not to think about what would have happened had they not come to his aid.

Shaking off the thought he turned to his father. "Please, take me home."

THE TRIP BACK to Glaslearg was slow and painful, and Quin soon found himself slumped over the back of his horse as it plodded slowly through the dark amidst the intermittent rainfall that accompanied them. Quin had tried to insist on walking with the other men, but his father would hear none of it, drily pointing out that Quin was in no state to stand on his own two feet, much less walk the whole way back to the estate. His body aching with Gambit's every movement and his eyes swollen mostly shut Quin quickly realised his father was right. He was grateful the baron had brought his mount—otherwise he might have ended up being transported on the wagon bed alongside a corpse.

This privilege already belonged to two other men, both far more gravely injured than Quin, one placed on either side of the deceased constable. Against all odds the second constable had not succumbed to his injuries, although he'd also been taken for a corpse at first. It was only when two of the tenants had tried to move him that it became apparent he was yet among the living. Whether that would remain so until he was delivered to the constabulary in Ballygawley was highly questionable.

In the end it was decided the man's odds would be increased if the corpse of his fellow was placed between him and Mr Murphy to prevent the latter from doing him further harm, Murphy's imminent demise having done nothing to improve his character. Between groans of agony Murphy continued to spew hatred, making Quin think his father had been correct in his assessment.

How many days could a man linger on the brink of death?

Unchristian as the thought was, Quin hoped he wouldn't have to bear witness to the event to answer that question. Having to deliver the wretch to his long-suffering wife wasn't any more appealing, though.

And then there was still the dreary business of arriving in Ballygawley with several rebels who may well hang for what they'd done, not to mention having to hand over one dead constable and another who was clinging to life by the merest of threads. Guilt over their fate had accosted Quin once more when he'd seen the two men up close. They were clearly young and inexperienced—which was probably why they'd gotten themselves caught at the abandoned cottage in the first place.

But they'd been there because of Quin.

Exhaustion pulled at him, and he wanted nothing so much as to ignore the world around him and sleep for a week.

"Alright, son?"

Quin lifted his head and painfully cracked open one eye as the baron rode up beside him.

"I'll do."

His father gave him a sceptical look but didn't say anything. Instead, he handed him the whiskey flask, which mercifully still contained a few drops. Although Quin thought it likely the spirits might cause him to slide headfirst off his horse he drained the remaining contents, hoping for the best.

They rode on in silence, Quin feeling oddly comforted by his father's presence, like a small child who believed all would be well with his sire beside him. It was a feeling Quin hadn't experienced in many years and he was suddenly grateful the two of them had resolved some of their differences.

If they hadn't, his father might never have come to visit him. And if he hadn't been there tonight...

Quin pushed away the thought.

"There's Ballygawley."

Grateful for the distraction Quin glanced ahead, where he could make out a few dim lights, all the illumination to be expected in a small town in the dead of night. Several more lights were struck as they made their way down the main street, the noise of their passage startling folks from their beds. A few faces appeared at windows, shocked at the sight of a large group of men descending upon their homes at this hour.

Once they reached the constabulary, the baron took charge, quickly dispatching a man to fetch the commanding officer while he lined up the prisoners and had the wagon brought to the front. When the bleary-eyed constable arrived the baron briskly explained the events of the night before leading the man to his fallen comrades. The constable clenched his jaws and threw Quin a brief glance as he sent the young officer who'd followed him to fetch the doctor.

It was all a blur to Quin after that, as the two constables were taken away and the rebels shoved into the building with obvious contempt. Quin was asked a few questions, but the sight of his bruises seemed sufficient evidence for now. Or perhaps it was the baron pompously throwing his weight around that prevented Quin from being more thoroughly interrogated. Whatever the reason, Quin was grateful he wasn't obliged to give an extensive statement in the small hours of the night and that their stay in Ballygawley remained relatively brief.

Brief though it was, by the time they finally made their way back to Glaslearg the first light of dawn was brightening the horizon, which was for once clear of clouds.

Reaching the courtyard, Quin was about to slide from his horse when he realised his work was not yet done. Mr Murphy still needed to be dealt with, which meant accompanying the rest of the tenants to their homes at the other end of the estate. He glanced at the man's pitiful form and sighed, trying to shake off his exhaustion.

"You go on up to the house."

His father's voice made Quin turn his head and blink at him. "But Mr Murphy…"

"I shall deliver him to his family."

"But he's my tenant."

The baron looked Quin up and down. "Considering how he's thanked you for that privilege I don't believe he deserves your consideration now."

"But…"

His father cut him off with a sharp wave of his hand that made his horse prance nervously. "Will you listen to me for once in your life, Quinton?" The baron glared at him with bloodshot eyes. "If you'd only…"

Quin braced himself for the inevitable beratement of his decision to stay in Ireland, a choice that had resulted in him being subjected to the violence that had nearly got him killed the night before.

But the baron only sighed. "Go up to the house, Quinton," he said softly. "Your wife will be anxious to see you." With that he turned his horse away and headed toward the tenants, who were huddled together, waiting for instructions. They followed the baron without question, no doubt eager to seek their own beds.

Quin watched them go for a moment before dismounting and leading Gambit to the stables.

"Let me, sir." John had come up next to Quin and now took Gambit's reigns.

"Thank you, John.—For everything." Quin clasped the man's arm, making the groom look deeply uncomfortable even as his face glowed with contentment.

As Quin turned away Finnian and Rupert materialised beside him. He struggled to recall whether the two of them had been there the whole time, the entire night starting to feel like a distant dream. He was grateful for their assistance, though, as he staggered up the steps to the front door.

He'd barely made it into the entrance hall when Alannah stumbled from the drawing room, looking dishevelled.

Catching sight of Quin, she gasped. Coming to stand in front of him, she reached up a hand but fell short of touching his cheek, her eyes filling with tears. With a cry she wrapped her arms around him, making him take a deep breath at the pain in his side.

"I'm sorry," she said, trying to pull away.

He drew her closer and kissed the top of her head. "It's all right."

They held each other for a moment, what remained of Quin's strength slipping away.

"Come," Alannah said, taking him by the hand. "You need to rest."

Quin nodded, letting her lead him toward the stairs, becoming dimly aware of the servants materialising around them, welcoming him home. He barely managed to lift his chin in acknowledgment as he took one heavy step after another, his body swaying with exhaustion. Leaning heavily on Rupert he made it to the bedroom, his head swimming while his surroundings came in and out of focus.

Hearing Alannah ask Rupert to prepare a bath he moved his head laboriously from side to side.

"Bed," he managed to mumble before collapsing onto the coverlet and gratefully sinking into oblivion.

QUIN'S HEAD HAD barely hit the pillow before he was fast asleep.

I swallowed heavily, my throat feeling tight at the sight of his damaged face. The violence it had taken to cause him such injuries made me ball my hands into fists. Given how many Irishmen were forced to live I could understand their hatred, but I could never condone their actions.

Rupert slipped off Quin's shoes and I started removing his jacket, pausing when he grimaced in his sleep. Between the two of us we got Quin undressed to his shirt, revealing more bruising as the layers were stripped away. He must have been in agony, with scarcely an inch of unmarred skin remaining.

Once Rupert left, I gently pulled the blanket over Quin and kissed his forehead before carefully lying down beside him. Although I was exhausted myself, I couldn't sleep. Watching Quin's chest rise and fall with each laboured breath I wondered for the first time whether we'd made a mistake staying in Ireland for all this time. It had never been easy living in a land steeped in such stark contrasts but since the onset of the famine its challenges had increased a hundred-fold. Surrounded by the misery and desperation of the wretchedly poor, was it inevitable for their despair to have turned into hatred? Should we have seen something like this coming and escaped to England where it was safer?

I sighed even as I knew the answer.

The baron had insisted on this course of action repeatedly, but Quin and I had never seriously considered it. Glaslearg had become our home and neither of us wanted to abandon the people who lived there during their time of need. Even if we'd had a reliable steward to oversee the running of the estate in our absence we still would have stayed.

It was our duty as much as it was our wish to take care of those who depended on us.

Quin moaned in his sleep, and I rolled closer to him, pressing carefully against his side. He had survived and we would get through this together, as we had done so many times before.

Slowly, as the dawning sunlight filtered through the curtains, I felt my lingering anxiety fade away and sleep overcome me at last.

# 36.

IT FELT LIKE only a moment later that I jerked awake, the sound of Eveline's cries pulling me out of a deep sleep.

I staggered toward the nursery, having to place a hand against the wall on more than one occasion to stop myself from falling.

Mechanically, I took Eveline from the crib and placed her to my breast, leaning against the back of the nursing chair as my eyes fell closed once more.

It was too much to hope for that she might want to sleep some more after she'd had her fill, but I took her back to the bedroom anyway, placing her between Quin and me and lying down beside her. Quin was tossing and turning, clearly in pain. I thought the presence of his daughter might soothe him but unfortunately it had the opposite effect.

Evidently ready to start the day Eveline was wide awake, on all fours and wanting to explore. She crawled closer to Quin, placing her pudgy hands on his chest and gurgling happily as she'd done so many mornings before. Quin cracked open one swollen eye and turned his head toward her, a small smile on his face.

Eveline froze, her eyes going wide. There was a moment of silence as she stared at Quin before her lower lip wobbled and she let out a great howl. She scampered away from him, completely distraught as she buried her face in my chest.

"Da-da," she whimpered, pressing close to me.

"Oh dear," I said, laying a hand on her back.

I met Quin's eyes over her curly head and had to admit, he did look a fright. Even knowing what to expect it was a shock to see his usually handsome features so disfigured.

I patted Eveline's back once more. "It's da, sweetheart. He got hurt but he'll be alright again in a little while."

Quin stroked her head, making her still. When she turned to look at him, though, she started to whimper once more.

Quin compressed his lips, clearly distraught himself at his daughter's reaction to him. She refused to look at him and clung to me like a barnacle, with no amount of coaxing able to convince her the frightening creature next to her was the father she adored.

I reached across to Quin, squeezing his hand. "She'll come around. Just give her a little time."

He nodded reluctantly, holding my eyes for a moment, making me suddenly long for answers.

There was so much he hadn't yet told me. The night before I'd been concerned only with his welfare but now I had so many questions.

What had he been doing in Ballygawley? How had he managed to get himself entangled with a group of rebels when he'd only wanted to go to the market?

What, in the name of God, had happened?

I felt a sudden surge of anger overcome me and had to look away.

I rose from the bed, holding Eveline in my arms. "If you're awake I'll send up Rupert to prepare a bath."

"Thank you. A bath would be wonderful."

At the sound of Quin's voice Eveline risked a peek at the bed but quickly looked away. Watching Quin's face fall in response made my anger slip away.

He didn't need my judgement, only my support.

"She'll come around," I said once more, sitting on the side of the bed and cupping his cheek. I suddenly felt my throat go tight. "We are so very glad you're home."

# 37.

DESPITE HIS EXTENSIVE injuries Quin recovered quickly. Any movement was painful, though, and so he spent most of his time in bed, dozing on and off throughout the day as his body healed.

Mrs O'Sullivan prepared teas and broths, poultices and healing salves, fussing over him interminably. The remaining staff members declared themselves wholeheartedly to be at his beck and call, a testament to the esteem in which they held their employer and the concern they, too, had felt during his absence.

While Quin recuperated I frequently brought Eveline to see him, until she got used to her father's bruises and was back to her normal bubbly self around him. When she was sleeping or being watched by Geraldine I often sat with Quin, bringing him something to eat or just keeping him company.

He told me how he'd been taken by the rebels and what had happened after they'd left Ballygawley. Hearing he'd already had the noose around his neck by the time the baron arrived—which the baron himself had conveniently left out of his account of events—made bile rise in my throat, thinking of what might have been.

Quin clasped my hand, holding my eyes until I had to look away.

I wanted to berate him for following his tenant into the cottage and putting himself in danger but clamped my mouth shut instead.

I might have done the same, after all.

"I was concerned for Mr Casey," Quin said, as if reading my mind. "I never could have imagined what happened as a result."

"No. I suppose not."

He squeezed my fingers once more but suddenly paused. "What happened to him? Joseph, Mr Casey's son. I hadn't thought to ask."

I was silent for a moment before answering. "He came home with his father. But…"

"What is it?"

I hesitated before responding. "Some of the tenants…they took objection to what he'd dragged his father and you into. They…ah…well they took justice into their own hands."

Quin's eyes went wide, and he swallowed visibly. "You mean…"

I hastily shook my head. "He's alive. But not much better off than you are yourself."

"I see." Quin's eyes were hidden beneath lowered lashes, and I couldn't tell his reaction. Did he think his tenants had meted out a just punishment? Or did he think the boy should have joined the other rebels in gaol?

I was about to ask when Quin spoke once more. "And Murphy?"

I took a deep breath at the question. I'd ridden to the tenants' cottages the previous afternoon. Besides calling on the Caseys I'd gone to see Mary, who'd barely been able to look at me in her shame at her husband's actions.

And the sight of Robert Murphy was one I wouldn't soon forget.

"He's alive."

This brief statement did little to encompass the horror of the man's condition. While his mind clung stubbornly to life his body was deteriorating around him, the stench in the cabin signifying the contagion that would soon be his end.

We were both silent for a time, contemplating the life of the man who'd caused us so much trouble. Did he deserve to suffer as he did now, after the way he'd treated the people around him during his lifetime? I didn't know and was glad I didn't have to sit in judgement.

"Only God can judge him now," I murmured.

FOR THREE DAYS Mr Murphy lingered in agony. When he finally stilled Mary gave a deep sigh of relief as silent tears ran down her cheeks. The children were subdued, sobbing quietly in the corner of the cabin, huddled together in their grief. Mary had wanted to spare them her husband's suffering, but they'd refused to leave, wanting to be there for the last moments of his life.

Whatever else Mr Murphy might have been, he'd been their father, a constant in their lives, and his children would mourn him.

I slowly pulled a sheet over the lifeless body before wordlessly moving around the cottage, tidying up here and there. I'd stayed with Mary and the children into the night, when it had seemed the end was finally near. Murphy had been incoherent, not recognising those around him and lashing out at anyone who came close. Together, Mary and I had forced him to take a few drops of laudanum—all the help the doctor had been able to offer—but his suffering had seemed little improved. At the last, he'd cried like a child, begging for relief.

The cabin seemed eerily silent now. But when I closed my eyes, I was sure I could still hear the man's tortured wails.

The sound followed me even when I staggered up the steps of the manor house as the first rays of sunlight appeared on the horizon. I stumbled through the entrance hall and up the staircase, overwrought from the events of the last few days, physically and mentally exhausted.

When I got to the bedroom, I quietly opened the door, not wanting to disturb Quin. I stopped next to the bed, a wave of emotions overcoming me at the sight of its occupants. Eveline was wrapped in Quin's arms, his body curled protectively around hers, her small mouth open in the absolute contentment of a deep sleep in the safety of her father's embrace.

I quickly changed into my nightdress and crawled into bed beside them, pressing myself against Eveline's back as I draped my arm around the two of them.

The two people dearest to me in all the world.

My throat felt tight, and tears started trickling down my cheeks.

Quin's hand came up against my back, warm and solid, running up and down my spine, soothing me, until at last my tears ran dry and I gratefully fell into oblivion.

# 38.

"WE'RE LEAVING."

"What?" I gaped at Mary Murphy as she hovered in the rear doorway, her eyes downcast.

"As soon as Robert's been buried. We'll be leaving Glaslearg then."

"Mary, come inside." I took her by the arm and she reluctantly allowed herself to be led into the kitchen where I deposited her on one of the benches. It wasn't even twenty-four hours since her husband had died and the woman looked exhausted. Feeling barely conscious myself after the dreadful night before I wondered how she was able to function at all.

Mrs O'Sullivan quickly placed a steaming cup of tea in front of her. Mary stared into it, her back rounded in despair. "We can't stay here," she said, slowly moving her head from side to side.

I sat down across from her and leaned toward her. "Of course you can. This is your home."

Mary continued shaking her head. "We can't stay here. Robert…" She swallowed heavily before going on. "Mr Williams almost died because of him…and the poor constable…"

"It's not your fault."

"He was my husband! I should have known what he would do!"

"But you didn't."

Mary's hands clenched into fists on the tabletop and colour rose in her cheeks. "Maybe I did," she whispered, finally looking up at me with red-rimmed and bloodshot eyes. "I knew how he felt. I knew the rage he had in his heart."

Quite unexpectedly I felt my own fingers curling in anger at her words, wanting suddenly and irrationally to berate her for doing nothing to prevent the events of the last few days, when surely she must have known that the man who lay in bed with her each night was capable of causing Quin physical harm.

Her eyes met mine and I held her gaze until my anger faded away as quickly as it had come.

"It's not your fault," I said once more, reaching out a hand to clasp hers. "Even if you knew his heart you couldn't have known what he would do."

"But…"

"Were you with him when he plotted with the others? Did he tell you of his plans?" She looked about to respond but I continued ruthlessly. "Were you there when he set out in rebellion and Mr Williams was caught in the middle?"

Mary was silent for a moment as a tear rolled down her cheek. "He never confided in me, and he'd never have let me come even if I wanted to. He didn't think I was important enough. I never mattered to him. Never." She wrapped her arms around herself and started rocking back and forth, her tears falling in earnest now.

With a quick glance in my direction Mrs O'Sullivan turned toward the sideboard, where she snatched up a bottle of brandy. Upending it over Mary's teacup she added a healthy dose before wrapping Mary's fingers around the handle.

Mary obediently brought the cup to her mouth, coming up sputtering.

"You matter to *us*, Mary," I said. "And that is why you'll stay."

Mrs O'Sullivan came to stand behind her and placed a hand on her shoulder even as I grasped Mary's fingers more firmly.

"You and the children will come here and live in the manor house with us," I decided. "There's plenty of room in the attic." I hadn't discussed the matter with Quin but I knew he would support my choice. "You won't have to travel so far each day to come to work and the change of scenery will do the children good." Although I doubted the scars of having a father like Robert Murphy would ever fade entirely I hoped their lives would be better now that he was gone—Unchristian though the thought may be.

I looked at Mary expectantly but a doubtful expression still marred her face.

"We are not to blame for other people's actions," I said softly, thoughts of Kieran flitting through my mind. "Only our own.—You have done nothing wrong, Mary, and you and the children deserve some happiness at last."

Mary silently removed a handkerchief from her sleeve and used it dab at her eyes. Finally, she gave a stuttering sigh. "We would like more than anything to stay," she whispered and burst into tears once more.

# 39.

MARY AND THE children moved into the manor house a few days later. While the children's natural exuberance soon emerged Mary remained quiet and subdued, barely able to meet Quin's eyes when he came downstairs to welcome them to their new home. Robert Murphy's funeral had taken place the day before, the small group of mourners present mostly for the family's benefit rather any strong desire to bid the recently departed farewell. Alannah had tried to prevent Quin from attending, claiming that Mary wouldn't appreciate his presence at the graveside, not needing to be reminded of Robert's transgressions on the day he was laid to rest. The baron had added his voice to the argument, pointing out that Quin was in no condition to walk the few steps to the stable much less travel any distance to the churchyard. But Quin had insisted, feeling duty bound to be present at his tenant's funeral, no matter what the man might have done.

Mary had watched the coffin disappear into the ground with dry eyes, clutching her children's hands. Her expression had clouded whenever she'd glanced at Quin's bruised face, making him think perhaps Alannah had been right in her insistence that he stay behind. By the time they'd returned to the manor house once it was all over Quin could only stagger up to his bed, being watched stiffly by his father, the baron's lips pressed firmly together as he tried to hold his tongue.

Remembering the scene now Quin lay back in the tub, leaning his head against the side of the large vessel. He closed his eyes as the warm water started to soothe his tortured body and his muscles slowly relaxed. Some of the smaller scrapes and cuts had already faded away but others were taking longer to heal, making his skin feel stiff and tight beneath the scabs. Bruising still mottled his body with colourful blotches, the green and yellow patches among the purple making him look a right sight indeed.

He was amazed Eveline had managed to see past all that and recognise him for the man he was in the end—there were times he barely recognised himself after everything that had happened.

The thought of his daughter made his heart swell with love, and he was overcome with gratitude at still being alive to see her every day.

Unfortunately, the vision of Evie's sweet face was obliterated suddenly and without warning by the flash of a bootheel coming toward him at speed. He opened his eyes with a start and shook his head to rid himself of the memory, even knowing it was futile. While his body would heal, a lifetime wouldn't be enough for him to forget the night's work.

He could only hope to live with the aftermath.

But he was home and he was whole. It was more than he'd hoped for standing atop the wagon bed with the noose around his neck.

His mind flitted once more to Robert Murphy and the role he'd played in his capture, making him feel a sudden onslaught of rage. But the man was dead and buried, he reminded himself, and he wouldn't have to worry about him anymore. Quin felt a little guilty about the uncharitable thought. Murphy had certainly paid the price for his hatred—as had his wife and children, who were innocent of any crime. Having wanted to take the drastic measure of leaving the estate out of guilt over her husband's actions, Quin wondered if Mary would ever be able to look him in the eyes again.

He sighed, taking hold of the washcloth and the bar of soap. Rupert had wanted to assist him with his bath but Quin had sent him away, wanting to be alone. Although he appreciated everyone's attention he was starting to feel suffocated, not wanting or needing to be coddled without end.

The gentle motion of running the washcloth over his skin soothed him and he slowly felt himself return to himself. When the water began to get cold he got up, reaching for the towel Rupert had placed on a stool next to the tub. He yawned as an overwhelming tiredness assaulted him and started drying himself clumsily. When he was finally dressed in a clean nightshirt he sank gratefully onto the bed, his body feeling heavy and weak. He closed his eyes and tried to empty his mind, dozing for several minutes.

The sound of the bedroom door opening a short while later made him look toward the threshold, where Alannah's head appeared as she looked in on him. Seeing he was awake she came inside and sat on the side of the bed.

Quin put a pillow behind his back and took her hand, smiling. Her lips twitched briefly in response but she quickly looked down. Her eyes were red-rimmed and her face was pale, the sight squeezing Quin's heart.

"Are you alright?" he asked, stroking the back of her hand.

She nodded but kept her head lowered. Despondency flashed across her features, making Quin hate himself in that moment for everything he'd put her through.

"I'm sorry for what happened," he said for the dozenth time.

"It's not your fault," she assured him as she always did, finally lifting her head.

He could see the depth of feeling in her gaze—the fear she'd felt for him when he was taken, the despair of seeing his injuries, and the horror of standing by Mary's side as her husband died an agonised death.

She shouldn't have had to deal with any of those things.

Quin tightened his jaws, still holding her eyes. He found no resentment there and yet, she looked deeply troubled.

"Everything will soon be back to normal," he said, squeezing her fingers, thinking perhaps she was still feeling subdued after Murphy's funeral.

She only shook her head, though, and one or two tears spilled down her cheeks.

Quin leaned forward to take her in his arms. "It will be alright, Alannah. Everything will be alright."

He ran a hand up and down her back but she continued to shake her head.

"Nothing will be alright," she whispered.

His heart gave a lurch and he took her by the upper arms so he could look at her. "What do you mean?" She looked down, refusing to meet his eyes. "What is it, Alannah?"

When she still didn't speak he gave her a shake. "Tell me," he demanded gruffly, a feeling of unease coming over him.

"It's the harvest." Her voice was so soft that he barely heard her but the words made the hairs on the back of his neck stand on end. "It's failed…again."

"No." His denial came out in a croak. "It can't have."

"It has." Her eyes flicked back and forth between his, their blue depths filled with desolation. "It was in the paper that arrived this afternoon. News has come in from the west…but it'll be spreading everywhere soon."

"How much…?"

"Officials say half the crop is likely to be lost."

Quin swallowed heavily, momentarily unable to speak.

"And the harvest season hasn't even begun," Alannah said, staring into the distance.

"What about our tenants?"

"They haven't noticed anything amiss."

Quin sighed in relief although it was short-lived.

"We can only hope it stays that way," Alannah said softly.

He pulled her to him once more, trying not to think about the fact that the destruction may yet reach his own land, reminding himself stubbornly that they had faced and dealt with similar hardships before, and would do so again now if needed. He pulled Alannah closer, ignoring the pain in his injured ribs as she clung to him in turn.

"I shouldn't have told you."

Quin leaned back to give her a quizzical look.

She ran a hand gently along his face, over the mottled bruising that covered his cheek and temple. "You're still recovering from your own ordeal. You shouldn't have to worry about anything else."

He gave a humourless laugh. "You could hardly have spared me for long." No doubt even now the news of yet another failed harvest was spreading across Glaslearg and the neighbouring estates. "Although I'm grateful for your concern," he added softly, her earlier hesitation making sense to him now. She had tried to relieve him of a burden—even if only for a brief time—while carrying several of her own.

"Should *you* have to worry about the fate of thousands of Irish people?" he asked, taking her face between his hands. "Were you not also burdened by my abduction...and everything that followed?"

Alannah nodded silently and he kissed her lightly on the lips.

"What's happening in Ireland..." Quin shook his head and sighed. "It's a fate neither of us can escape, no matter how hard we may try."

He ran a hand over her hair and she closed her eyes, leaning into his touch. He urged her gently to lie down beside him with her head on his chest. He held her close and kissed her forehead, wishing the world around them could disappear.

AS I LAY in bed that night I felt dazed, my mind unable to make sense of reality.

A third failed potato harvest, it was unthinkable—after everything the people in Ireland had already gone through.

I shoved aside the blanket and rolled onto my side, unable to sleep.

Quin seemed to be having no such trouble. His eyes were closed, his chest rising steadily in slumber.

A stab of irritation lanced through my heart at the sight.

How could he be sleeping so peacefully amidst the tragedy that continued to play out around us?

I flopped angrily onto my back once more, crossing my arms in front of my chest. After a moment I forced myself to take a few deep breaths and glanced over at Quin. Even in the darkness I could make out some of the bruising that still marred his face.

My throat constricted and I had to swallow heavily.

Hadn't I wanted to spare him this further burden while he recovered from his own ordeal?

He had done so much for the Irish people on his land, more than many Irishmen had done for their own countrymen. And he'd done it for me, because he'd stayed here for my sake, because he loved me.

A flood of emotions came over me at the thought of what his decision to stay in Ireland had cost him. He'd almost died a few nights ago being caught up in the Irishmen's hatred—a hatred he didn't even resent them for because he understood their plight and commiserated with them.

I sighed, rolling back onto my side, wondering whether I'd ever be able to sleep again.

Suddenly I envied Quin's ability to put aside his troubles when he went to bed, to focus solely on getting the rest he needed to face the challenges that came inevitably with the next dawn.

I closed my eyes and tried to empty my mind, to focus on the here and now, but it was no good.

I tossed and turned, exhausted but unable to find the blessed relief of sleep.

I finally stilled at the touch of Quin's hand, his fingers running gently along my side before pulling me against his chest.

I took a deep breath and he stroked the back of my head and kissed my cheek, trying to brush away my fears. I turned so my mouth met his and felt a sudden, desperate need overcome me—the need to lose myself in his arms to forget, if even just for a moment, the gloomy future that awaited the Irish people once more.

I crushed my lips against his and dug my fingers into the muscles of his back, wanting—needing—to get closer. Quin yanked aside the layers of fabric that separated us, the same urgency seeming to overtake him as he rolled me onto my back and sheathed himself within me in a single thrust. Amidst the chaos that surrounded us our bodies moved in unison, their joining the only thing that made sense in these troubling times—the ancient need to seek life in the presence of death driving us, compelling us to become one, to seek that single instant that allowed us to forget everything else around us.

Our cries merged and we clung to each other, desperate to hold onto that moment before it faded away and our bleak reality returned.

Long afterward we lay in each other's arms, not speaking just being, Quin's heart beating steadily beneath my ear, his breath warm across my cheek. After a time his arms went slack as he fell asleep. When I finally drifted off myself I sank into a gloriously dreamless void, unencumbered by the endless worries that plagued me during the day, allowing me to get the rest I so desperately needed to face all that was to come when the sun rose above the horizon once more.

# 40.

SEVERAL DAYS LATER Quin was sitting in the drawing room, reading the newspaper with a frown on his face. As his strength had returned he'd been spending more time downstairs. But while he was undoubtedly enjoying the slow return to his normal life and his normal self, he was also feeling increasingly conflicted about his family's circumstances. He'd told Alannah they couldn't escape Ireland's fate and yet it wasn't infrequently that he wished they could do exactly that—to get on a ship and sail to England where they could pretend ignorance of the Irish people's plight.

But even if they didn't forget about the Irish altogether, should they leave the land behind anyway, for their daughter's sake? Was it their responsibility as Evie's parents to remove her from a land filled with despair, when they had the means to do so? Were they putting her at risk by choosing to stay?

The baron's voice at the doorway broke in on Quin's thoughts.

"I beg your pardon?"

"The rebels are being transported to Van Diemen's Land," the baron repeated, forgoing any preliminary greetings.

Quin's brows rose in astonishment. "They've already been tried?" It had barely been two weeks since his capture.

The baron gave a curt nod as he took a seat in one of the wingchairs. "The courts have dealt with them swiftly.—And kindly, according to them, finding their retribution quite magnanimous compared to what it might have been."

"I suppose it is." The men might very well have been hanged for treason. Instead, they were being sent to an unknown land half a world away—a place they'd probably never return from. "It seems to be the government's approach to dealing with troublesome Irishmen these days," Quin said after a moment, passing the baron the newspaper. "Page 16."

The baron paged to the article Quin had read only a few minutes before. With tensions heightened throughout Ireland as they were, it had only been a matter of time until attempted risings sprung up here and there. Just a few weeks earlier crown forces had ended one such attempt, clashing with a group of poorly prepared rebels in the Widow McCormack's cabbage patch in County Tipperary, while several co-conspirators were arrested in Dublin. Like so many times before over the course of Irish history, even the most ardent country folks simply had little hope of staging a successful insurrection against the far superior military forces of their oppressors.

Unlike on previous occasions, though, the British had no wish to martyr any of the attempted rebels, at least not in the midst of the ongoing famine. And thus, the leaders of the Irish Confederation—formerly called the Young Irelanders—who'd attempted to raise the revolt, were being transported, although a few had reportedly fled to America or France. Whether they would try to stage another rebellion from afar remained to be seen.

"I suppose the judiciary in Omagh was inspired by these events," the baron said, waving the paper in the air.

"Did you go to Omagh?" Quin didn't know when his father might have gone to the courthouse in the county town, although it might have slipped his notice with Quin spending much of the last week in bed.

The baron shook his head. "I simply requested the chief constable in Ballygawley to keep me informed."

"So he let you know the verdict had been reached?"

"Indeed. The letter arrived only a short while ago."

Quin was silent for a moment. His mind felt strangely addled, as if it hadn't quite recovered from the physical ordeal he'd endured. "Why wasn't I informed of the trial and asked to testify?" he asked at last.

His father shrugged. "It wasn't necessary."

"It wasn't necessary?"

"The constable who survived the night gave an extensive statement. Yours wasn't needed."

"But I'm the one who was abducted," Quin pointed out.

"And he's the one who was almost beaten to death," the baron countered.

Quin was not deterred, though. "I'm relieved to hear the man is sufficiently recovered to have given his testimony. Still, it seems peculiar that a statement wasn't required of me—when I'd been with the rebels from the time they set out from Ballygawley."

Quin gave his father a pointed look. When the baron dropped his gaze, Quin sat up straighter in his chair. "You told the chief constable not to call on me, didn't you?"

The baron sniffed. "I simply asked him to make do without your input."

"You *asked* him?" Quin scoffed. "More likely you intimidated the man and informed him he'd do well to follow a baron's demands."

His father pursed his lips but didn't answer—which was all the answer Quin needed.

"Did you even consider what *I* wanted?" he asked, trying to suppress his growing irritation.

"I was protecting you."

"I didn't need your protection!"

The baron narrowed his eyes as he leaned closer to Quin. "That's not the impression I got when I found you with a noose around your neck!"

"And I am deeply grateful you came to my rescue." Quin held his father's eyes for a moment. "But I had a right to speak at the trial of the men who meant to see me killed."

"It wouldn't have made a difference. And as my son..."

"I am no longer a child!" Quin interrupted, his irritation turning rapidly into anger. How typical of his father to decide what was best for Quin—and then be disappointed in his son for disagreeing with his views.

The baron clenched his jaws, stubbornly refusing to budge.

Quin took a deep breath and briefly closed his eyes, until he felt he could speak without shouting. "Are all the men to be transported?" he asked, deciding there was no point in arguing further.

The baron took a moment to answer. "All but one."

The tone of his voice made Quin give him a sharp look. "Who?"

"The leader's son."

Quin recalled a gangly youth, filled with a raging anger as he followed his elders to attempted rebellion. "What will happen to him?"

"He is to hang for the murder of the second constable."

Quin's eyes flew open in shock. "But he's only a child!"

"Fourteen, or so I'm told."

"But..."

"According to the chief constable at Ballygawley the boy damned himself from the start, hurling insults at the judge, trying to incite further insurgence in the crowd, and defending his father—who, you will recall, did not survive the night's events."

Quin compressed his lips, recalling full well what had happened to the father. The sight of the man's ruined face on the wagon bed next to him was one he was unlikely ever to forget. He shook his head to rid himself of the memory. "Even so, how can he have been held accountable for the constable's death? Any number of the rebels laid into the two police officers and contributed to their injuries."

The baron sighed. "He confessed," he said softly, holding Quin's eyes. "Perhaps he wanted to die."

Quin stayed silent, letting what his father had said sink in. The baron may well be right, he thought, remembering the leader's angry words so filled with despair. The rest of the boy's family was dead, his home destroyed. And with his father now also gone, perhaps a quick death on the scaffold was preferable to a long and frightening journey to an unknown destination followed by a lifetime of lonely servitude.

"Will you *now* reconsider your choice to stay in Ireland, Quinton?"

His father's voice pulled Quin back to the present, and he took a deep breath. He'd been pleasantly surprised that he hadn't yet been berated by the baron following his abduction but clearly that respite had come to an end.

"I told you before, father, this is our home."

"And are recent events not enough to change your mind?" the baron demanded. "Look around you, at what's happening across Ireland, at what's to come following yet another failed harvest. Who's to say you won't be caught up in the next surge of violence?" He leaned forward, giving Quin a penetrating look. "You have a wife and child to think of now."

The statement made Quin's nostrils flare in annoyance. While he did appreciate his father's concern and was immensely grateful that the baron had saved his life just a few days ago, he did not appreciate being accused of ignorance.

"I am well aware of that, I assure you," he forced the words out between his teeth. "I am doing the best I can to care for them."

As recently as a few minutes ago thoughts of his family's welfare had been plaguing him, as they did every day, vacillating constantly between the need to stay and the need to leave. At that very moment he found himself fervently wishing they could simply live in blissful ignorance either way.

"And how will you care for them if you're dead?" The baron lifted his chin and stared down his nose at his son, clearly meaning to shock Quin into submission.

Instead, Quin gave a snort. "Staying in Ireland is hardly more dangerous than fighting with the British army, which is what you would have had me do for all these years," he countered, suddenly resigning himself to his father's disapproval. It was something he'd been well versed in for years, after all. "Or had *you* forgotten *that*?"

The baron's lips quivered ever so slightly. "No, I had not forgotten."

They were both silent for a moment. Finally, the older man sighed. "If you insist on staying here, Quinton, you should at least know...the families of your rebellious tenants will pose no danger to you in the future."

His father's eyes were hard as steel as they held Quin's, the expression on his face speaking volumes.

"I suppose you put the fear of God into the people living on my land." Quin inhaled deeply as he pictured Glaslearg's newest residents cowering under the baron's wrath. Having already lost numerous relatives through hunger and disease, and with several more now being transported, Quin was sure they'd been thoroughly browbeaten indeed. He ran a hand over his face, feeling suddenly terribly tired, weighed down by the horrors that seemed to be everywhere around them.

The baron got up and clasped Quin's shoulder. "Is it not better for some of these burdens to have been taken from you? For you to have been spared the details of the trial and everything to do with it whilst you recover from your own ordeal?"

Quin slowly shook his head, thinking of Alannah not wanting to tell him about the latest failed harvest. "It is not possible to be spared from the misery that surrounds us," he said, "only to pretend ignorance of its existence."

"But you do not," the baron said. "You have gone above and beyond what your tenants ever expected of you.—And even if I disagree with your decision to stay in Ireland I do know you will care for them again now."

"That is of little comfort to the thousands who are not so fortunate."

"You cannot save everyone."

Quin's lips twitched at his father's words, which echoed those he'd himself often said to Alannah when she'd despaired over the fate of the countless, desperate Irish people—a despair she would feel once more in the coming months.

"And yet we continue to try."

# 41.

AS NEWS OF the famine's return spread far and wide so, too, did the misery that accompanied the blight. By the time summer turned to autumn and the months of the baron's visit were coming to an end it was clear that the Irish would continue to starve, the potatoes that should have fed them for the next year having turned into sludge once more. Even as the last of the bruising faded from Quin's skin, the scars on the land he called home deepened with each passing day, unlikely to dwindle as easily. And with the devastation caused by three failed harvests in four seasons, the catastrophic consequences of the blight were unlikely to dwindle at all, whether in Quin's lifetime or the decades thereafter.

Glaslearg's tenants had been lucky, with most of their harvest unspoiled, the damage in the north being less pronounced than elsewhere in Ireland, as it had been before. And so, despite all the horrors surrounding them, life on the estate went on much like it had before—as it had to, for everyone's sake.

Quin looked around the courtyard, where the baron's carriage was being prepared to take him back to England, Glaslearg's staff lined up in front of the house to see him off. He smiled at Geraldine and Rupert, who were standing close together, their hands almost touching, whispering to each other as if they were the only two people in the world.

They'd been married in a simple ceremony the week before and had just returned to their duties that morning, clearly pleased with their newfound intimacy and most reluctant to give it up.

Catching sight of their employer watching them they both blushed, standing up straighter and looking carefully ahead. Rupert's expression remained one of dreamy contentment, though—the same he'd worn almost permanently since Geraldine had announced their betrothal in the dining room several weeks before.

"Are you sure you don't want to come with me?"

Quin turned toward his father, who was eyeing him expectantly. The baron looked from Quin to Alannah and back again, his expression softening as his eyes settled on Eveline, who was being held on her mother's hip. Even as the last of his luggage was being secured on the carriage roof his father was still hopeful that Quin might change his mind about staying behind.

"Yes, father, I'm sure," Quin said patiently.

Alannah came to stand next to him and gave him a soft smile, making Quin feel grateful for her support. Whether their decision to stay in Ireland was right or wrong, at least they'd made it together.

His father's lips compressed in disapproval and Quin braced himself for one last argument. To his surprise, though, the older man gave a great sigh as his shoulders drooped. "You'll take care, won't you, Quinton?"

The baron's eyes searched his, with a depth of feeling Quin had seldom seen in his father—a depth of feeling Quin hadn't known his father was capable of for much of his life. He gave a curt nod, feeling rather unsettled by such unaccustomed sentimentality.

He wondered suddenly how many more opportunities they would have to reminisce about shared experiences, how much more time his father would have to spend with his son and granddaughter. The thought made Quin swallow heavily, feeling even more torn than usual about their decision to stay in Ireland, when what natural family he had was in England.

"The carriage is ready, sir."

John's voice pulled Quin back to the present and the reality of having to bid his father goodbye, not knowing when—or if—they would see each other again.

"Farewell, father," he said, drawing him into a tight embrace. The baron froze briefly before returning the gesture. Soon, though, he thumped Quin on the back and stepped away. Clearing his throat he quickly turned toward Alannah before Quin could see the expression on his face.

Taking Eveline into his arms he looked at her sternly. "Darling, you'll be sure to take care of your parents, won't you?"

Evie stared back at her grandfather with big eyes and slowly placed her thumb into her mouth.

The baron laughed. "That's my girl." He held her close for a little longer and kissed her cheek. Handing her back to Alannah he laid a hand on her arm. "You take care, too. All of you." He looked briefly back at Quin, who thought he saw a tear glistening in his father's eyes—but perhaps it was only from the wind that had picked up and was blowing softly across the courtyard.

With his jaws tight the baron bowed his head in farewell to Glaslearg's staff and stepped into the carriage. He waved back at them only once before signalling for the door to be closed and his driver to get underway.

Quin stood next to Alannah, taking Evie from her as the carriage started rattling away. He looked after it for a long time before turning back to the house, a strange feeling of emptiness in his chest.

Evie's pudgy hands suddenly slapped the sides of his face, making him smile. At the welcome reminder of the many blessings in his life despite the turmoil surrounding them he felt his heart slowly lift once more. As if in unison a sliver of sunlight appeared, lightening the courtyard as the autumn breeze blew away the scattered clouds.

Quin placed a kiss on his daughter's nose, making her giggle. She started babbling to herself and waving her arms, and Quin turned to Alannah with a cock of his head. "Would you like to go for a walk?" he asked as a sudden gust of wind lifted the ends of her hair.

"Oh!" The exclamation behind them distracted Alannah from answering and they turned toward the house and the servants, who were still waiting to be dismissed.

Mary was reaching for her mobcap, which the breeze had lifted off her head, hurrying after it as it was carried toward the stable in a merry dance. Stepping in front of the errant headwear John snatched it out of the air with one hand. He dusted it off against his leg before presenting it to Mary when she came up next to him.

"Thank you, Mr Mullen," she said, taking it from him a little shily.

She gave him a brief smile, which made the groom look rather startled. They looked at each other for a moment as if seeing each other for the first time before they both abruptly looked away. Mary's cheeks turned a soft pink as John gave a gruff response, visibly flustered. His eyes slid sideways toward Mary's face once more before he quickly bobbed his head and headed back to the stable.

Looking at Quin, Alannah quirked her brows, making him grin. Perhaps John and Mary might get to know each other a bit better in the coming months—Lord knew they both deserved a little happiness.

Feeling his spirits lift still further Quin told the servants they were free to go before turning toward his wife once more.

"Yes, I would like to go for a walk," she said before he'd opened his mouth.

With his daughter balanced on one hip and his wife on his other side Quin ambled slowly across the courtyard and toward the fields, enjoying the gentle warmth of the sunshine on his skin. The few trees that were scattered across the estate were decked in oranges and reds, the autumn foliage clinging stubbornly to their branches. The breeze picked up the occasional fallen leaf, whirling it around their feet. With the soft sunlight shining onto the land the muted colours surrounding them seemed to glow, like polished amber holding hidden secrets, while the winter crops provided a splash of colour as they peeked their hopeful green heads above the surface.

They crossed over the bridge to reach the other side of the river, where Quin placed Evie onto the fading grass along the bank. She tugged on the tufts for a minute or two before crawling toward a cluster of nearby stones. Picking up a pebble she threw it toward the water, falling well short.

"Look." Quin selected a flat stone and launched it carefully so that it skipped several times across the stream before going under with a soft plop.

Evie clapped her hands together in delight and he did it a few more times. When she tired of the game she crawled to one of the larger stones and pulled herself to her feet.

"Ma-ma, ma-ma," she chanted as she started making her way around the boulder, slapping the surface with her palms as she held herself upright.

Alannah laughed and Evie looked toward her mother with a grin. She bobbed her knees up and down before suddenly letting go of the boulder and taking a step forward, a look of intense concentration on her face. She took another and another, gaining momentum until she toppled into Alannah's outstretched arms.

"Oh, you clever girl!" Alannah exclaimed, lifting Evie up into the air, making her giggle.

Quin ran a hand over the top of Evie's head, beaming from ear to ear. "You can walk," he said, filled with immense pride at her achievement.

"Wa, wa, wa," Evie echoed, making her parents laugh.

Still smiling, Quin put his arms around his wife and daughter, kissing each of them in turn and pulling them close. His earlier apprehensions had faded away and instead, he felt only a deep sense of gratitude for the blessings in his life. He tightened his hold on the two people dearest to him in all the world—a world that was filled with hardships but one that was also filled with the possibility of an immense amount of joy, if one only had the courage to find it and the good fortune to keep it.

THE END

Thank you for reading *Amid the Oncoming Storm*!

If you enjoyed this book, please consider posting a short review on Amazon or Goodreads. It takes me about two years to write one of these books and a little encouragement from my readers goes a long way toward keeping me motivated! Reviews and telling your friends about the book also help to get the word out. For an independent author, this is vital to the book's success. Thank you for your help!

# Escape to 19th century Ireland in the first book of the Irish Fortune Series

## *Under the Emerald Sky*

*He's come to Ireland to escape his past. She's trying to run from her future.*

Ireland, 1843. Irishwoman Alannah O'Neill is feeling trapped. Under the thumb of her controlling brother she finds herself contemplating the meaninglessness of her existence. When the Englishman Quinton Williams arrives on the neighbouring estate, Alannah feels drawn to him. Knowing that her brother hates the English for their role in Ireland's bloody history, Alannah keeps her growing relationship with Quin a secret. But it's a secret that can't be kept for long from those who dream of ridding Ireland of her English oppressors.

Among the stark contrasts that separate the rich few from the plentiful poor, Under the Emerald Sky is a tale of love and betrayal in a land teetering on the brink of disaster – the Great Famine that would forever change the course of Ireland's history.

"*Under the Emerald Sky* reaches another level in storytelling, the kind where the characters remain with you long after you have closed the book"
**THE HISTORICAL FICTION COMPANY**

"Intelligently plotted and atmospheric"
**READERS' FAVORITE**

# The gripping sequel to
*Under the Emerald Sky*

## *Beneath the Darkening Clouds*

*In a land on the brink of ruin, their past can't be outrun.*

They've overcome obstacles and endured heartache, but their biggest challenge is yet to come.

It's 1845 and Ireland is plagued with unrest when the unthinkable happens — the potato harvest on which most Irish peasants depend fails, leaving thousands desperate for food. Unease and fear ripple across the land, along with hunger and disease. With the government's response inadequate, it's up to Quin and Alannah to save the people living on their estate.

But all the while, danger lurks from other quarters, as Quin delves into mysteries from his past, incurring the wrath of powerful enemies.

Amid the hardships of the Irish Famine, Beneath the Darkening Clouds sweeps the reader on a heart-wrenching journey of love and loyalty in a myth-shrouded land.

"From the first line, Weber captivates the reader"
**THE HISTORICAL FICTION COMPANY**

"A sweeping saga with plenty of romantic tension, historical drama, and deeply emotive moments"
**READERS' FAVORITE**

# Author's notes

BEING A FORMER scientist I enjoy adding bits of science to my books, fascinated as ever by discoveries both then and now. And so, after I'd read a National Geographic article about bog bodies, I just knew I had to include something about the topic in this book! While the body discovered by Mr Lewes is fictitious, it is based on real ones that have been unearthed in bogs across northern Europe, such as Tollund Man and Grauballe Man, who were indeed several centuries old and incredibly well preserved, as well as being presumed victims of human sacrifice. Several such bodies had been discovered by the middle of the 19th century, including in Ireland, and naturalists have long speculated about their origins.

Another topic that quite fascinated me was mummy unwrapping parties. These were, in fact, a popular pastime of 19th century British aristocrats and would have followed proceedings similar to those described by Quin's father. Even the invitation he received was based on an actual invitation to one such event.

Sadly, the newspaper article about the mother and children that so upset Alannah is also factual, as is the article reporting the disastrous sea voyage of the *Exmouth*. Both are difficult to contemplate as they brutally bring to light the horrors so many Irish people experienced during the famine. The attempted rebellion of 1848 that ended in the Widow McCormack's cabbage patch is also factual, as is the relatively lenient punishment received by those involved. The trial following that attempted rebellion only took place about two months after the fact, though. I have shortened this period following Quin's capture for the purposes of the story. I hope you can forgive me.

As always, the historical details included in this book are based on extensive research and are portrayed as accurately as such a thing is possible when obtaining information from historical records, scientific papers, expert opinions and the like. Political figures and historical events, as well as existing scientific knowledge mentioned are based on this research, and I have made every attempt to provide a balanced view wherever possible. The political situation leading up to and during the Great Famine is a complex one, and naturally not all aspects thereof can be included in a single novel, or even a series, which is meant foremost to entertain (although I do hope it also informs). For a succinct look at the situation in Ireland during the Famine I can recommend:

*Gray, Peter. The Irish Famine (New Horizons). Thames & Hudson Ltd, London, 1995.*

# Acknowledgments

THE AUTHOR WOULD like to thank:

My faithful readers, who encourage me to keep writing with their positive feedback; Members of the Historical Fiction Club and Friends of the Coffee Pot Book Club for their vast knowledge of all things historical fiction and for their ongoing encouragement, not just of me but many other writers wanting to get their stories out there; Dee Marley at White Rabbit Arts for yet another stunning cover and her unending enthusiasm for my books; my parents and extended family, as well as friends far and wide, for their unerring support of my writing; my dearest friend, Nikola Schmidt, for reading everything I write (more than once!) and for the endless discussions, useful suggestions and feedback that have helped get this book to its final stage; my children, for always believing in me; and my husband, for his unfailing support and encouragement and, last but not least, for coming up with the charmingly descriptive "reactions of a dead horse", which have finally found their way into one of my books.

# About the author

JULIANE WEBER IS a scientist turned historical fiction writer, and author of the Irish Fortune Series. Her stories take readers on action-packed romantic adventures amid the captivating scenery and folklore of 19th century Ireland. The first book in the series, *Under the Emerald Sky*, was awarded bronze medals in The Coffee Pot Book Club 2022 Book of the Year Contest and The Historical Fiction Company 2021 Book of the Year Contest. The second book in the series, *Beneath the Darkening Clouds*, was selected as an Editors' Choice title by the Historical Novel Society and was awarded a bronze medal in The Historical Fiction Company 2022 Book the Year Contest.

Juliane spent most of her life in South Africa, but now lives with her husband and two sons in Hamelin, Germany, the town made famous by the story of the Pied Piper.

www.julianeweber.com

https://www.facebook.com/JulianeWeberAuthor

https://x.com/Writer_JW

Printed in Great Britain
by Amazon